Jacobite Ireland, 1685–91

J.G. SIMMS

This detailed study traces the course of a critical period of Irish history: from the accession of James II to the surrender of Limerick, which made William of Orange master of the whole country. It takes the story from the Catholic revival that followed the accession of James II to the treaty of Limerick, which led to a century of Protestant ascendancy and penal laws. Much of the book is concerned with 'the war of the two kings', which coincided with a struggle for power between the Protestant settlers and the older inhabitants who were Catholic.

The siege of Derry and the battle of the Boyne are still commemorated, and Dr Simms shows how the tensions of modern Ulster have their origins in the seventeenth century. Considerable attention is paid to the European implications of the conflict, which is shown as part of the contest between Louis XIV and the Grand Alliance. French, Danish and Dutch sources are used to illustrate the course of events in Ireland and, in addition to the military narrative, problems of religion, politics and landholding are discussed.

'Dr Simms treats with brilliant erudition and admirable impartiality of the complex constitutional, religious, agrarian and military problems in Ireland from 1685 to 1691 ... This book is a major contribution to the study of seventeenth century Ireland' *Irish Sword*.

'He provides students of Irish history for the first time with a critical study of James II's campaigns, but the main theme of the book is the final decline of the Catholic Anglo-Irish gentry, whose roots went back to the fifteenth century and before. ... The main attraction of the book will be in the glimpses it provides of politics on both sides' H.F. Kearney, *History*.

J.G. Simms read Classics in Oxford, and after a career in the Indian Civil Service he re-entered academic life in 1950 in the History Department of Trinity College, Dublin. His publications include The Williamite Confiscation in Ireland 1690-1703, *as well as many historical articles and substantial contributions to* The New History of Ireland.

J.G. SIMMS

Jacobite Ireland, 1685–91

FOUR COURTS PRESS

Published by
FOUR COURTS PRESS
Fumbally Lane, Dublin 8, Ireland
email: info@four-courts-press.ie
http://www.four-courts-press.ie
and in North America by
FOUR COURTS PRESS
c/o ISBS, 5804 N.E. Hassalo Street, Portland, OR 97213.

First published 1969 by Routledge and Kegan Paul Ltd
First paperback edition 2000

This new paperback edition of *Jacobite Ireland*
does not include the two illustrations which appeared
n the original printing. These illustrations were portraits
of Richard Talbot, duke of Tyrconnell and
Patrick Sarsfield, earl of Lucan.

ISBN 1-85182-553-3

A catalogue record for this title
is available from the British Library.

The cover design, by Terry Foley, incorporates a detail of an
engraving by Romeyn de Hooge titled *King James II takes ship
for France after his defeat at the Boyne in July 1690.*

Printed in Ireland
by Colour Books Ltd, Dublin.

PREFACE

~~~~~~~~~~~~~~~~~~~~~~~~~~~~~~~~~~~~~~~

THIS BOOK traces the course of events in Ireland from the accession of James II to the treaty of Limerick. No detailed history of the period has appeared for over fifty years, and much new evidence has meanwhile become available. It was a critical time in Irish history, in which the older inhabitants who were Catholic made a strong bid to recover power and land from the Protestant settlers, but finally succumbed to the forces of William of Orange. Considerable attention has been paid to the international significance of the war in Ireland, which formed part of the contest between the France of Louis XIV and an alliance of lesser powers.

I am glad to acknowledge the assistance I have received from the fine collection of microfilms, taken from many countries, in the National Library of Ireland. My thanks are also due to Mrs Mary Davies, who drew the maps. I take this opportunity of expressing my gratitude to those who have given me advice on specific points, and in particular to Dr L. M. Cullen, Fellow of Trinity College, Dublin; Mrs Maureen Wall, Lecturer in History, University College, Dublin; Dr G. A. Hayes-McCoy, Professor of History, University College, Galway; and Dr Sheila Mulloy. Above all I am grateful to Professor T. W. Moody and Professor J. C. Beckett, who read the whole work in typescript and made many valuable criticisms and suggestions. I also thank the Board of Trinity College, Dublin, for a generous grant in aid of publication.

Dublin, May 1969   J. G. SIMMS

v

CONTENTS

~~~~~~

Contents

Contents

ABBREVIATIONS

The following abbreviations have been used in the citation of sources:

Anal. Hib.	*Analecta Hibernica* (I.M.C.)
B.M., Add. MS	British Museum, Additional MS
B.M., Eg. MS	British Museum, Egerton MS
B.M., Harl. MS	British Museum, Harleian MS
Bodl.	Bodleian Library, Oxford
Cal. S.P. dom.	*Calendar of state papers, domestic series*
Clarendon corr.	*Correspondence of Clarendon and Rochester,* ed. S. W. Singer
Clarke corr.	Correspondence of George Clarke (T.C.D., MSS K. 5. 1–13)
Coll. Hib.	*Collectanea Hibernica*
Danish force	*The Danish force in Ireland, 1690–1,* ed. K. Danaher and J. G. Simms (I.M.C.)
D'Avaux	*Négociations de M. le comte d'Avaux en Irlande, 1689–90,* ed. J. Hogan (I.M.C.)
D'Avaux, supp.	Ditto, supplementary volume
H.M.C.	Historical Manuscripts Commission
I.H.S.	*Irish Historical Studies*
I.M.C.	Irish Manuscripts Commission
Jacobite narrative	*A Jacobite narrative of the war in Ireland,* ed. J. T. Gilbert
James II	*The life of James the second,* ed. J.S. Clark

Japikse	*Correspondentie van Willem III en Hans Willem Bentinck*, ed. N. Japikse
King	[W. King], *The state of the Protestants of Ireland under the late King James's government*
Leslie	[C. Leslie], *An answer to a book intituled The state of the Protestants of Ireland*
Min. guerre	Bibliothèque Nationale, Paris, archives anciennes, ministère de la guerre
N.L.I.	National Library of Ireland
O Bruadair	*The poems of David O Bruadair,* ed. J. C. MacErlean
O'Kelly	C. O'Kelly, *Macariae excidium, or the destruction of Cyprus,* ed. J. C. O'Callaghan
P.R.O.	Public Record Office of England
P.R.O.N.I.	Public Record Office of Northern Ireland
R.I.A.	Royal Irish Academy
R.S.A.I. Jn.	*Journal of the Royal Society of Antiquaries of Ireland*
Stevens	*The journal of John Stevens,* ed. R. H. Murray
Story	G. Story, *A true and impartial history*
Story, *Continuation*	G. Story, *A continuation of the impartial history*
T.C.D.	Trinity College, Dublin

Dates are given in the old style, except that the year has been treated as beginning on January 1. For letters originally dated in the new style, both styles of dating have been shown.

I

IRELAND AT THE DEATH
OF CHARLES II

~~~~~~

I. A DIVIDED COUNTRY

THE CONFLICT between James II and William of Orange had dramatic and lasting consequences for Ireland. It made her an important theatre in a major European war, and it accentuated internal tensions which have continued to the present day. The annual celebrations of the siege of Derry and the battle of the Boyne keep alive traditions of the struggle between Catholic and Protestant, which, in the Irish context, was the central issue of the war. The result of the struggle was to establish a structure of society of which traces still remain. The Jacobite war in Ireland was closely linked to the English revolution of 1688 and to the European ambitions of Louis XIV; but it was also a result of the unstable conditions of Irish society at the accession of James II in 1685, and of the tensions created by the Catholic revival of the next four years.

The twenty-five years of Charles II's reign had been a period of peace, recovery and comparative prosperity for Ireland, but they had not solved the Irish problem. That problem was no longer one of Gaelic separatism, which had ceased to be a practical issue as a result of the Elizabethan conquest. The principal issues of the seventeenth century were land and religion, and since Cromwell they were inseparably linked. Cromwellian policy had treated all Catholics alike, whether their origins were Gaelic or English. With very few exceptions the lands of 'Irish papists' on the hither side of the Shannon were seized, and a reservation was created for them on the Connacht side of the river. The Catholic church was ruthlessly suppressed, its buildings destroyed, its friars 'knocked on the head', its priests transported to the Barbadoes.

The restoration of Charles II gave new hope to Irish Catholics, who had declared themselves to be on the royalist side in the civil war, and many of whom had shared Charles II's exile. They looked forward eagerly to the recovery of their lands and the revival of their church. But their efforts to get back their estates and to obtain toleration for their religion were matched by the determination of Protestants to hold what they had gained and to prevent the Catholic church from securing more than a suppressed existence, dependent on the connivance of the establishment. The official attitude was disapproval of both Catholics and Protestant dissenters. In particular, the Ulster Scots were regarded as a potential danger to both church and state; their treatment depended on the current relations between their brethren in Scotland and the English government.

Apart from these internal tensions, the relations between Ireland and England were often strained, largely as a result of the development of the Irish economy and the consequent restrictions imposed on Irish trade by English laws. The administration of Ireland was subject to frequent change as a result of political developments in England, caused either by Charles's dealings with his parliament or by the jostling for power that was characteristic of his court.

For most of the reign the duke of Ormond was the dominant figure on the Irish scene. He had immense prestige, derived from his ancient lineage, his large estates and the experience he had gained in the service of the crown since the beginning of the civil war. He maintained an unwavering attachment to the established church, but all his relatives were Catholics. He had kept close contact with them in his negotiations with the Kilkenny confederates and at the court of the exiled king, where royalism counted for more than the distinction between Catholic and Protestant. Ormond was a committed royalist and had no sympathy for puritanism or for the republican views of some of those who had come to Ireland under the commonwealth. If Catholics would make an unequivocal declaration of loyalty he was prepared to grant them toleration. Among Catholics he distinguished between those who had come to terms with him at the close of the confederate war and those – mainly Gaelic Irish – who had taken the side of Rinuccini and had refused to accept the peace terms.

During his first period as Charles II's viceroy, which lasted from 1661 to 1669, the principles of the land-settlement were laid down in the act of settlement of 1662 and the act of explanation of 1665.[1] His removal from the viceroyalty in 1669 was partly due to the intrigues at Whitehall that brought about the fall of Clarendon. But the efforts of Buckingham and his friends were assisted by financiers in Ireland, who proposed to 'farm' the revenue for the mutual profit of themselves and the crown, and found Ormond an obstacle to their policy.[2] Charles showed little appreciation of Ormond's loyalty and faithful service; for some years he was out of favour and his advice on Irish questions was not sought.

The next two viceroys, Robartes and Berkeley, had very brief tenures. Essex, who held the office from 1672 to 1677, was a capable and moderate governor; but he was constantly frustrated by the intrigues of unscrupulous financiers, which eventually resulted in his recall. Ormond was restored to favour and in 1677 returned as viceroy for a second period which lasted till the end of the reign.

2. THE RESTORATION SETTLEMENT

Charles owed his restoration to the commonwealth army, and the maintenance of the Cromwellian settlement in Ireland was part of the bargain. He made a declaration in which, with characteristic flexibility, he promised that Irish Catholics who had come to terms with Charles I should get back what they had lost, and that their Cromwellian supplanters should keep what they had. Ormond dryly remarked that a new Ireland would have to be found to meet the king's promises. The restoration land-settlement was a compromise which resulted in Catholics getting back about a third of what they had held when the war

[1] See below, p. 4.   [2] For the 'farm' see p. 15, below.

in Ireland began in 1641. They had then owned the greater part of Munster and Leinster and almost all Connacht. Their total share of the land was about 60 per cent in 1641; between 8 and 9 per cent (almost all of it in Connacht or Clare) when the commonwealth ended in 1660; and a little over 20 per cent in 1685.[3]

The restoration compromise pleased neither side. Catholics were disappointed at having recovered so little; Cromwellians objected to giving up part of what they had so recently been granted. Legal effect was given to the king's declaration in the act of settlement, passed by an all-Protestant Irish parliament in 1662. It provided for the immediate restoration of 'innocents' and for the 'reprisal', or compensation, of the Cromwellian holders with equivalent lands elsewhere. The act also named a large number of individual Catholics whose loyalty to the crown recommended them for special consideration, provided that the Cromwellian occupants had first been reprised. This policy was apparently devised in the belief that there was much unowned land available for reprisals. The belief was without foundation, and the problem was made more difficult by fresh assignments of land, notably the grant to Charles's brother James, duke of York, of the large estates that had been granted to the regicides, those who had signed Charles I's death-warrant.

The act of settlement set up a court of claims to decide who should be restored; a number of decrees were issued, but the difficulties of dislodging the Cromwellians appeared insuperable. To resolve the deadlock a fresh act was passed in 1665, the act of explanation. It explained its predecessor by introducing a new principle: Cromwellians (with a few named exceptions) were to give up one-third of their holdings and thus make available a pool for the restoration of Catholics and the reprisal of their supplanters. The land thus made available was not nearly enough to meet the demand. A favoured minority recovered their estates in whole or in part, but many of the smaller claimants were left unsatisfied. Ormond, the viceroy, favoured the 'old English' (those of Norman or English stock), particularly if they were connected with the Butler family. The Gaelic Irish

---

[3] For a summary of the restoration settlement see Simms, *Williamite confiscation*, pp. 14–20. The commonwealth figure is based on W. Petty, *The political anatomy of Ireland*, pp. 3–4.

of Ulster, who had opposed Ormond's negotiations with the confederate Catholics, came off worst of all.

The restoration settlement was regarded by most Catholics as a breach of faith, and they were ready to take the first opportunity of upsetting it. It was strongly criticized by a Catholic bishop, writing in the character of a Protestant gentleman. *The narrative of the settlement and sale of Ireland* made Chancellor Clarendon the villain of the piece, and accused him of betraying Catholic royalists for Cromwellian gold.[4] It declared the acts of settlement and explanation to be repugnant to the laws of God and nature, sound policy and reasons of state; and it called for their repeal. It was ingeniously suggested that it was in the interest of England to restore Irish Catholics as a bulwark against Scots Presbyterians. Another writer who condemned the settlement was David O Bruadair, the poet, who described the events of Charles II's reign under the title 'The sum of the purgatory of the men of Ireland'. He particularly deplored the low social standing of the Cromwellians. Elizabethans had at least been gentlemen; Cromwellians were 'roughs formed by the dregs of each base trade, who range themselves snugly in the houses of the noblest chiefs as if sons of gentlemen'.[5]

Protestants were well aware that Catholics had not accepted the settlement as final. Sir William Petty regarded the land question as the main cause of friction in a divided country. He noted that those Catholics who had recovered their estates tended to side with their dispossessed co-religionists against the newer Protestant landowners. The old distinction between Gaelic Irish and old English was 'asleep now because they have a common enemy'.[6] Petty's friend Sir Robert Southwell wrote of the dispossessed owners haunting their old estates and reckoning the day when they should again possess them.[7] Some of them took to the woods and hills and, as it was called, turned tory. Among the celebrated tories of the period were Redmond O'Hanlon in Armagh and the three Brennans in Kilkenny.

[4] Published in Louvain in 1668, and attributed to Nicholas French, bishop of Ferns.

[5] *Poems of O Bruadair*, ed. J. C. MacErlean, iii. 15 (hereafter cited as O Bruadair).

[6] W. Petty, *Political anatomy of Ireland*, p. 43.

[7] B.M., Eg. MS 917, f. 88.

Tory-hunting was a Protestant pastime, and many of the tories met a violent end.[8]

Protestants also were dissatisfied with the land-settlement. They considered themselves guardians of the English interest in Ireland. Catholics in general were branded with the iniquities of the 1641 rising, the outbreak of which was annually commemorated with church services and more secular celebrations. To recent colonists the Gaelic Irish were treacherous savages, while the old English were degraded by popish superstition and by long association with the Irish. The more extreme Protestants violently resented the restoration of Catholic landowners. To them Catholics were rebels who richly deserved to be stripped of their possessions; that the victorious Protestants should have to hand back even part of their land was both inequitable and unwise. Some 'furious spirits' on the Protestant side thought that another rebellion was needed, so that the Irish could be completely crushed.[9]

The land question continued to dominate the Irish scene throughout Charles II's reign. The legislation of 1662 and 1665 was followed by inquiry commissions and by a series of crown grants which, by the end of the reign, resulted in a notable improvement of the Catholic position. But numbers of those who at last succeeded in recovering estates did so only after a rancorous and expensive contest with the Cromwellian occupants; as a result many estates were heavily encumbered and much ill-feeling was generated. The reign ended with a 'commission of grace', which allowed some five hundred individuals, Catholic and Protestant, to compound for defective titles by paying the crown for fresh patents.[10]

Much of the improvement in the Catholic position was due to Richard Talbot, a cadet of a famous Norman family, who had gained the favour of the future James II and whose energy and court influence were effective in restoring many dispossessed owners. This earned him a high reputation as a Catholic

[8] J. P. Prendergast, *Ireland from restoration to revolution*, pp. 57–164; T. W. Moody, 'Redmond O'Hanlon' in *Proc. Belfast Nat. Hist. and Phil. Soc.*, 2nd series, i. 17–33 (1937).

[9] Petty, p. 26. The most sensational example of Protestant reaction was Blood's plot of 1666 (see Bagwell, *Ireland under the Stuarts*, iii. 35–7).

[10] See R. C. Simington, ed., *Books of survey and distribution* (I.M.C.), i. pp. xvii, xviii.

6

champion, and made him a wealthy landowner into the bargain. He and a number of Catholics – lawyers and men of affairs – made good use of an unsettled market in land to acquire large estates under the restoration settlement.

Nevertheless Protestants still enjoyed a clear superiority at the end of the reign. They owned nearly all Ulster, where the only Catholic magnate was Lord Antrim. They had four-fifths of Leinster and Munster and over half of Connacht. Galway was the only county in which Catholics owned the greater part of the land. But outside Ulster there were everywhere enough Catholic nobility and gentry to cause apprehension to Protestants and to provide the nucleus of a Catholic revival if a favourable opportunity arose.

3. THE CHURCHES

For the Church of Ireland the restoration meant the recovery of former privilege and a return to the monopoly of church revenues and official recognition. The reign of Charles II was for it a period of rebuilding after war-time devastation and of increasing revenues. By the end of the reign the see of Derry was worth £2,000 a year, and some other sees approached it in value.[11] Bishoprics were eagerly sought after. But since the deaths of Bramhall and Jeremy Taylor there had been no bishops of distinction. The patronage of the state gave promotion to viceroys' chaplains and to members of great families. At the close of Charles II's reign the primate was Michael Boyle (a kinsman of the earl of Cork), whose successive tenure of the archbishoprics of Dublin and Armagh stretched over forty years; for the last twenty years of the reign he was also lord chancellor, the revival of a former link between church and state. Two other Boyles were bishops during the reign. With the exception of William Sheridan at Kilmore, all the bishops at the time of Charles's death bore English names. The Elizabethan act of uniformity, reinforced by a similar act of 1666, gave recognition to the Church of Ireland alone and conferred comprehensive powers on its bishops. Tithes were payable to its clergy by adherents of every creed. The Church was conscious of its dependence on state support and its weakness as a small

[11] *Tanner letters* (I.M.C.), p. 456.

minority in hostile surroundings. In 1641 and the following years it had suffered heavily from Catholic violence, but the puritan régime of the commonwealth fell almost as heavily on it. Many of the higher clergy were new arrivals from England, and upheld the Caroline traditions of alliance between church and state and of passive obedience to the monarch.

Petty estimated that in 1672 there were 800,000 Catholics and 300,000 Protestants, of whom something over 100,000 belonged to the established church. Half of the latter were in the cities, leaving only about 50,000 for the countryside. Even in Ulster they were heavily outnumbered by Presbyterians.[12] In Dublin the established churches were crowded, and the cathedrals were repaired and embellished. In other parts of the country the work of restoring ruined churches and devastated glebes progressed irregularly. There was much absenteeism on the part of the clergy and congregations were sparse.

The treatment of the Catholic church varied from toleration and semi-official recognition to extreme persecution. These variations were linked to the fluctuations of English politics and the degree to which a tolerant king was obliged to give way to an intolerant parliament. There was little in the way of penal legislation, and the legal position of Catholics in Ireland was considerably better than that of their brethren in England. The principal laws that affected them were the acts of supremacy and uniformity. Both of these had, somewhat mysteriously, been agreed to by a largely Catholic parliament at the beginning of Elizabeth's reign. The act of uniformity had been repeated in 1666 to bring it into line with a revision of the prayer book; advantage was taken of the opportunity to make further regulations, such as that requiring schoolmasters to be licensed by a Protestant bishop and to take the oath of supremacy. The two acts had far-reaching effects on the Catholic clergy and laity. The oath imposed by the act of supremacy acknowledged the king's authority in things spiritual as well as temporal, and Catholics could not conscientiously take it. It was required of all holders of public office, civil or military. It had already to be taken by members of the newer corporations and in the course of the reign was applied to the rest, unless special exemption was given by the viceroy in individual cases. There were

[12] Petty, pp. 6, 16.

8

periodical minor relaxations of the requirements, but for most of the reign the army and the administration, both central and local, were completely under Protestant control. The act of uniformity prescribed the form of religious rites to be used, and laid down penalties for using any other form of 'open' prayers. The Catholic clergy performed their ministrations under great difficulties and in conditions of extreme poverty. Their congregations were themselves poor, and the obligation of paying tithes to the Protestant clergy left little over for their own priests. Those who absented themselves from the official services were liable to fines, but these were seldom collected during Charles II's reign.

The problem of finding a basis of agreement between the Catholic church and a Protestant state was never satisfactorily solved in the seventeenth century. Just as Catholics baulked at acknowledging the ecclesiastical claims of the sovereign, so Protestants were apprehensive of the temporal claims of the pope, and in particular of his claim to absolve subjects from their allegiance. An attempt to get round this difficulty was the celebrated 'remonstrance', sponsored by the Franciscan Peter Walsh, in return for which Ormond was prepared to grant practical toleration of the Catholic church. The terms of the remonstrance required the Catholic clergy and laity to acknowledge the king's sovereignty in temporal affairs 'notwithstanding any power or pretension of the pope'; they were to disclaim 'all foreign power, be it either papal or princely, spiritual or temporal' that professed to release subjects from their allegiance.[13] Walsh found some supporters, but Rome declared against the remonstrance and it was rejected in 1666. But even after that relations between the state and the Catholic church were not wholly disrupted. For parts of the reign the hierarchy was able to function more freely than it had done for over a century. Archbishop Oliver Plunkett of Armagh co-operated with successive viceroys. Archbishop Peter Talbot of Dublin was well-known to the court, apart from being Richard Talbot's brother.

The persecution suffered by the church in the latter part of the reign was a by-product of the 'popish plot' and the hysteria

[13] For the text of the remonstrance see P. Walsh, *History of the remonstrance*, pp. 7–9.

that accompanied it in England. Executive action was taken to expel bishops and regular clergy, and those who remained in the country were hunted remorselessly. Plunkett and Talbot were both implicated in the plot. Talbot died in prison; Plunkett met a martyr's death at Tyburn, in spite of some attempt by Ormond to save him. Plunkett was generally respected by Protestants, but Talbot was regarded as a political figure on whom suspicion could more easily fall. The anti-Catholic fervour that flared up in England had its counterpart among Protestants in Ireland, and for some years the life of the Catholic hierarchy and lower clergy was harried and troubled. Memories of the 'plot' and of the persecution were still fresh in James II's reign and account for much in the reciprocal relations between Protestants and Catholics.

As the excitement associated with the popish plot died down, Catholics ventured to practise their religion more openly, but the toleration accorded them was severely limited. In 1683 the Galway Catholics were rebuked for their presumption in maintaining a priory and a nunnery near the town and four mass-houses in it. They agreed to remove these public manifestations of Catholicism, but asked to be allowed to practise their religion privately in their houses.[14] In the same year Ormond noted with displeasure that the 'insolence and indiscretion' of the regular popish clergy had led them to construct no less than four chapels in Kilkenny. He gave directions for them to be closed and forbade the celebration of mass within the town walls. The superior of the Jesuits was arrested and the rest of the regular clergy fled.[15]

The Catholic laity showed great loyalty to their faith and church. Members of the aristocracy were under considerable government pressure to conform to the established church, but during Charles II's reign very few of them did so. The Catholic religion provided a strong bond of social solidarity, and many observers commented on the religious zeal to be found in Ireland. The war of 1689–91 had some of the elements of a crusade, in which priests were active in stimulating a spirit of militancy and of obstinate resistance. On the Protestant side the same crusading atmosphere was perceptible in Derry, but else-

[14] *Ormonde MSS* (H.M.C.), n.s., vii. 115–16.
[15] Ibid., p. 139; P. Power, *A bishop of the penal times*, p. 77.

where it was observed that ministers were markedly less effective than priests in stirring up belligerent emotions.

Much the largest group of Protestant dissenters were the Scots in Ulster. Some of them belonged to families that had arrived in James I's reign, either to the official plantation or to the more thriving unofficial settlements in Antrim and Down. Their numbers had been substantially increased in Charles II's reign. Petty reckoned that by 1672 80,000 'new Scots' had settled in Ireland, and they continued to arrive during the following years.[16] They brought with them the traditions of their home-land, both ecclesiastical and secular. Most of them sympathized with the covenanters, and at the time of Bothwell Brig and later they were suspected of active plotting against the established order. Some of their ministers were imprisoned and meeting-houses were closed. Their relations with the bishops of the established church were very strained. Their great patron was Sir Arthur Forbes, marshal of the army, who as earl of Granard was to figure prominently in James II's reign. Forbes was instrumental in obtaining the *regium donum*, the celebrated subsidy to Presbyterian ministers which first appeared in 1672 as a secret service grant in Forbes's name. It is doubtful how often it was paid, and in the last years of Charles II's reign and throughout James II's it was not paid at all; but it formed a precedent for William's grant and its successors.[17]

There were considerable numbers of dissenters in other parts of Ireland, chiefly in Dublin and the larger towns. They were referred to as fanatics and were objects of suspicion to the authorities, particularly after the Rye House plot of 1683. Conventicles were suppressed in Cork, Limerick and elsewhere.[18] Quakers were regarded as less dangerous by the civil authorities, but their unwillingness to pay tithes often involved them in conflict with the established church. Although both dissenters and Catholics were victims of official disapproval, there were no signs of them forming a common front. Ormond thought that if

[16] Petty, p. 17.

[17] For the *regium donum* see J. S. Reid, *History of the Presbyterian church in Ireland*, ii. 416–18.

[18] *Ormonde MSS*, n.s., vii. 121. The Rye House plot was a plan, devised by extremist whigs, to assassinate Charles II on his way from Newmarket to London.

Catholics came to power they would draw no distinction between Protestants, no more than the fanatics would distinguish between Catholics and members of the established church.[19]

4. ECONOMICS AND POLITICS

Charles II's reign was a time of great economic expansion in Ireland. During the latter years of the Commonwealth there was already some recovery from the devastation caused by twelve years of war. At the restoration the process was accelerated by the return to more normal political conditions. Agricultural production increased; there was a revival of commercial confidence; the return of Catholics and the arrival of new Protestant settlers from England, Scotland and continental Europe led to a sharp rise in population. Petty estimated that between 1652 and 1687 the population rose from 850,000 to 1,300,000. His figures have been criticized as underestimates, but we can accept his presentation of the trend.[20] There was a particularly striking rise in the population of Dublin. During the reign its numbers almost trebled. By 1685 it held an unchallenged position as the second city in the British dominions, with about 60,000 inhabitants.[21] It was the chief centre of the trade with England. A new and socially ambitious class of rising country gentry looked to it for skilled craftsmanship and imported consumer goods. It was estimated that the amount of such goods must be 'prodigious to supply not only the necessities but the vanity and luxury of so opulent and populous a kingdom, the rate of whose expenses was in no way regulated by thrift'. The standard of expenditure on clothing, wine and tobacco was denounced as wickedly extravagant by the puritan Lawrence.[22] Ormond and Orrery set an ostentatiously high standard of luxurious living; the extreme cheapness of provisions and labour was an encouragement to expenditure on inessentials.

[19] *Ormonde MSS*, n.s., vii. 152.

[20] Petty, *Political anatomy*, p. 17; *Petty papers*, ed. Lansdowne, i. 64; K. H. Connell, *The population of Ireland*, pp. 259–60.

[21] For a discussion of Dublin's population see my article 'Dublin in 1685' in *I.H.S.*, xiv. 212–26.

[22] G. Phillips, *The interest of England in the trade of Ireland*, p. 22; R. Lawrence, *The interest of Ireland in its trade and wealth stated*, p. 18.

Sheep and cattle were the chief sources of wealth, in spite of the commercial restrictions imposed by English laws. The most notable of these was the act of 1667 prohibiting the import of Irish cattle into England. At the time this was regarded as a mortal blow to Irish prosperity, and it was accordingly resented by all classes. In fact the cattle trade was less profitable than is usually supposed, and after an initial period of dislocation, to which the Dutch war contributed in large measure, the restriction did little damage to the economy. There was a marked growth in the export of salt beef to the West Indies and a thriving butter trade developed with the continent.[23]

Cork was the second port in the kingdom, though its trade was a long way behind that of Dublin. The customs returns of 1668 showed that 39 per cent of the revenue was produced by Dublin and 12 per cent by Cork. The trade of Cork expanded rapidly in the latter part of Charles II's reign, and by 1685 it was reported that the customs establishment was quite inadequate to control it. The harbour was well wharfed, so that the merchants could ship their goods at their own doors, which made it difficult to prevent evasion of duty.[24] The business of the city was mainly in the hands of new Protestant merchants, who had eclipsed the old Catholic trading families. Most of the leading merchants were Quakers.[25] In the customs returns for 1668 Waterford took third place with 9 per cent of the revenue, followed by Limerick and Galway with 7 per cent and 6 per cent respectively. Belfast was not yet a major port, though it grew rapidly in the latter half of the seventeenth century, and by 1700 it eclipsed Limerick and Galway to become the fourth port of Ireland.[26] During Charles II's reign Galway was the only port in which Catholic merchants appear to have recovered the bulk of the trade. Their wealth, which was also derived from lands in Connacht, was a conspicuous feature of an economy in which most of the commanding heights were occupied by Protestants. The defeat of the Jacobites in 1691 was to have a

---

[23] L. M. Cullen, *Anglo-Irish trade, 1660–1800*, p. 33.

[24] *Cal. S.P., Ire. 1666–9*, pp. 672–3; *Cal. S.P. dom., 1685*, p. 122; W. O'Sullivan, *Economic history of Cork city*, p. 125.

[25] *Ormonde MSS*, n.s., vii. 121.

[26] Cullen, *Anglo-Irish trade*, p. 17.

depressing effect on the trade of Galway, which suffered a marked decline in the eighteenth century.

Much land was turned over to sheep-rearing during the reign. This was as much due to the demand for wool created by the expansion of the English woollen industry as to the prohibition of cattle exports. There was a ban (imposed by an English act) on the export of raw wool except to England.[27] The policy was to prevent continental rivals making cloth from the excellent Irish wool, and to reserve it for English cloth-manufacturers. It was a policy easier to formulate than to enforce; smuggling was rife and much Irish wool found its way to France and Flanders, though the greater part went to England under licence. The export of friezes was not restricted, and they found a ready market in England and on the continent. Irish wages were half those of England, and this gave an enviable advantage to the trade, which was largely in the hands of recent immigrants from the English west country.[28]

The linen industry was encouraged by Ormond, who imported workers from the continent and set up manufactures at Chapelizod, County Dublin, and at Carrick-on-Suir, County Tipperary. But when Ormond was recalled in 1669 these enterprises languished. The main development of the trade centred in Ulster, where flax-spinning became an important domestic industry. Lurgan, County Armagh, was a busy linen market, in which Quakers took a leading part.[29] Fish was a profitable export; salmon from the Bann was sent as far as Spain and Italy.[30] The navigation acts had an erratic effect on direct trade between Ireland and the American colonies. A period of restriction was followed in 1681 by free trade consequent on the expiry of a particular act.

Rents rose steadily during the reign of Charles II, and land increased in value from ten to fifteen years' purchase. It was noted that money was plentiful and land scarce, so that loans could often be raised at lower rates of interest than the standard

[27] 14 Charles II, c. 18, which made such export a felony; it was already a misdemeanour.

[28] *A letter from a gentleman in Ireland*, 1677.

[29] C. Gill, *Rise of the Irish linen industry*, p. 8; W. H. Crawford, 'The rise of the linen industry' in L. M. Cullen, ed., *The formation of the Irish economy*, p. 25.

[30] T.C.D., MS I. 4. 17, f. 77.

10 per cent.[31] Landholders prospered, and there was all the more reason for the dispossessed to feel resentful.

The Irish revenue expanded greatly during the reign. The restoration land-settlement provided a substantial revenue from quit-rents, and also the opportunity for a bargain with parliament by which a perpetual grant was made of customs and excise, hearth-tax and other sources of revenue in exchange for the surrender of feudal revenue, notably from the court of wards. Having secured this 'new hereditary revenue', the crown did without a parliament in Ireland for the last eighteen years of the reign.[32]

With growing prosperity the yield from these sources expanded, and an Irish income was of some help to Charles II in his efforts to resist English parliamentary pressure. The collection of the whole revenue was handed over in 1669 to 'farmers', who contracted for an annual payment of £204,500. Superimposed on the farm was a scheme devised by Richard Jones, Viscount and then earl of Ranelagh, by which the financial administration was entrusted to undertakers who contracted to pay a fixed amount to the crown. A typical restoration intrigue provided for the payment of a secret amount in addition, much of which went to the king's mistress, the duchess of Portsmouth, who was one of Ranelagh's supporters.[33] Another was Richard Talbot, whose price was Ranelagh's help in getting the land-settlement modified in favour of Catholics.[34] Ormond was throughout an opponent of the farm, and his recall in 1668 was an essential step in getting the farm policy approved. The results were deplorable; the collection of taxes was highly irregular and the establishment was left unpaid. Charles alone profited, as a number of unpublicized remittances were made to his privy purse. In return he protected Ranelagh from the indignation of the Irish executive. A second experiment in farming, which was not much better, ended in 1682.

This was a satisfaction to Ormond, who had returned to the

[31] B.M., Eg. MS 917, f. 89.

[32] T. J. Kiernan, *Financial administration of Ireland to 1817*, p. 86.

[33] M. Twomey, 'Charles II, Lord Ranelagh and the Irish finances' in *Ir. Comm. Hist. Sc. Bull.*, Apr. 1960; J. C. Beckett, *The making of modern Ireland*, pp. 130–1.

[34] *Cal. S.P. dom., 1673–5*, p. 162.

viceroyalty in 1677 and who worked hard to expose the iniquities and incompetence of both undertakers and farmers.[35] In the concluding years of the reign the finances were directly administered and much was done to build up Ireland as a source of financial and military strength for the crown. The position was not unlike that which Wentworth had tried to create for Charles I, and it excited the same suspicions on the part of those opposed to the crown. Southwell, writing in 1684, summed up some English reactions to Irish prosperity:

and though it sound harsh to the merchants in England to hear that Ireland thrives and that the revenue makes near £300,000 per annum, yet it is much more so to those that are discontented at his majesty's prosperity, since his royal authority is there more absolute and his power on that side does by consequence make him more powerful on this [i.e. in England].[36]

Ormond took particular interest in the Irish army and was concerned to make it a reliable force, properly paid and politically sound. As the potential dangers were from 'fanatics' and Catholics he was determined to exclude both; all ranks were required to take the sacrament according to the rites of the established church. The correspondence of Ormond and his son Arran (who acted as deputy in Ormond's absence) shows what trouble they took over the organization and equipment of the army. In the early part of 1685 it consisted of three regiments of horse, commanded respectively by Ormond himself, his son and his grandson; and seven regiments of foot. The whole amounted to about 5,500 men. The officers were almost all drawn from the seventeenth-century settlers.[37] Their replacement was to be one of the most controversial parts of the Jacobite programme.

The fact that commercial restrictions were imposed on Ireland by English acts of parliament raised the constitutional question of the legislative independence of Ireland, which was later to be pressed by both Catholics and Protestants. During Charles II's reign it was a grievance particularly felt by Protestants as they had so great a share of the trade. Petty pointed out the

---

[35] *Ormonde MSS*, n.s., vi. 285.
[36] B.M., Eg. MS 917, f. 89.
[37] *Ormonde MSS*, ii. 361; ibid., i. 400–6.

absurdity of a situation in which the inhabitants of Ireland were left in doubt as to which parliament they should obey; he thought it wrong that Englishmen in Ireland should be bound by laws in the making of which they were not represented.[38]

The importance of Ireland as an economic and military source of independent power to the crown was to be significant in the next reign as James progressively alienated the affections of his English subjects. Suspicion that the crown would use Ireland to support an absolutist policy was of less account while the administration was steadily Protestant and under the conservative control of Ormond. The political difficulties of Ormond himself sprang directly from his middle-of-the-road policy. Whigs denounced him as a favourer of Catholics and made much of his large circle of Catholic relatives. Catholics, on the other hand, complained of his repression of their religion, and their chief spokesman, Richard Talbot, was on particularly bad terms with him.

Talbot had no liking for Ormond's Ireland. Its prosperity, taxable capacity and military resources were too completely under Protestant control, and might be dangerous if there were a political crisis. He was in Ireland in 1684, collecting material to make a case for a complete overhaul of the civil and military administration. An essential step towards this was the removal of Ormond, who was known to be rigidly opposed to the admission of Catholics to civil or military office. Talbot was able to enlist the support of James, who had lived down the exclusion crisis and had re-established his position at court. James appears to have been convinced that in the event of Charles's death there was a real danger of a Protestant *putsch* in Ireland.[39]

Since the spring of 1682 Ormond had been in England as one of Charles's principal advisers, leaving Ireland in charge of his son Arran. In the summer of 1684 he was suddenly ordered to return to Dublin, and very soon after he had left London reports reached him that he was to be removed from the viceroyalty. Talbot's complaints of Cromwellian influences in Ireland counted for more than Ormond's long and faithful

[38] Petty, p. 32.
[39] T. Carte, *Life of Ormond*, iv. 668–9; J. P. Kenyon, *Robert Spencer, earl of Sunderland*, p. 101.

service to the crown. The plan that now emerged was the replacement of Ormond by James's brother-in-law, Lawrence Hyde, earl of Rochester, who could be expected to be more amenable than Ormond, and whose removal from the English stage suited the purposes of Sunderland, the secretary of state. Sunderland's influence was therefore added to that of James and Talbot.

Ormond had not been long back in Dublin before he was surprised to receive a letter from Charles to the effect that 'very many and almost general alterations should be made in Ireland, both in the civil and military parts of government': Ormond was to be spared the embarrassment of carrying them out, but could choose his own time to leave. He was to be replaced by Rochester, who explained to Ormond that the king was determined that none who had fought against the crown should be retained in his service.[40] The French ambassador reported to his Government that commissions were to be granted to loyal and deserving Catholics.[41] Shortly before Charles's death it was reported that Talbot and Justin MacCarthy had been given regiments in Ireland.[42] MacCarthy had commanded Monmouth's regiment in France and his nephew, the earl of Clancarty, had just married Sunderland's daughter.[43]

These signs of impending change in Ireland, alarming to Protestants and welcome to Catholics, were soon followed by Charles's death, which took place on 6 February 1685. Rochester's appointment to Ireland was cancelled as a result, but Ormond's recall was maintained. For Protestants his departure and the accession of Catholic James meant the end of an era, and the prospect before them was one of anxiety and gloom.

[40] Carte, v. 166 (19 Oct. 1684).
[41] Kenyon, p. 101.
[42] *Cal. S.P. dom., 1684–5*, p. 287.
[43] For a recent account of MacCarthy see J. A. Murphy, *Justin MacCarthy, Lord Mountcashel*, 1959.

II

TYRCONNELL AND THE CATHOLIC REVIVAL

~~~~~~

I. A SLOW BEGINNING

PROTESTANT FEARS of what was in store for them in the new reign were increased by clear signs of excited expectancy on the part of Catholics. The Catholic reaction is described by Charles O'Kelly, whose *Destruction of Cyprus* is a contemporary account, in classic terminology, of Irish affairs from the viewpoint of a Gaelic gentleman: 'the Cyprians exulted in the assured hope that their sovereign . . . would forthwith restore to the heavenly powers their temples and altars and also to the natives their properties and estates of which they had been for so many years unjustly despoiled'.[1]

But James had to take account of English opinion. He was well aware of the strength of Protestant feeling and knew that any indiscreet affront to it would play into the hands of his opponents. Ormond was ordered to hand over his charge without further delay to lords justices who were to administer the government until a new lord lieutenant was appointed. But the position and character of the lords justices were clearly intended to be reassuring to Protestants. They were Michael Boyle, archbishop of Armagh and lord chancellor, and Arthur Forbes, earl of Granard, marshal of the army. A new privy

[1] C. O'Kelly, *Macariae excidium, or the destruction of Cyprus*, ed. J. C. O'Callaghan, p. 15; hereafter cited as O'Kelly.

council was appointed, all of whose members were Protestants of good standing. A disquieting instruction reserved to the king the granting of military commissions and stated that lists were under preparation.[2] A week later the commissions were announced, and it became clear that the army had been selected as the first area to be reorganized. The cavalry regiments of Ormond and his grandson Ossory were left almost unchanged, but Arran's regiment was taken from him and given to Talbot, though most of the Protestant officers remained. What had been Ormond's infantry regiment was given to Justin MacCarthy, and a scattering of Catholic officers appeared in other regiments. Individual Catholic officers were exempted from taking the oath of supremacy.[3] The use of the dispensing power that this involved was less controversial in Ireland than it was in England. There was no counterpart in Ireland to the English test act of 1673, and the relevant law was the Elizabethan act of supremacy, exemption from which had many precedents. MacCarthy had seen active service in Turenne's campaigns in the 1670s and had won a good reputation as a soldier. Talbot's experience was more patchy. In his youth he had been a cornet in the Catholic confederate army and had survived the siege of Drogheda. During the commonwealth period he had become lieutenant-colonel of James's regiment in the Spanish service, an unusually rapid promotion gained by his own pugnacity and James's support. Although the introduction of Catholics into the army began on a very limited scale, it soon aroused Protestant opposition and James was accused of going against his promise not to harm the established religion.[4]

It was soon evident that Talbot was to be given an important role in initiating the new order. In the middle of 1685 he was created earl of Tyrconnell and the lords justices were ordered to consult him on questions relating to the army.[5] He lost no time in sending Sunderland his proposals for reform: officers who had served the commonwealth should be investigated;

[2] *Cal. S.P. dom., 1685*, p. 59. Commissions were ordinarily granted on the recommendation of the chief governors of Ireland.

[3] Ibid., pp. 76–7, 149.

[4] Campana di Cavelli, *Les derniers Stuarts*, ii. 39.

[5] *Cal. S.P. dom., 1685*, p. 149 (12 May 1685).

soldiers should be given an oath unobjectionable to Catholics; he himself should have blank commissions to use in filling his regiment; Catholics should be admitted to the privy council. The last of these proposals was clearly designed to meet his own case, but James was not prepared to go so far at that stage.[6]

Talbot's elevation was highly unwelcome to Protestants. He had an arrogant manner, a hot temper and a violent vocabulary. His portrait shows a proud and fleshy figure, well-built and with the remains of good looks; but the general impression is not attractive. In earlier life he had the reputation for rakishness that was common among members of the restoration court. But he seems to have been a faithful husband to Frances Jennings, the sister of Lady Marlborough; and during James's reign it was his manners, not his morals, that incurred criticism. His role of 'popish champion' had frequently brought him into conflict with Protestants, and he had plenty of old scores to pay off. Many Catholics disapproved of him and thought him too violent, but his vigorous campaign for the removal of Catholic disabilities had naturally won him much support from both clergy and laity. The clergy petitioned the king to entrust the government of Ireland to him 'to the terror of the factious and the encouragement of your faithful subjects here'.[7] But this was going too fast for James and his English advisers, who had their hands full clearing up after the risings of Monmouth and Argyll. There were signs of unrest among Ulster Protestants, who might have given serious trouble by joining the Scots covenanters. Granard, a Scot whose loyalty could be counted on, was ordered north with a body of troops and directions were given to disarm suspected Protestants. All over Ireland the militia were ordered to hand in their arms, which produced complaints that tories were taking advantage of the situation to plunder the countryside.[8] In Tipperary a rumour of an Irish rising in the manner of 1641 brought out a number of Protestants to keep watch by night; this was reported as a conspiracy against the crown, and was followed by a prosecution. A Protestant account of the trial describes the crown witnesses as 'mere scullogues, scarce a cravat about their necks'. Most of the

[6] Ibid., p. 236 (30 June 1685).
[7] W. King, *State of the Protestants*, pp. 294–5.
[8] *Cal. S.P. dom., 1685*, pp. 176, 187, 405.

accused were discharged, but ten were found guilty, fined and imprisoned.[9]

The choice of the new viceroy was to depend on political manœuvres in England. Ireland was an unpopular assignment for leading politicians. Rochester, who had escaped that fate and secured the treasury at the accession of James, tried to repay Sunderland in his own coin by suggesting him for the vice-royalty. Moderate Catholics in England supported the proposal as less objectionable than the appointment of Tyrconnell. Sunderland countered by proposing Rochester's brother, the second earl of Clarendon, who was ready enough to take this chance of restoring his shaky finances. James approved, and Clarendon's appointment was announced in August 1685. He was a high-tory Anglican whose loyalty was assured; he was also acceptable to Protestants and to most English Catholics.[10] The appointment was a severe blow to Tyrconnell, who had himself hoped to get the post. He wrote to James that Clarendon's nomination

does so terrify your Catholic subjects here they seem more struck with this last change than any that hitherto hath been . . . and all these methods by which your authority as well as the worship of God began to take firm root in the kingdom seem utterly disappointed by lodging your authority in a person from whom they have so little reason to expect any favour.[11]

Clarendon was suspect in Ireland as the son of a father on whom the chief blame for the restoration land-settlement had been laid.

2. CLARENDON IN IRELAND

Clarendon reached Dublin early in 1686. His correspondence is an invaluable source for the events of that year, and a revealing picture of a well-meaning man in a situation that was too much for him.[12] He was not unintelligent; he belonged to the Royal Society and was interested in history and antiquities. Macaulay

[9] *Ormonde MSS*, n.s., vii. 367; viii. 344.
[10] J. P. Kenyon, *Robert Spencer, earl of Sunderland*, p. 120.
[11] Tyrconnell to James, 29 Aug. 1685 (B.M., Add. MS 32,095).
[12] Edited by S. W. Singer; cited as *Clarendon corr.*

called him an obsequious courtier; but he put his own interpretation on royal policy and tried to insist that concessions
to Catholics should not overthrow the English interest in Ireland.
He had no previous experience of the country and little sympathy for the expectations of Irish Catholics; his temperament
and outlook were, like those of James himself, invincibly
English. To him the Irish were a conquered people, to whom it
would not be safe to give military or judicial power.[13] His
appointment was a setback to Tyrconnell's ambitions and
indicated a policy of moderate reform unwelcome to majority
opinion in Ireland. Clarendon was ready to grant Catholics a
limited share in the administration and the army, and he hoped
to arrive at a compromise on the land-settlement that would go
some way to meet Catholic demand without expropriating
Protestants. He came armed with an assurance from James
which he made known in his first speech to the council: 'I have
the king's commands to declare on all occasions that, whatever . . . apprehensions any men may have, his majesty hath no
intention of altering the acts of settlement'.[14] Tyrconnell made
his hostility to Clarendon clear from the start. He left Ireland
while Clarendon was on his way there, and avoided the opportunity of calling on him at Holyhead.

With Tyrconnell in London, Clarendon's position in Ireland
was not going to be easy. He found Dublin a very 'tattling town';
the tattle was of Tyrconnell coming back to take command of
the army, bringing new commissions with him, and of changes
in the judiciary. With every mail-boat Clarendon's office was
besieged by a shoal of Irishmen asking whether the new commissions had arrived. Dubliners got letters from England with
news of old officers to be dismissed and new ones put in their
places. Rumour named three of the judges as due for replacement by Catholic barristers. Clarendon complained that he was
not being consulted, and ventured to propose to James that if
Catholics were to be appointed to military or civil office they
should be Englishmen from England: such a policy would be in
line with James's own view that the real division was between
English and Irish, not Catholic and Protestant. James, however, answered curtly that he did not see what harm it could do

[13] *Clarendon corr.*, i. 357; Macaulay, *History of England*, i. 613.
[14] *Clarendon corr.*, ii. 475.

to English interests to employ some Irish Catholics, so long as the land-settlement was maintained, 'which it must always be, though many ill and disaffected persons are secured in their possessions by it'.[15] Clarendon's letters to his brother Rochester show obvious distaste for Tyrconnell: 'a man of monstrous vanity as well as pride and furious passion'. He wrote that the current rumours had alarmed Protestants in Ireland and that businessmen were talking of selling up and retiring: 'very little business has been done this last week upon the exchange, but men look dejectedly one upon another'.[16]

Rumours of Tyrconnell's return were followed by official intimation of his appointment as lieutenant-general and that of MacCarthy as major-general. This was accompanied by first-hand information from England that Tyrconnell was to come over 'in great glory' with a commission to command the army independently of the viceroy; nothing was to be done in matters military, civil or ecclesiastical except with Tyrconnell's advice.[17] Tyrconnell returned to Ireland on June 5, and Clarendon found his presence even more trying than his absence had been. There were daily conferences in which Tyrconnell ranted, swore and changed his ground in endless arguments. Clarendon unburdened himself to his brother: 'whether my lord Tyrconnell will continue to be so terrible as he is at present nothing but time will determine; you will give me leave to be proud that I have so far mastered my natural unfortunate temper, though the treatment I daily receive would perhaps justify another man's being provoked'.[18]

Tyrconnell's first aim was to purge the army. Numbers of Protestant officers and men were replaced by Catholics. Dublin was crowded with incomers from the countryside, eager to join the army; they were jeered at by the Protestant proletariat, who derided their imperfect English.[19] Quarrels broke out between dismissed Protestant soldiers and the Catholics who took their place. Clarendon showed his sympathy for the cashiered officers and reported some of the harder cases to Sunderland. Nearly two years later some cases were still under inquiry, but we do not hear that the victims obtained redress

---

[15] *Clarendon corr.*, i. 270, 276, 299, 339.

[16] Ibid., pp. 291, 296.   [17] Ibid., pp. 343, 376.

[18] Ibid., pp. 430–5, 463–4.   [19] *Ormonde MSS*, n.s., viii. 346.

from the Jacobite Government.[20] Clarendon found much to disapprove of in the changes: many of the new officers were indiscreet in their talk, and there were boasts that by Christmas there would not be a Protestant left in the army; Protestants were alarmed to see commissions given to the sons of those who had been most active in 1641. The purge was extremely drastic; Clarendon talks of 400 men being turned out of a single regiment in one day.[21] By the end of September 1686 out of a sanctioned strength of 7,485 there were 5,043 Catholic privates. The replacement of officers was not so rapid. There were still only 166 Catholics out of a total of 406 officers, but the number was to be steadily increased, until by 1688 the great majority of the officers were Catholic.[22]

While Tyrconnell was still in England changes were made in the judiciary, which consisted of the lord chancellor and nine judges – three each in the courts of king's bench, common pleas and exchequer. Archbishop Boyle was removed from the chancellorship; his successor was a not very successful member of the English bar, Sir Charles Porter, a Protestant, who later came into prominence in the Williamite administration. One Protestant judge was removed from each of the three courts and replaced by a Catholic. The dismissed judges had held office 'during pleasure' and the question of compensation does not seem to have been considered. The new judges were Thomas Nugent, of a well-known 'old English' family, Denis Daly, and an English barrister named Ingleby who declined the post and was replaced by Stephen Rice. They were specifically exempted from taking the oath of supremacy. Clarendon disliked the appointments: he thought little of Nugent's ability; Daly was 'one of the best lawyers, but of old Irish race and therefore ought not to be a judge'.[23] Daly was later to be a controversial figure during the war. Sunderland explained to Clarendon that he had not been consulted on these developments as he had so recently assumed office: information from persons of undoubted integrity and loyalty (in other words, Tyrconnell) had convinced the king that such changes were urgently necessary.

[20] *Clarendon corr.*, i. 423, 429–30; Sunderland to Tyrconnell, 8 March, 3 May 1688 (P.R.O., S.P., 63/340, ff. 137, 144).

[21] *Clarendon corr.*, i. 476, 534.

[22] *Ormonde MSS*, i. 431–5.   [23] *Clarendon corr.*, i. 356–7.

Clarendon was hurt at not being consulted, and, somewhat tactlessly, tried to enlist the support of the queen: he pointed out to her how embarrassing it was for him to receive the first news of administrative changes from the letters which Dubliners got from their friends in England.[24] The new judges were later commended by Clarendon for their conduct on circuit: they took every opportunity to steady public opinion and to dissuade Protestants from leaving the country. They took care to have mixed juries, half English and half Irish. Daly behaved with extreme fairness in trying a case against a Protestant at Trim for seditious remarks made five years earlier. Nugent took the same attitude at Drogheda.[25]

Another change of importance was the admission of eleven Catholics to the privy council. They included Tyrconnell himself, Justin MacCarthy, the three new judges and some Catholic peers.[26] Clarendon's choice of sheriffs was severely criticized by Tyrconnell, and Clarendon was asked to explain his selection of Cromwellians. One of them was said to be the son of Cromwell's baker; Clarendon admitted that the father was a baker, but protested that the son was a baronet and an honest magistrate. Others were described as 'of Cromwell's race and principles', 'a caballing whig', 'son of an old Oliverian'. Clarendon was told that the king wanted some Catholics to be appointed sheriffs and magistrates, and that they should have the same privileges in corporations as Protestants. He complied with the last point by sending a circular to the corporations telling them to admit Catholic merchants and traders, their widows and apprentices as freemen without taking the oath of supremacy. This produced replies from a number of corporations indicating that they had complied or would comply with the direction; some places which had two bailiffs agreed to appoint one of each religion.[27] But these modest measures fell far short of the aspirations of Catholics, who wanted much more control of local administration. Judge Nugent reported to Sunderland that Clarendon had rejected his advice to issue a proclamation promising free admission to corporations of all Catholics who wished for it;

[24] *Clarendon corr.*, i. 321, 342–3.
[25] Ibid., p. 520.
[26] *Ormonde MSS*, n.s., viii. 345.
[27] *Clarendon corr.*, i. 285–6, 294, 461–2, 487.

this would have attracted Irish merchants from abroad.[28] In October 1686 a number of Catholics were appointed magistrates, Protestants being removed to make way for them. In the same month Clarendon was ordered not to make any appointments of sheriffs for the coming year.[29] There was in future to be a much more thorough catholicization of the administration.

The emergence of the Catholic church from a position of grudging toleration was surprisingly gradual. The primate, Dominick Maguire, went over to England with letters from the hierarchy pledging loyalty to the crown and asking for protection. He returned in March 1686 and was recommended to Clarendon, who was asked to see that the Protestant clergy and magistrates did not molest the Catholic clergy. Royal permission was given to the Catholic bishops to wear their episcopal dress in public ('long black cassocks and long cloaks') but they were not to wear their pectoral crosses; the primate acquiesced in this restriction, but evidently thought it unreasonable.[30] The king authorized payments on a modest scale (from £150 to £300) to be made to Maguire and eleven other Catholic bishops. The official order did not come through till August 1686 when a warrant was issued to pay £2,190 per annum to Dominick Maguire for secret service; bureaucracy succeeded in delaying the payment still further.[31] There are references to the restive conduct of the lower clergy, and Clarendon was asked to refer to the hierarchy before any civil proceedings were taken against them. He later reported that there were a number of cases in which priests had advised their flocks not to pay tithes to the Protestant clergy. He had informed the Catholic bishops, who expressed their disapproval and promised to rebuke the offending priests.[32] In May 1686 the king wrote to the primate commending the Capuchins, and later we hear of them establishing a house in Dublin for the rent of which an annual grant of £30 was authorized. When the friars first appeared in their habits Protestant youths mocked at them and police

---

[28] *Cal. S.P. dom., 1686–7*, p. 182.

[29] *Ormonde MSS*, n.s., viii. 347; *Clarendon corr.*, ii. 22.

[30] Ibid., i. 313, 395; *Cal. S.P. dom., 1686–7*, pp. 89, 112.

[31] Ibid., pp. 79, 249, 351. The money was ordered to be paid out of the revenue of the vacant bishoprics of the Church of Ireland (*Clarendon corr.*, i. 576).   [32] Ibid., i. 313, 535.

protection for the friars was called for.[33] Clarendon evidently believed himself to have treated the hierarchy with every consideration. He refers to a courteously conducted interview with Maguire about the subsidy and to 'a very civil visit' he had from the archbishop of Cashel. When the bishops met in Dublin they all called on him in the evening, two or three at a time, 'in a modest style', wearing ordinary dress.[34] But it is clear that the Catholic clergy were not satisfied with him and would not rest till Tyrconnell had taken his place. Bishop Tyrrell of Clogher (an able Franciscan who later became Tyrconnell's secretary) wrote to James in August 1686, warning him not to trust Protestant advisers: men of truth like Tyrconnell would serve him faithfully without trimming. The task remaining was to make the Irish army larger and wholly Catholic, to place Catholics in authority in all posts military and civil, to reform the corporations and to call a loyal parliament to free Ireland from all the restrictions that hindered her prosperity.[35]

James's policy for the Church of Ireland was at this stage one of passivity: bishoprics that fell vacant were to remain unfilled and the crown was to enjoy the revenue. There were three such vacancies, the archbishopric of Cashel and the bishoprics of Clonfert and Elphin. Clarendon made elaborate recommendations for filling the Cashel vacancy, but was told that the king was going to keep the see and its revenue in his own hands. Rumours spread that the pope had been written to about the appointment. Clarendon also wrote to the archbishop of Canterbury about the general condition of the Church of Ireland. He found it in much worse order than other Irish institutions: most churches were melancholy ruins; absentee clergy employed pitiful curates, which obliged people to resort to a 'Romish priest or non-conformist preacher, and there are plenty of both'. The archbishop of Tuam had been away from his see for three years and the bishop of Down for six. The latter was the notorious Hackett, known as 'bishop of Hammersmith'. The one redeeming feature was the Dublin churches, 'for the most part very well served and infinitely crowded'. Clarendon hoped for more clergy from England; if the king would fill the

[33] *Cal. S.P. dom., 1686-7*, pp. 148, 374; *Ormonde MSS*, n.s., viii. 350.
[34] *Clarendon corr.*, i. 402, 529; ii. 6.
[35] King, pp. 303-9.

vacant bishoprics it would be excellent; but that was too much to hope for.[36]

Tyrconnell went back to England at the end of August 1686. His departure freed Clarendon of unpleasant personal contacts; but his influence at court was soon felt in reports of royal dissatisfaction with the Irish administration and in rumours of Clarendon's impending recall.

3. THE COVENTRY LETTER

Clarendon's correspondence makes it clear that Protestants leaned heavily on the act of settlement as a guarantee of English control and thus a security not only for landowners but for merchants and traders as well. His solution of the question was another commission of grace; landowners should get confirmation of their titles and in return a charge should be levied from them, the proceeds of which could be used to compensate those Catholics who had been left unsatisfied in the settlement.[37] Declarations on James's behalf that the settlement would be maintained had created little confidence in the face of the mounting demand from Catholics for its revision. From the time of James's accession Petty and his friend Southwell were anxious for the fate of the settlement. The republication in 1685 of the *Narrative of the settlement and sale of Ireland* added to their anxiety, and Petty tried his hand at a reply: 'Another more true and calm narrative of the sale and settlement of Ireland.'[38] Another anti-settlement pamphlet which Petty tried to answer was *Twelve quaeries relating to the interest of Ireland.* Southwell asked Petty whether he had any ground for anxiety and whether there was any evidence that the government was 'fond of a new scramble or to be pestered with some years' tinkering to form a new settlement and put all trade, improvement and exchange in the meantime to a stand'. In the course of a discussion with Tyrconnell, Petty, unexpectedly, admitted that the settlement had its defects: 'I told him that there were things in it against the light of nature and the current equity of the world, but whether it were worth the breaking I doubted; but if it were broken by parliament I offered things to be mixed with

[36] *Clarendon corr.*, i. 252–4, 294, 407–9.
[37] Ibid., pp. 351, 414.   [38] *Petty papers*, i. 49–55.

those acts as should mend the condition of all men'. Petty later went to Windsor to interview James and was glad to be assured that the king would not break the settlement; but not long after that news came of a fresh attack and he told Southwell that the settlement like St Sebastian was stuck full of arrows.[39]

Much would depend on Tyrconnell's attitude to the settlement. He had done very well for himself out of it, but his reputation as champion of Catholic interests was largely based on his attacks on the settlement and the degree to which he had got it modified. He could not openly contradict the assurances given in James's name, but Clarendon found him ready to use violent language in private: 'by God, my lord, these acts of settlement and this new interest are damned things; we do know all those arts and damned roguish contrivances which procured these acts'. However, he admitted that the acts must be maintained, and apparently agreed with proposals to charge the new owners a third or a half of the value of their lands to compensate dissatisfied claimants.[40]

James was not in favour of Clarendon's proposals for a commission of grace or for the issue of a proclamation confirming the settlement. He preferred to have a session of parliament to confirm the acts and at the same time raise more money than a commission was likely to produce. Clarendon was told to consult Tyrconnell, but found him elusive: he was against a commission and said much would have to be done before a parliament was summoned – a hint of the project for remodelling constituencies. Subsequently Clarendon gathered that Tyrconnell wanted parliament to modify the acts by restoring the old owners to their estates and compensating the new owners with money.[41] When Tyrconnell left for England he took with him an able Catholic barrister, Richard Nagle, and the talk of the town was that they were going to propose a parliament and an alteration of the settlement. Clarendon warned his brother that Tyrconnell and Nagle would pretend to be in favour of confirming the settlement, 'but with so many exceptions and alterations as will in truth overthrow it'.[42]

[39] *Petty–Southwell correspondence,* ed. Lansdowne, pp. 147–50, 215, 234, 264.
[40] *Clarendon corr.,* i. 432.
[41] Ibid., pp. 447, 507, 560, 581–2.   [42] Ibid., pp. 555, 562.

When Tyrconnell reached England he had little difficulty in convincing James that Clarendon was soft on Cromwellians and a half-hearted exponent of the king's policy, and that he would have to be recalled. It was harder to get a decision that Tyrconnell should himself be the next viceroy. There was strong opposition to him on the grounds that he was too violent and too unpopular with Protestants; various members of the English Catholic nobility were suggested for the post, but after much manœuvring, Tyrconnell succeeded in getting Sunderland's backing and this, together with his long-standing association with James, proved decisive.[43] In the course of the negotiation Sunderland had proposed that, to allay the fears of Protestants, the change of viceroys should be accompanied by a proclamation in favour of the act of settlement. This was the context of the famous letter sent from Coventry by Nagle, who was on his way back to Ireland, to Tyrconnell, who had remained in London.[44] Nagle objected strongly to the issue of a proclamation in support of the settlement. He maintained that no such reassurance was required by landowners: they had not tried to sell out at panic prices. It would not serve to encourage trade: Protestant traders had no real estates; Catholic traders would be disheartened by the issue of such a proclamation. If James died, he would be followed, as the succession then stood, by his Protestant daughter Mary, and Catholics were likely to be more oppressed than ever. Their only hope was to make their position safe by securing a larger share of the land. If the settlement were confirmed the new arrivals would be established and the old Catholic families kept out of their ancestral property. James, as a pious Catholic, must not take on himself the guilt of confirming such an iniquitous settlement: 'he that hath a resolution to establish Catholic religion cannot imagine that the way of doing the same is to confirm the most considerable interest there in the hands of the Protestants and to take away all the hopes of the Catholic proprietors'.

Nagle's proposal was that the king should declare that the acts of settlement and explanation had not been properly put into effect and that they should be modified by a fresh act of

---

[43] *Life of James II*, ii. 61 (hereafter cited as *James II*). The book is discussed in the Appendix, pp. 281–4. below.

[44] *Ormonde MSS*, n.s., vii. 464–7.

parliament, particularly in favour of the numerous 'innocents' whose cases had never been heard.

4. A NEW DEPUTY

Though Clarendon heard many circumstantial reports that he was to be recalled and replaced by Tyrconnell, it was not till January 1687 that an official communication from Sunderland was sent to him. It was exceedingly abrupt: he was to be replaced almost immediately by Tyrconnell, who would arrive before the end of January; Clarendon was to hand over to him a week after his arrival.[45] The one consolation was that Tyrconnell was not to have the style of lord lieutenant, but that of deputy. Otherwise there was no ray of comfort, and Clarendon was left in no doubt that he had incurred the royal displeasure. When he began to realize this he protested plaintively that he had not deserved such treatment: the king had specifically commissioned him to support the English interest in Ireland; the Irish were to get some advantage from having a king of their own religion, but it was to be made clear to them that the king regarded them as a conquered people and was determined to maintain the settlement.[46] Clarendon was satisfied that he had been as helpful to Catholics as was compatible with the security of Protestants. He clearly had little idea of Irish aspirations; even with James's backing, Clarendon's policy would not have satisfied the leaders of Catholic opinion, clerical or lay.

The news of Tyrconnell's appointment created consternation in Dublin, and many families got ready to leave for England; it was rumoured that there was no time to spare as the new deputy would stop their departure.[47] There was talk of Trinity College students plotting Tyrconnell's assassination. Adverse winds that held Tyrconnell's arrival up till February 6 were regarded as a belated intervention of providence in favour of Protestants. Catholics, on the other hand, were naturally jubilant about the appointment. Their excitement was mocked in Wharton's famous doggerel of Lilliburlero which, to Purcell's rousing tune, became the marching-song of the revolution:

[45] *Cal. S.P. dom., 1686–7*, p. 332.
[46] *Clarendon corr.*, ii. 25–6.   [47] *Ormonde MSS*, n. s., viii. 347.

Ho, brother Teig, dost hear the decree
Dat we shall have a new debittie:
Ho, by my soul, it is a Talbot,
And he will cut all de English throat.[48]

The *London Gazette* made the most of Tyrconnell's triumphant return: his reception at the waterside, the ringing of bells, the lighting of bonfires, and other demonstrations of public rejoicing.[49] Malicious insinuations, put about by fiery Protestant preachers, that the deputy intended to oppress a section of the population were indignantly denied, and those who spread them were threatened with the rigour of the law.[50] A number of Catholics were added to the privy council and further changes were made in the judiciary. The Protestant Porter was replaced by the English Catholic Fitton, whose chequered career had included a term in jail. Each of the three courts now had two Catholic judges and only one Protestant; it was remarked that the Protestant was kept for show and could always be outvoted.[51] An important appointment was that of Nagle as attorney-general. He thus became the chief law-officer; if there was a parliament he would be designated speaker, which boded ill for the act of settlement.

The catholicization of the army was stepped up. Tyrconnell brought over a number of fresh commissions, and more Protestants were displaced to make room for Catholics. The Catholic primate was appointed chaplain-general and authorized to approve regimental chaplains.[52] The purge was not complete; up to the end of 1688 there were some Protestant officers left, and a few of the new commissions were given to Protestants. Though most of the officers appointed since 1685 were without military experience, there was a nucleus of veterans who had served in France during Charles II's reign, in Hamilton's regiment, which had later become the duke of Monmouth's. Those who had seen active service in this way between 1671 and 1678 included Patrick Sarsfield, Justin

[48] The words are taken from Colm O Lochlainn, *Irish street ballads*, p. 72; the tune is still familiar as that of 'The Protestant boys'. See also J. Carswell, *The old cause*, pp. 353–8.

[49] *London Gazette*, 10 Feb. 1687.

[50] Ibid., 7 March 1687.　　　　　　　　　　[51] King, p. 67.

[52] *Cal. S.P. dom., 1686–7*, pp. 339–40, 353.

MacCarthy and a number of others who were to take a leading part in the war in Ireland.

Both Gaels and 'old English' appear in the lists of commissions. Most of them were members of families that, at any rate up to the beginning of the seventeenth century, were landed gentry. A soldier's life was a traditionally appropriate occupation for gentlemen, and the opportunity of returning to it was naturally gratifying to the Catholic upper class. The poet O Bruadair expressed hopes that the new army would recover the lost land; he praised a fellow poet, Eoghan Ruadh O Sullivan Mor, who came up from Kerry to Dublin to get a cavalry commission, performed remarkable feats of horsemanship in front of Tyrconnell, and then was fatally stricken with small-pox.[53] Another Munster poet produced a hymn of joy to celebrate the new order:

> Behold there the Gael in arms every one of them,
> They have powder and guns, hold the castles and fortresses;
> The Presbyterians, lo, have been overthrown,
> And the fanatics have left an infernal smell after them.
> Whither shall John turn? He has now no red coat on him,
> Nor 'Who's there?' on his lips when standing beside the gate.
> 'You popish rogue' they won't dare to say to us,
> But 'Cromwellian dog' is the watchword we have for him.[54]

Other ranks were recruited at fairs and holy wells, and at this stage there seems to have been no difficulty in getting them.[55] A proclamation of February 1687 suggests that discipline was weak, and that there were brawls between the army and the civil population. Part of the trouble was irregularity in paying the troops, and another proclamation laid down rates of subsistence money, pay and clothing. To train the army it was decided to have a large camp at the Curragh in the summer of 1687, and Tyrconnell asked for arms to be sent from England for the purpose.[56] A similar camp was held in the following summer, and Tyrconnell took a personal interest in the training.

The substitution of Catholics for Protestants in the civil

[53] O Bruadair, iii. 39–43, 45–59.

[54] Ibid., p. 97; the poem is 'A hundred thanks to God' by Dermot MacCarthy.

[55] *Clarendon corr.*, i. 476.

[56] *Ormonde MSS*, i. 371–3, 373–5; *H.M.C. rep. 11, part 5*, p. 132.

administration was less rapid. The majority of the Protestant revenue-commissioners remained until the revolution, and most of the local revenue-officers in Dublin were retained throughout the Jacobite régime.[57] A different policy was followed for the sheriffs: the nominations made soon after Tyrconnell's arrival were almost all of Catholics. William King remarked that there was only one Protestant – in Donegal – and that he had been confused with a Catholic namesake.[58] These appointments were made to ensure appropriate returns to the contemplated parliament. With the same object in view steps were almost at once taken to call in the charters of corporations by *quo warranto* proceedings.[59] This seems to have had James's approval: Sunderland wrote to Tyrconnell that the king was very pleased about the issue of *quo warrantos* and hoped that the remodelling of corporations and everything else relating to the holding of a parliament would be hurried up.[60] Some of the corporations tried to avert their fate. Dublin hastily changed its by-laws to remove the oath of supremacy, and sent a petition to the King in which they stated that Catholics would be treated on a complete equality with Protestants. A legal member of the corporation was briefed to contest the case in court. The effort was to no purpose. Dublin lost its charter, and a fresh one naming new members was issued in November 1687; it was an impressive document with a portrait of James and the escutcheons of some of the newcomers. The lord mayor, sheriffs and the majority of the corporation were Catholics, but Protestants were given substantial representation. Ten of the twenty-four aldermen were Protestants, and fifteen of the forty-eight burgesses. The new aldermen included Bartholomew van Homrigh and two Quakers, Samuel Claridge and Anthony Sharp.[61] In Belfast negotiations with a Presbyterian merchant, Thomas Pottinger, produced a charter in which Pottinger

[57] King, p. 323.   [58] Ibid., p. 85.

[59] The term for a writ by which the crown could compel a corporation to show that it had exercised its powers according to its charter.

[60] *Cal. S.P. dom., 1686-7*, p. 405.

[61] *Cal. anc. rec. Dublin*, v. 427, 436; *Facs. nat. MSS Ire.*, part iv (ii), plate lxxxiv. Van Homrigh, a Dutch merchant, settled in Dublin, was the father of Swift's Vanessa; he later became commissary-general for William (see p. 137, below). Sharp was a wool merchant (see O. Goodbody, 'Anthony Sharp' in *Dublin Historical Record*, xvi. 12–19).

himself was named as the first sovereign and half the new burgesses were Protestants.[62]

There seems little doubt that the court proceedings in these corporation cases were a foregone conclusion, supported by a show of legal technicalities. William King expressed indignation about them and summarized the Derry case, which involved the rights of the London companies. *The life of James II* mentions Derry as the most obstinate contestant – 'a stubborn people, as they appeared to be afterwards'.[63] There was precedent for the *quo warrantos* in the similar proceedings that Charles II had taken in England, and James himself was to repeat the process by a fresh remodelling of the English corporations. King contended that it was necessary for Protestants to have the power to choose their own representatives in parliament to protect themselves against arbitrary (in other words, anti-Protestant) government. While the corporations remained Protestant bodies, Protestants had nothing to fear from an Irish parliament. But his argument that the remodelling of the corporations undermined the constitution is not altogether tenable. It is true that rules, which had the force of law, had been made by the Irish government in 1672, which obliged members of corporations to take the oath of supremacy; but the rules expressly permitted the viceroy to dispense with the requirement at his discretion.[64] According to King the change was directly responsible for Protestants leaving the country: 'it was intolerable to them to live under the government of their footmen and servants, which they must have done had they stayed'. This was propaganda; most of the new members were merchants or lawyers or had the status, if not the incomes, of gentry. But there is no doubt that Protestants were seriously alarmed by the change, and that some migration took place in consequence. Eleven of the Protestant burgesses in Dublin were named as having failed to take their seats in the new corporation.[65]

[62] W. Benn, *History of Belfast*, pp. 156, 224, 730.

[63] King, p. 316; *James II*, ii. 96.

[64] *Stat. Ire.*, iii. 205 ff.

[65] King, pp. 87–93; *Cal. anc. rec. Dublin*, v. 475. The composition of the new corporations is given in W. Harris, *The life of William III*, app., pp. iv–xvi.

5. TYRCONNELL AND THE KING

There was much apprehensive speculation about the coming parliament. How far could Tyrconnell follow an extreme Catholic policy at the expense of Protestants and the established church? His speech and actions had clearly alarmed Protestants and encouraged the bolder Catholics. An official, but hardly convincing, attempt was made to allay Protestant fears: Tyrconnell's English ancestry and his English wife were advanced as grounds for the English in Ireland to feel secure under his administration.[66] In estimating his real intentions we have to consider what weight to attach to the conflicting accounts which were later written at the Jacobite court. The account that forms the basis of the *Life of James* is highly favourable to this period of Tyrconnell's career. According to it he surprised his critics by his impartial conduct and by the care he took to restrain the exuberance of the new army: 'his zeal for the good and welfare of the country appeared no less, and whatever their jealousies might be in reference to religion it is certain that kingdom was never in a more flourishing way than during the time he governed it'.[67] A less flattering account is that of Thomas Sheridan, one of the remarkable family founded by a former priest, who had collaborated in the production of Bishop Bedell's Irish bible. Thomas was educated at Trinity College, Dublin (of which he became a fellow), but was later involved in the 'popish plot' and by this time had become a Catholic. He came over to Ireland as Tyrconnell's secretary and first commissioner of the revenue. A year later he was dismissed on charges of corruption, but after the revolution he was appointed private secretary to James and spent the rest of his life in the service of the Stuarts. Sheridan's account is clearly designed to exonerate James from responsibility for Tyrconnell's policy in Ireland, and it has provided much ammunition for historians hostile to Tyrconnell.[68]

Sheridan, according to his own account, was specially selected by James for the post of viceroy's secretary in order to

[66] *A vindication of the present government of Ireland.*

[67] *James II*, ii. 96–8.

[68] For Thomas Sheridan see *D.N.B.*; his account is in *Stuart MSS* (H.M.C.), vi. 1–75.

keep a check on Tyrconnell; Sheridan was to see that no man was to be put out of, or into, any employment, civil or military, on account of religion, and that particular care was to be taken 'not to disoblige' the king's Protestant subjects. James told Sheridan, it is alleged, that no English peer would be as well fitted as Tyrconnell to act the 'rough part' of reforming the army and remodelling the corporations, but the king knew Tyrconnell too well to allow him a free hand; Tyrconnell would have to consult Sheridan and the lord chancellor, and if he departed from their advice Sheridan must let Sunderland know.[69] He goes on to say that Tyrconnell failed to take advice, pursued a reckless and extravagant policy, and falsely gave out that he was complying with the king's wishes. The story is not altogether convincing: the 'rough part' could not be played without disobliging the Protestants, and particular examples of Tyrconnell's extremism seem to have had royal approval.[70] Sheridan is in any case a suspect witness, and the corruption proceedings do not give a favourable impression of him. James and Sunderland took care to give no sign of supporting Sheridan against Tyrconnell, and their attitude does not agree well with Sheridan's claim to be a royal watch-dog in Ireland.[71] Caution is needed in accepting his evidence unless it is corroborated. Some points of corroboration are to be found in Sunderland's letters to Tyrconnell, which often have a tone of rebuke. In several instances James refused to agree to Protestants being dismissed, one of them being the Dublin postmaster, whom Tyrconnell suspected of tampering with the letters; Tyrconnell was also forbidden to disarm the Ulster Protestants. But when his proposals were turned down attempts were made to mollify him by saying that the king was generally satisfied with his administration.[72]

James seems to have hoped to get the best of both worlds: Tyrconnell would give him a Catholic army and a well-disposed Catholic parliament, while he himself would appear as an impartial ruler, extending what protection he could to his

[69] *Stuart MSS*, vi. 14.
[70] E.g. the appointment of a second Catholic judge to each court and the hurrying up of *quo warranto* proceedings.
[71] *Anal. Hib.*, i. 46–57; S.P. 63/340, ff. 133, 137 v.
[72] *Cal. S.P. dom., 1686–7*, pp. 421, 442; S.P. 63/340, f. 144.

Protestant subjects. Tyrconnell was well aware that Catholics would resent the maintenance of the Protestant ascendancy, and that they welcomed the administrative changes and hoped for great things from a parliament. He was certainly in favour of modifying the act of settlement, but his plans at this stage seem to have stopped short of outright repeal.

In August 1687 Tyrconnell was told that the king was coming to Chester and wanted to see him there for a general discussion of English and Irish affairs. There was speculation whether he was to be rebuked for his conduct in Ireland, but nothing of the sort seems to have occurred when Tyrconnell met James at Chester; the French ambassador reported that James expressed his entire satisfaction.[73] Another French report said that Tyrconnell had a plan in the event of James's death to put Ireland under the protection of France so as to keep it from William of Orange (as James's son-in-law), and that James had agreed to this in order to provide an asylum for Catholics. The authority for this information was said to be 'a person of quality' at the court who was in Tyrconnell's confidence. Sheridan has a similar story, but puts it a year earlier (before Tyrconnell's appointment as deputy), and he implies that James objected to the scheme.[74] There is no direct evidence that Tyrconnell put forward such a plan, and in any case the queen's pregnancy soon altered the situation.

There is enough evidence to show that the act of settlement was discussed at Chester, but there are variations in the accounts. Sheridan's version is that in discussion with the king Tyrconnell pressed for modification of the act and proposed that it was 'in part to be broken and in part to be confirmed by a new act that should cut off a half or a third from all the new interested men and divide what should be so cut off among some particular sufferers to be named, reserving a sufficient fund of reprisals for all bona fide Catholic purchasers'. Sheridan disagreed 'adding that he judged it necessary for his majesty's honour to break the act entirely and form such a new one as should best answer the ends Charles II proposed'. According to Sheridan the king ordered two drafts to be prepared, one on Tyrconnell's lines and

[73] Ibid., f. 124; Ailesbury, *Memoirs*, i. 149.
[74] Bonrepos to Seignelay, 25 Aug./4 Sept. 1687 (P.R.O., Baschet, p. 172); *Stuart MSS*, vi. 8–10.

one on Sheridan's, which should be brought over at Christmas. The French ambassador reported that Sunderland had told him that James was determined to reverse the settlement, though this was being kept a close secret: English opinion was that it would mean the entire separation of Ireland from England.[75]

In February 1688 Tyrconnell suggested sending over two judges, Nugent and Rice, with proposals for legislation. Sunderland replied that the king approved of their coming 'with the drafts of such bills as were approved at Chester'.[76] The judges took with them a letter from Tyrconnell to James saying that he was sending two draft bills 'in which all imaginable care hath been taken to preserve your majesty's intentions in giving as little disturbance as is possible to the Protestant interest and to restore the Catholics to no more than what seems absolutely necessary to render them any way considerable or capable to serve your majesty here'.[77] Tyrconnell's letter shows that the two drafts were alternatives, which corroborates Sheridan's account. The French ambassador was wrongly informed that the settlement was to be repealed. The first alternative, which came nearer to Sheridan's proposal, provided that the restoration settlement should be reopened. Those whose claims of innocency had not been heard for lack of time were now to have their claims admitted for hearing. If they were adjudged innocent, they were to get back their ancestral lands by paying three years' purchase to the Cromwellian occupier; a common fund would pay another three years' rent to the Cromwellian, who would thus get nearly half the value of the property as compensation for eviction. Those who were not adjudged innocent, but had been named in the act of settlement as entitled to recover their lands after the Cromwellian occupants had been given lands elsewhere, were to get half of their ancestral property, the Cromwellians keeping the other half. It could be argued that this scheme corresponded to Charles II's intentions to be fair to both sides, while giving preferential

[75] *Stuart MSS*, vi. 28; J. Dalrymple, *Memoirs of Great Britain and Ireland*, iii. 262–3.

[76] Sunderland to Tyrconnell, 21 February 1688 (S.P. 63/340, f. 137).

[77] Tyrconnell to James, 28 March 1688 (B.M., Add. MS 32, 095, ff. 259–60).

treatment to innocents – intentions that had been frustrated by the time-bar on innocents' claims and by the fact that lands were not available for compensation to Cromwellians. Tyrconnell admitted that this was a plausible argument in favour of the first draft, but he himself was in favour of the second which did not involve the reopening of old claims or the complete eviction of Cromwellians. The second draft bill, which Tyrconnell favoured, provided that all estates in the possession of Cromwellians should be divided equally between the old owners and the new, and that the division should be made in such a way that all improvements should be included in the half that was left with the new owner. He argued that this alternative would settle things quickly, would be more satisfactory to Protestants, and would decide the question once for all. Tyrconnell's letter has a note of studied moderation. He states the arguments for each alternative and comes down on the side of concession to Protestants, opposed to outright repeal of the settlement.

When the judges reached London the mob is said to have demonstrated, carrying potatoes impaled on sticks and shouting 'make way for the Irish ambassadors'. Sunderland, in an account written after he had joined William, claimed to have frustrated the holding of an Irish parliament and the alteration of the act of settlement. He said he was offered £40,000 for his support, but disclosed the offer to James and told him that the proposal was unjust and would do harm to Ireland.[78] His version is an attempt to commend himself to William and is incompatible with a letter sent to him in May by Tyrconnell, who expresses pleasure that his proposal has been accepted by James and Sunderland and says that the settlement bill and others are being got ready for the coming parliament: all the new charters would be given to the corporations by the middle of June. Subsequently Sunderland informed Tyrconnell that the king had not decided when parliament should meet, 'but you will easily judge it cannot be very soon'. This was in August, when there were already signs of impending trouble.[79] The evidence as a whole suggests that Tyrconnell's proposal for a compromise

---

[78] *Full and impartial account of all the secret consults . . . of the Romish party*, pp. 119–20; Sidney, *Diary*, ii. 379.

[79] *Anal. Hib.*, i. 38; S.P. 63/340, f. 145.

on the settlement was agreed to. A bill on these lines was introduced in the house of lords in 1689, but was discarded in favour of the more radical repeal bill on which the commons insisted.

Up to the autumn of 1688 Tyrconnell's administration, steadied to some extent by James, did much to improve the status of Catholics without driving Protestants into open opposition. Catholics had a dominant position in the army, the judiciary and the local administration. But the land-settlement had not yet been touched, and James discouraged the hearing of individual land-cases in the meantime.[80] The Church of Ireland has been left intact, though the new chapel in the Kilmainham hospital had, with James's approval, been taken over for Tyrconnell's own devotions. The chapel of Dublin castle was also taken over, and £789 was authorized for suitable furnishing.[81] The royal policy of leaving Church of Ireland vacancies unfilled continued, the latest case being the deanery of St Patrick's.[82] The Catholic primate was rebuked for trying to interfere with a Protestant church in Drogheda. Tyrconnell's proposal to admit Catholic bishops to the privy council was not accepted.[83]

Although the status of the established church was not at this stage officially attacked, its practical position was affected by the Catholic revival, and there seem to have been many cases of refusal by Catholics to pay dues to the Protestant clergy. A notable feature of Catholic church life was the return of the religious orders. Brenan, the Catholic archbishop of Cashel gives a striking account of the part they played in his diocese. There were houses of Dominicans, Observantine Franciscans and Jesuits, each with its own public chapel and school. The numbers were very few, but the friars went about in their habits and had begun to repair the old buildings. The orders were a valuable supplement to the work of the secular clergy, who were

[80] *Cal. S.P. dom., 1686–7*, p. 432.

[81] Ibid., pp. 383, 432.

[82] S.P. 63/340, f. 143 v. When a vacancy occurred otherwise than by promotion the chapter of St Patrick's claimed the right under their charter to elect the dean. The chapter pointed this out to Tyrconnell and after some ineffective negotiations proceeded to elect William King on 26 Jan. 1689 (W. M. Mason, *History of St Patrick's Cathedral*, pp. 206–7).

[83] S.P. 63/340, f. 145.

few in number and handicapped by extreme poverty.[84] A sensational piece of educational policy was adopted in June 1688, when the king ordered that Jesuits were to be appointed as masters of government-controlled schools whenever vacancies occurred. The first such appointment was made at Cashel at the end of August.[85] Trinity College, Dublin, was involved in some conflicts with the administration. Clarendon had authorized the college to send a quantity of plate to England. Tyrconnell seized it from the ship, and refused to return it until he got an assurance that it would be used for the improvement of the college and would not be removed without permission.[86] James tried to obtain a fellowship for a graduate named Doyle who had become a Catholic, but the college succeeded in resisting this and apparently satisfied Tyrconnell that Doyle was not a desirable character. Tyrconnell objected to the election of the second duke of Ormond as chancellor of the university, but was overruled by James.[87]

Protestants were certainly uneasy during this period, but migration seems to have been on a comparatively small scale up to the autumn of 1688. There were signs of a trade recession, but there was no catastrophic fall in the revenue. Catholics had received enough encouragement to enable them to restrain their impatience for a complete reversal of the previous position. By the middle of 1688, with so much political and administrative power in Catholic hands and with the dynasty apparently assured, they could hope for great things from the forthcoming parliament and trust that the rest of their demands would soon be satisfied.

[84] P. Power, *A bishop of the penal times*, pp. 85–6.

[85] S.P. 63/340, ff. 144, 146–7.

[86] *Cal. S.P. dom.*, 1686–7, p. 376; J. W. Stubbs, *History of the University of Dublin*, pp. 124–7.

[87] Ibid., p. 122; S.P. 63/340, f. 150.

III

IRELAND AND THE
ENGLISH REVOLUTION

~~~~~~

I. BIRTH OF AN HEIR

UP TO THE AUTUMN of 1687 Mary of Orange was looked on as the natural successor to James, whose second wife, Mary of Modena, had no surviving child and had not given birth for several years. Catholics in Ireland were anxious about the future and tried to prepare for it by improving their status and economic position. Protestants felt able to endure with comparative patience what they hoped would be the temporary discomforts of Tyrconnell's administration. Reports of the queen's pregnancy gave fresh courage to Catholics, and produced in Protestants mixed feelings of disbelief and despondency. The importance of the news, of course, depended on whether the baby would prove to be a boy; but Catholics saw no reason why providence should stop at half measures. Official thanksgivings were ordered, and a Dublin diarist noted that Catholics, who had dreaded a Protestant successor more than doomsday, were suspiciously confident that a son would result.[1]

The birth, which aroused controversy in England, was made the occasion for Irish celebrations in the grand style: a vice-regal cavalcade proceeded from Kilmainham Hospital to the Castle, where high mass was celebrated by the Catholic archbishop in pontifical robes; the conduits ran with wine,

[1] *Ormonde MSS*, n.s., viii. 352.

44

largesse was scattered in the streets, and fireworks on the river wound up the festivities. The day's events were fulsomely reported in the *London Gazette*, which must have riled many of its readers.[2]

The prospect of an heir apparent led to a growing estrangement between James and William of Orange. One result of this was a move (apparently initiated by Tyrconnell) to recall the English regiments that had, by a long-standing arrangement, been seconded for service in Holland.[3] Although some of the officers and men were Catholics, James seems to have been suspicious of the use that William might make of the force. He had tried hard to get William to accept an Irish Catholic commander, the earl of Carlingford, but had met with a firm refusal.[4] At the beginning of 1688 James wrote to William that he found it necessary to recall the regiments for service at home.[5] The States General reluctantly agreed to let the officers go, but were unwilling to part with the men, though they later let some of them go. In the event, most of the Protestants stayed in Holland and those who returned to England were mainly Catholic; their places were taken by Protestants dismissed by Tyrconnell from the Irish army, who are said to have urged William to active opposition to his father-in-law.[6] Those who returned to England formed the nucleus of three additional regiments, paid for by Louis XIV.

2. TEIG IN ENGLAND

Ireland was an obvious source of recruits to man the new regiments, and Tyrconnell was asked to send over men selected from the Irish army, ten from each company. They were, in the first instance, earmarked for Colonel Roger MacElligott, a Kerryman who had commanded one of the regiments in Holland, many of whose officers were Irish Catholics.[7] The coming of the Irish soldiers caused much stir and resentment in

---

[2] *London Gazette*, 12 July 1688.
[3] J. Dalrymple, *Memoirs of Great Britain and Ireland*, iii. 174–7.
[4] *Cal. S.P. dom., 1686–7*, pp. 220, 246, 248, 255, 263.
[5] Dalrymple, p. 181.
[6] *Stuart MSS*, vi. 21.
[7] Tyrconnell to Sunderland, 9 May 1688 (*Anal. Hib.*, i. 39).

England, and was one of the reasons for growing opposition to James. In August 1688 Tyrconnell warned James that a *coup d'état* was being planned in Holland, a warning which was at first rejected: 'as to the noise of the preparations made by our neighbours, the king is very well assured that whatever the design may be it is not against him'.[8] But the French ambassador kept urging that Irish regiments should be brought over to strengthen the king's position in England, and in the last week of September Tyrconnell was ordered to send three regiments of infantry and one of dragoons to Chester or Liverpool: they were to be given an advance of one month's pay and to bring no wives or other women with them. An equivalent number of new regiments was to be raised to bring the Irish army up to strength. The infantry units were the Guards and the regiments of Anthony Hamilton and Lord Forbes.[9] The Guards and Forbes's men created a surprisingly good impression. The Guards were described as 'tall, sprightly young men, their clothes also very fresh and fashionably made, each man having a frock to keep him clean'. Forbes's men were 'expert at their arms' and 'behave themselves very civilly'. A much less favourable impression was created by MacElligott's regiment, which was the terror of Portsmouth. The soldiers robbed, drank and beat up the inhabitants; there was a riot after an Irish soldier had fired a shot into a Protestant church.[10] Portsmouth was a key position, providing communication with France. The infant prince was sent there with an escort of Irish dragoons, but the naval authorities refused to let him embark.[11] James's natural son, the duke of Berwick, was made governor of Portsmouth and tried to incorporate into his regiment some of MacElligott's surplus Irish. This led to a flat refusal on the part of five captains to take 'raw, undisciplined Irishmen': their consequent cashiering caused general indignation, and William made effective use

---

[8] Sunderland to Tyrconnell, 8 Sept. 1688 (S.P. 63/340, f. 150).

[9] Same to same, 25, 29 Sept.; 4, 12 Oct. 1688; S.P. 63/340, ff. 151 v, 152, 152 v); Dalrymple, pp. 202–6. Anthony Hamilton, author of the *Mémoires de Grammont*, was a well-known figure of the restoration court and a brother of Lt-Gen. Richard Hamilton; Forbes was son of the earl of Granard and remained loyal to James even after his father had joined William.

[10] *H.M.C., rep. 12*, app. vii. 213–18.

[11] *H.M.C., rep. 11*, app. v. 210; *rep. 12*, app. vii. 225.

of the incident in the propaganda he addressed to James's army.[12]

In October London was disturbed by a riot which began with Irish troops attacking a crowd of jeering boys.[13] English opinion was expressed in lampoons, one of which, written while the Dutch invasion was imminent, contained the following lines:

> Now while we are hearing and telling of lies,
> A cloud from the west does quite darken our eyes.
> All Egypt's ten plagues do at once on us fall,
> For in naming the Irish that comprehends all.
> > To what purpose they come
> > Is no secret to Rome,
> And to guess at the consequence we may presume.[14]

The affront given to the English army by the importation of Irish Catholic regiments undoubtedly contributed to its abandonment of James. His reliance on Catholics had its corollary in the alienation of Protestants. The situation had echoes from fifty years earlier, when Strafford was accused of plotting to 'reduce this kingdom' with an Irish Catholic army. William, who landed in Devonshire on November 5, advanced with deliberation and met singularly little resistance. Jacobite publicity had to make the most of a minor success gained by Colonel Patrick Sarsfield at Wincanton in Somersetshire.[15] When Churchill deserted on November 24, James had little to hope for.

After the collapse of James's cause the Irish regiments were ordered to be disbanded, but their disposal presented a major problem to the Williamite government. About 1,800 men from MacElligott's regiment and other units were interned in the Isle of Wight, but a number, including MacElligott himself, escaped to France. Arrangements were made to send to Hamburg two ship-loads of men intended for the imperial service to fight against the Turks. But four or five hundred of them made their way from Hamburg to France and seem to have got back to

[12] Dalrymple, i. 227; *Ellis corr.*, ii. 184.

[13] *H.M.C.*, *rep. 12*, app. vii. 216.

[14] Collection of poems, lampoons, etc., 1670–90 (Austrian National Library, MS 14090, f. 442).

[15] *London Gazette*, 24 Nov. 1688.

Ireland.[16] Other units marched north, making for Liverpool to the accompaniment of sensational reports of burning and massacre.[17] The 'Irish night' was one of terror in London and elsewhere, caused by rumours of an intended massacre. An Irish commentator later described London as 'all in a tremblement' at the approach of the Irish, and regretted that there was no ground for the panic: if the Irish had burned the city, it would have been fit punishment for its rebellion and would have saved James's throne; 'but sparing of blood, as well in this occasion as afterwards in Ireland, proved his ruin'.[18]

A great many of the Irish got away either to Ireland or to France. William was none too certain of his position and took no effective steps to stop them. A Dublin letter of February 1689 refers to 1,200 Irish troops having been brought back by Chester packet boats, and we hear of others being shipped off from Liverpool.[19] Some of the fugitives were arrested, but they were few in comparison with those who got away. William and his government were criticized for their leniency in allowing Sarsfield and other Irishmen of note to leave England: they should have been held as hostages for the proper treatment of Protestants in Ireland.[20] Bringing Irish troops to England had not made James secure and did much to give the ordinary Englishman an unfavourable impression of the Irish.

3. REACTIONS IN IRELAND

The overthrow of James created much confusion in Ireland. Tyrconnell was in a very difficult position. Nearly half his army was in England, trade had come to a standstill and his finances were at a very low ebb. Protestant sympathy for the revolution was evident, and an immediate Williamite attack was expected. Both in Dublin and the north there were large numbers of armed Protestants and there was a serious risk that they might

[16] *London Gazette*, 6 June 1689; J. Macpherson, *Original papers*, i. 330; J. L. Garland, 'The regiment of MacElligott, 1688–9' in *Irish Sword*, i. 121–7.

[17] *H.M.C., rep. 12*, app. vii. 229.

[18] 'A light to the blind' (N.L.I., MS 476, p. 385).

[19] *The present miserable condition of Ireland*; *Cal. S.P. dom., 1689–90*, p. 14.

[20] B.M., Eg. MS 917, f. 104.

overthrow the Jacobite régime. A plan was made to seize Dublin Castle and arrest Tyrconnell, but it was abandoned because of the opposition of Lords Granard and Mountjoy, two Protestants still in high command in the army.[21] Overtures from Ulster were made to William,[22] and there was open defiance at Derry, where the gates were shut on December 7 against Lord Antrim's regiment. At the same time there was widespread panic among Protestants and fear of another 1641. The alarm was largely due to the circulation of an anonymous warning that the Irish were to rise on December 9 and start a general massacre. There was a hurried exodus of frightened Protestants to England, Scotland and the Isle of Man. A Dublin diarist noted the number of ships that left each day, 'laden mostly with women, children and such goods as they could get on board'.[23]

On December 8 Tyrconnell issued a proclamation, promising protection to loyal subjects and denouncing false reports, whether of Catholics massacring Protestants or vice versa. He threatened to punish those who met 'at unseasonable times with fire-arms in great numbers'. This particularly referred to the Dublin Protestants who had posted themselves in such places as Trinity College and the earl of Meath's liberties, where they kept armed guard.[24] Tyrconnell's policy was to calm the fears of Protestants and stop the flight. He persuaded the Protestant archbishop of Dublin to have a reassuring message read in the churches. At the same time, he decided to bring his own forces up to a substantial level and is reported to have issued at this stage commissions for raising 20,000 men, a figure that was to be greatly exceeded in the following months.[25]

The news of James's flight (which finally took place on December 24) and rumours of a Williamite invasion of Ireland caused alarm to Catholics, and a number of them were reported to have sent their property to France and other places.[26] Meanwhile, in spite of Tyrconnell's efforts, the Protestant

---

[21] *True and impartial account.*

[22] [C. Leslie], *Answer to a book intituled The state of the Protestants*, p. 77 (hereafter cited as Leslie).

[23] King, pp. 101, 345; *Ormonde MSS*, n.s., viii. 356.

[24] Ibid., ii. 388–9; n.s., viii. 356.

[25] Ibid., p. 357.   [26] Ibid.

exodus continued. In the rural areas outside Ulster many abandoned their farms and livestock and fled to the north or to England. Others banded together for protection against a restive Catholic population. In Bandon the Protestants turned out the Catholics and held the town for a considerable time till they were brought under control by Justin MacCarthy, who listened to the representation of the Rev. Nicholas Brady (the hymn-writer) and let them off with an indemnity of £1,500. MacCarthy was equally successful in reducing other centres of militant Protestants in Munster.[28] In the north the Protestants formed themselves into armed associations, which openly sympathized with the revolution and established effective control over wide areas. In Sligo the association declared its determination to 'unite with England and hold to the lawful government thereof and a free parliament'. In Down the declared object was to preserve 'the public peace of the nation . . . in these distracted times wherein no lawful government is established in the kingdom of Ireland'.[29]

Tyrconnell played a difficult hand with much skill. He entered into negotiations with the Ulster Protestants, using two ministers to reassure the Presbyterians and himself holding talks with an influential Antrim landlord, Sir Robert Colvill.[30] Relations with rebel Derry were restored by letting it be garrisoned by Protestant troops of Mountjoy's regiment. Mountjoy himself was allowed to bargain on behalf of his fellow Protestants in the north on surprisingly stringent terms. He proposed that, pending orders from James, Tyrconnell should cease to levy fresh troops; that no more troops should be sent into Ulster; and that there should be no arrests 'for any tumultuous meetings or arming of men'.[31]

There was much speculation whether Tyrconnell would come to terms with William. Some of his council considered that resistance was hopeless and that negotiation was the only prudent course. Tyrconnell's own conversation gave many, both Catholics and Protestants, the impression that he was willing to

[28] *A true and impartial account*; J. A. Murphy, *Justin MacCarthy*, p. 16.
[29] M. O Duigeannain, 'Three seventeenth-century documents' in *Galway Arch. Jn.* xvii. 154–61; *Montgomery MSS*, p. 273.
[30] *Faithful history of the northern affairs of Ireland.*
[31] *Ormonde MSS*, n.s., viii. 14.

submit. Communication with William was begun by a letter from Keating, one of the remaining Protestant judges, to Sir John Temple, the Irish solicitor-general, who had gone to England. Sir John was a brother of Sir William Temple, who had been ambassador at the Hague and was well known to William. Keating reported that Tyrconnell was taking every opportunity to declare, in public as well as in private, that he was ready to disband the army and give up the government; Catholics were willing to return to the position in which they were at the end of Charles II's reign, but wished to be assured that they would be no worse off. The letter was taken seriously and, on the recommendation of Sir William Temple's son, Richard Hamilton was sent to Ireland to negotiate on William's behalf. He was one of the celebrated Hamilton brothers, Catholic nephews of the first duke of Ormond. He had served as a soldier in France and then in James's army; he was made a major-general in November 1688 and soon after was taken prisoner by William. He was on intimate terms with Tyrconnell, whose wife had previously been married to George Hamilton.[33] Danby, the leading English politician, was opposed to the Hamilton plan, and suggested that a squadron of ships would be a more effective way of getting Tyrconnell to surrender. But William had no confidence in the English navy and thought that 'the business of Ireland was in a fair way to be settled'.[34] When Hamilton reached Dublin he failed to execute his commission and was believed to have urged Tyrconnell to hold out. A Protestant observer remarked that 'the papists lit bonfires when Dick Hamilton came over; they said he was worth 10,000 men'.[35]

Was Tyrconnell really prepared to hand over to William? Protestants in Dublin were convinced that he was, and the Catholic population apparently formed the same opinion; according to the French ambassador they threatened to burn him in his house if he tried to make peace with William.[36] The official Jacobite view was that Tyrconnell had made 'a prudent show of wavering'; that he 'strove to amuse the Prince of Orange's agents with a feigned disposition of submission till he

---

[32] King, pp. 347–52.   [33] R. Clark, *Life of Anthony Hamilton*.
[34] A. Browning, *Thomas Osborne*, i. 424.
[35] *H.M.C., rep. 12*, app. vi. 141.   [36] D'Avaux, p. 50.

could put himself and the kingdom in a position not to be forced to it'.[37] This was a reasonable conclusion to draw after Tyrconnell had clearly come out for resistance. But later events were to reveal his adaptability to circumstances. His tentative approach could well have been developed, had William succeeded in making effective intervention in Ireland before the arrival of James. He told Sir Robert Colvill that he was weary of the sword, but added 'what shall I do with it? There is no one to receive it. Shall I throw it into the kennel?'[38]

The refugee Protestants in England constantly pressed for a force to be sent to Ireland without delay. Clarendon was their spokesman, but found William indifferent: 'it is certain the prince has very little curiosity, or sets a very small value on Ireland'.[39] When the convention parliament met on 22 January 1689, each member was presented with a set of aphorisms on Ireland, drawn up by Richard Cox, a County Cork lawyer who later became lord chancellor of Ireland. The theme was the importance of maintaining the connection between the two countries, the practicability of military intervention, and the prospect of making the operation self-financing by confiscating the estates of James's supporters.[40] William's address to the convention referred to the dangerous condition of the Protestants of Ireland, 'requiring a large and speedy succour'.[41] But no speedy steps were taken. The army was unreliable and money was short; Scotland was undecided and English politicians were wrangling about the constitution. The hoped-for invasion of Munster did not take place; no help reached Ulster until after James had landed in Ireland. Jacobites thought that William had lost an opportunity: had he sent a few troops to Ireland immediately, he would have 'easily effected what afterwards cost him so much blood and treasure'.[42]

4. TYRCONNELL TAKES CONTROL

Encouraged by the coming of Hamilton, Tyrconnell continued to build up his position with subtlety and skill. Mountjoy's

---

[37] *James II*, ii. 319. [38] *H.M.C., rep. 12*, app. vi. 139.
[39] *Clarendon corr.*, ii. 319.
[40] *Aphorisms relating to the kingdom of Ireland.*
[41] W. Harris, *William III*, p. 164. [42] *James II*, ii. 322.

military experience and local influence marked him out as a potential leader of the Ulster Protestants. He was sent off to France, ostensibly to ask James's permission for Tyrconnell to make terms, the alternative being to turn Ireland into 'a heap of rubbish'.[43] With him went Judge Rice with secret instructions that sent Mountjoy to the Bastille. Shortly afterwards, two officers, a Frenchman and an Irishman, arrived from France to report on the Irish situation and promise a limited quantity of French arms. At the end of January Tyrconnell informed James that he had recently given out commissions for nearly forty regiments of foot, four regiments of dragoons and two of horse, making a total of nearly 40,000 newly raised levies.[44] The army was now virtually all Catholic; most of the Protestants who had remained up to the revolution had since left of their own accord or had been dismissed.[45] The French officer, Pointis, noted that about half the new levies were armed with muskets or worm-eaten pikes; the rest had sticks tipped with nails. He was, however, struck by their enthusiasm, which kept them going without pay or uniforms: they were resolved to perish rather than submit to Protestant domination; Tyrconnell could have raised 100,000 if he had wished, and the soldiers showed great attention to arms drill.[46] Protestants gave the Catholic clergy credit for much of the enthusiasm: 'the popish party arm themselves with great vigour by the instigation of the priests, and were not to have mass unless they had skeeans or some other weapons'.[47] Pointis's account is borne out by Tyrconnell's statement that the men were 'unclothed' and mostly without arms, and that up to the end of February they were being maintained by their officers 'to the ruin of most of them'; after that they would have to live off the country.[48]

Though Tyrconnell had been promised arms from France, his chief need was money and there had been no indication that he was to get it. He asked James to impress on Louis the urgent need for 500,000 crowns, which with his own resources would last him for a year; he added that, if Louis wanted security for

[43] *Ormonde MSS*, n.s., viii. 14.
[44] Campana de Cavelli, *Les derniers Stuarts*, ii. 532.
[45] *Ormonde MSS*, n.s., viii. 359.
[46] Campana de Cavelli, ii. 538. [47] *Ormonde MSS*, n.s., viii. 359.
[48] Campana de Cavelli, p. 532.

repayment, it would be worth handing over Galway or Waterford to him.[49]

The natural consequence of not paying the troops was that they fended for themselves, and there were frequent complaints of robbery and cattle-driving. A Protestant critic complained that the soldiers had 'already plundered, slaughtered and destroyed as much as would, right managed, have fed an army of 40,000 for a whole year: . . . some papists . . . do openly say that there needs no army to conquer them, for famine will destroy them before August'.[50] Tyrconnell received many protests and tried to remedy matters by a proclamation, addressed to army commanders, in which he denounced 'the depredations committed by loose and idle people which are by some imputed to the new levies, to the great dishonour of the army'.[51] The breakdown of law and order was a major factor in the Protestants' decision to safeguard themselves by armed associations. Feelings between the communities were very strained and the Catholic population had many old scores to repay, though there was much less violence than there had been in 1641 and the more responsible Catholics tried to restrain their co-religionists. Centres such as Petty's iron-works at Kenmare were clearly organized for protection; where Protestants were stronger, as in Sligo, self-defence was accompanied by active aggression against the Catholic population.[52] Protestants continued to leave the country in large numbers, and Tyrconnell noted with displeasure that the ships which took them away had brought no goods to Dublin, which was running short of coal and other commodities. He therefore ordered that no passengers should leave unless their ships had brought in cargoes.[53] Shipping between England and Ireland seems to have been subject to little interference up to this time, but the mails were censored: 'here is no public news-letter nor gazette suffered to be in any coffee-house, only the *Dublin Gazette* which is a legend of their own composition.'[54]

[49] Campana de Cavelli, p. 534.

[50] *The present dangerous condition of the Protestants.*

[51] *Ormonde MSS*, ii. 392.

[52] *An exact relation . . . of the Protestants of Kilmare*; J. G. Simms, 'Sligo in the Jacobite war' in *Ir. Sword*, vii. 124–6.

[53] *The present dangerous condition of the Protestants.*

[54] *An account of the present miserable state of affairs.*

Towards the end of February Tyrconnell felt strong enough to disarm the Dublin Protestants. The orders were to send the arms to the parish churches; those who failed to comply would not only be punished but 'must run the risk of the ill consequences which may fall upon them by the disorders of the soldiers'. Gentlemen, however, were allowed to keep their swords. Trinity College was searched as well as a number of Protestant charities. The search was said to have revealed several thousand weapons, which were thus made available for the army. Orders were also given for the seizure of all serviceable horses. These actions were justified by the imminence of a Williamite invasion and the risk that arms and horses in private ownership would fall into the invaders' hands.[55] They were soon followed by a proclamation commandeering arms and horses throughout the country. It referred to the 'treasonable associations' that had harassed loyal subjects and committed acts of hostility against the government. Payment was to be made for serviceable horses and those unfit for military use were to be returned to the owners, who were also to get back horses used for ploughing or the carriage of goods. The poet O Bruadair rejoiced at the humiliation inflicted on Protestants by the seizure of their horses; but his hymn of triumph was quickly followed by a poem of disillusion, regretting the return of the unwanted horses.[56] In all these proclamations Tyrconnell was concerned to present the image of a reasonable and impartial governor whose object was the preservation of order and the protection of all loyal subjects. The orders for the seizure of arms and horses make no mention of religious distinctions. In practice those of Catholics were already available for the army, and it was Protestants who were adversely affected. But Protestants seem to have sensed that Tyrconnell was trying to govern impartially, and they believed that he had had special orders from James to be 'kind to his Protestant subjects that were loyal'. Tyrconnell himself assured James that he had been very tender of Protestants, knowing his majesty's 'pious care' of them.[57]

By the beginning of March 1689 Tyrconnell had established control of all Ireland outside Ulster, with the exception of Sligo

[55] *Ormonde MSS*, ii. 392–3; n.s., viii. 360–1.
[56] Ibid., ii. 393–5; O Bruadair, iii. 116–25.
[57] *Ormonde MSS*, n.s., viii. 360; Campana de Cavelli, p. 533.

where a militant association remained until later in the month. It then withdrew in response to a message from Lundy, commander of the Derry garrison, who urged its members to join him.[58] Elsewhere the Protestants generally were disarmed and a Catholic administration, supported by a large but ill-equipped army, was in full command.

William's declaration of 22 Febuary 1689, which called on Irish Jacobites to lay down their arms and submit to him by April 10, met with no response. It promised pardon and toleration for Catholics who obeyed, and threatened military action and confiscation of estates against those who resisted.[59] Tyrconnell's vigorous administration was a major factor in the French decisions to send James to Ireland and contribute officers, money and arms to his cause. With these prospects in view, Catholics had no incentive to listen to William's promises and threats.

In Derry the citizens, after their initial defiance, had accepted a garrison which nominally owed allegiance to James, under a commander whose allegiance was more than nominal. But in January an envoy from Derry was sent to England who succeeded in interviewing William and obtaining a promise of military aid. This aid arrived not long after James had reached Ireland. In Enniskillen the local Protestants had formed their own garrison in December under an experienced soldier, Gustavus Hamilton, and had driven off a small detachment of Tyrconnell's army. They maintained their position without challenge for some months, and in March proclaimed William and Mary. In eastern Ulster the centre of resistance was at Hillsborough, County Down, where representatives of several counties formed a 'supreme council' with the earl of Mountalexander at its head and regiments of horse and foot at its disposal.[60] They sent an agent to ask William for protection and military aid and received a reply assuring them that William was resolved to take early steps to rescue them from the 'oppression and terrors' to which they were being exposed, but no material aid ever reached them.[61] Mountalexander was an ineffective leader and his associates quarrelled with one another.

[58] *Irish Sword*, vii. 126.   [59] *H.M.C. rep. 12*, app. vi. 164–5.
[60] *Faithful history of the northern affairs of Ireland.*
[61] *Montgomery MSS*, p. 278.

In January the Protestants had plotted to disarm the Catholic troops in Belfast and Carrickfergus, but divided counsels resulted in the complete failure of the scheme. It was followed in February by another move against Carrickfergus. This also was a failure, but resulted in a truce that on paper appeared to be satisfactory to the Protestants: one of the Jacobite regiments was to be disbanded, and the townsfolk of Carrickfergus were to be allowed to organize their own defence without interference from the garrison. One of the conditions, however, was that the earl of Antrim, the Jacobite commander, was to communicate the terms to Tyrconnell, who was thus kept informed of the Ulster situation.[62]

Tyrconnell's next move was to send Richard Hamilton, whom he promoted to lieutenant-general, northwards with a force of 2,500 men, including cavalry, dragoons and a few pieces of field-artillery. On 14 March 1689 Hamilton easily routed Mountalexander's forces in an engagement known as 'the break of Dromore'. The Protestants appear to have mismanaged matters; the pick of their cavalry did not arrive in time, and the infantry, in danger of being surrounded by Hamilton's horse, saved themselves by flight.[63] The defeat was a severe blow to the morale of the Protestants and completely broke up their organization in eastern Ulster. Mountalexander escaped to the Isle of Man; Hillsborough and other Protestant garrisons in Down and Antrim offered no resistance; and the Jacobite force was not checked until it reached Coleraine, where it was repulsed by Major Gustavus Hamilton (not to be confused with his namesake at Enniskillen). A second attempt, in which boats were used to cross the Bann and threaten the defenders in the rear, was more successful and the Protestants fell back on Derry.[64] Thus by the end of March, soon after James had reached Dublin, his authority extended over the whole country, with the exception of the area covered by Derry and Enniskillen. Tyrconnell had deserved well of his master.

[62] Ibid., pp. 275–6.
[63] Ibid., pp. 280–1; *James II*, ii. 327; D'Avaux, supp., p. 7.
[64] D'Avaux, p. 91.

IV

THE COMING OF JAMES

~~~~~~

I. PREPARATIONS IN FRANCE

THE REVOLUTION was a shattering experience for James. The shock showed itself in severe attacks of nose-bleeding, which came on when he advanced to meet William and left him dazed and unable to act with decision. Nothing seemed left of the courage and energy that he had shown as soldier and sailor in earlier life. His first attempt at flight ended ignominiously with detection and return in captivity to London, where his presence was an embarrassment to William. It was debated whether he should be kept as a prisoner in order to put pressure on Tyrconnell to hand over the government of Ireland, or whether he should be sent to Holland as security for the safety of the Irish Protestants. William rejected both courses, which would have put an unbearable strain on James's daughter, Mary.[1] A second flight was deliberately encouraged, and James finally left the English coast on 24 December 1688.

When he reached France he gave the impression of contented apathy. One account describes him as 'tranquil and insensible; he would rather stay in France occupied with devotional exercises and hunting, but he is driven to Ireland not only by Tyrconnell but by the French'.[2] Louis received him and his attendants with friendliness and generosity, establishing him at

[1] G. Burnet, *History of his own time*, iii. 336–7.
[2] Campana de Cavelli, ii. 528.

58

St Germain with a liberal income. This treatment might in part be due to sympathy for a brother monarch in distress, but it was clear that James could also be used as a pawn in the European game. Louis was faced with opposition on all sides: from Holland, Spain, the emperor and the pope. William's seizure of power in England was a severe blow to Louis's ambitions, and the restoration of James would be in the French interest. The question was how much effort France should make to achieve it. She was already heavily involved in Europe, and an expedition to the British Isles would be a major extension of her commitment. James himself seemed likely to be an inert passenger and, once restored, might be the tool of English politicians and forget his French benefactor.

The situation was complicated by differences between Louis's advisers. Louvois, the minister for war, had a continental outlook and did not wish to divert his resources from the mainland. Seignelay (Colbert's son) was minister of marine and was ready to exploit French naval strength in an overseas enterprise. Louis held the balance between them. His own experience was purely military; left to himself he would probably have decided against an overseas expedition. But Louvois was out of favour. His military operations had not been going well and, what was more important, Madame de Maintenon disliked him and preferred Seignelay.[3] The best prospect for an expeditionary force seemed to be Ireland. Tyrconnell had written to James in December to say that all was quiet and that William had not so far attacked.[4] Seignelay decided to send a naval gunnery officer, the marquis de Pointis, to Ireland to report on the situation and on the prospects for a successful expedition.

Pointis arrived in Ireland on 15 January 1689, together with an Irish officer, Captain Michael Roth, who brought a letter from James to Tyrconnell. The letter was not encouraging. James hoped that Tyrconnell would be able to defend himself 'till summer at least'. All Louis had been persuaded to promise was seven or eight thousand muskets; any further French commitment would depend on the information received from Ireland.[5] There was no indication that James himself might come. Tyrconnell replied with detailed information on the state of the

[3] E. Lavisse, *Histoire de France*, viii. 150; Burnet, iv. 30–1.
[4] *James II*, ii. 320.   [5] Ibid.

country and strongly urged James to come: 'if, sir, your majesty will in person come hither and bring with you those succours necessary to support the country . . . I will be responsible to you that you shall be entirely the master of this kingdom and of everything in it; and, sir, I beg of you to consider whether you can with honour continue where you are when you may possess a kingdom of your own'.[6] Pointis sent a report to Seignelay that without help the Jacobite forces could not hold out against William, but that if they were supplied with arms, officers and money they could easily repel an invasion and could also carry the fight into England.[7] Tyrconnell in a second letter to James stressed the need for early help. He seemed to sense reluctance on James's part to come to Ireland: 'if your majesty would take a step here to arrange our affairs, you could again return afterwards if you found it necessary'.[8]

The French naval archives contain a memorandum, evidently based on Pointis's report, entitled: 'Reasons why the king of England should go to Ireland'. It laid great emphasis on the psychological effect of James's presence in Ireland and of the value to France of being able to ruin English trade and divide William's forces. An interesting point was that English Jacobites would prefer James to be in Ireland rather than in France, to which they had an absolute repugnance.[9] Louvois's reluctance to support an Irish expedition was strengthened by the fact that Lauzun wanted to command it. Lauzun was a courtier, whose varied career had included imprisonment and a proposal of marriage to Louis's cousin. He had volunteered to escort Mary of Modena and her baby on their flight from England, and had thus earned her good opinion and a promise that he should command the Irish expedition. Mary was much more alert and active than her husband, and those who wished to influence James often enlisted her support. Lauzun failed to get the Irish command in 1689 but, to the detriment of the Jacobite cause and of his own reputation, obtained it in the following year.

There were several changes of French policy in regard to Ireland. Louvois's earlier plan envisaged a small expedition under the French major-general, Maumont, to bring money and arms to Tyrconnell, and also transport the units that had been

---

[6] Campana de Cavelli, ii. 531.   [7] Ibid., pp. 538–9.
[8] Ibid., p. 536.   [9] Ibid., pp. 524–5.

formed from Irish and British subjects of James who had made their way to France; these units would be under the command of the duke of Berwick, James's natural son, who had enrolled the men as they came over. In the improbable event of Tyrconnell having made terms with William, Maumont was to return without landing; otherwise he was to co-operate with Tyrconnell. He was to find out what Tyrconnell proposed to do if there was a Williamite invasion: the best course seemed to be to engage the invaders at once before the Protestants joined them. He was to urge Tyrconnell to confiscate the Protestants' property and use it to maintain his army. He could assure him that if he held out till the winter Louis would send a French corps which would be able not only to resist William but to invade Scotland or England. As the preservation of Ireland was a paramount French interest, more money would be sent, altogether up to a million livres (*c.* £80,000) by the end of July. A ministry of war memorandum emphasized the importance of speed and secrecy in organizing the expedition. Neither document mentioned the possibility of James accompanying the expedition.[10] But Seignelay was already assured that James would go, and the decision was reinforced by some cogent arguments from Vauban, the celebrated military engineer, who wrote to Louvois: 'I have an idea that when a man plays his last stake he ought to play it himself or to be on the spot. The king of England seems to be in this condition. His last stake is Ireland; it appears to me that he ought to go there, where with the help that the king can give him he can get on his legs again and be supported by those of his subjects who remain loyal to him'.[11]

Louvois's first letter to Maumont was followed by a second, informing him that James was to go to Ireland and that Maumont was to be subordinate to Rosen, now designated as military commander.[12] Rosen was a German from the Baltic who had been forty years in the French service and had reached the rank of lieutenant-general. He had a rough manner and was not an ideal choice for the mission. An important member of the expedition was to be the comte d'Avaux, an able diplomat who had been ambassador at the Hague, where he had been quick to report William's designs. His correspondence is an invaluable

[10] *Anal. Hib.*, xxi. 10–11, 18–19; Campana de Cavelli, ii. 501.
[11] F. C. Turner, *James II*, p. 463.   [12] *Anal. Hib.*, xxi. 22–3.

source for events in Ireland for the first twelve months of James's stay.[13] His instructions had already been drawn up by Seignelay. They informed him that James was to leave for Ireland immediately and that Louis wished him to be accompanied by an ambassador capable of giving good advice and of reporting back full information. D'Avaux was to do his best to reconcile Protestants to Catholics and to convince them that James would treat both alike with mild benevolence. He was also to smooth out differences between James's chief supporters and to establish contacts with Jacobites in England and Scotland. He was to be given 500,000 livres (*c.* £40,000), of which 300,000 were to be paid under James's instructions and the rest kept in reserve.[14]

2. JOURNEY TO IRELAND

James left St Germain on 15/25 February 1689. Louis's farewell to him is said to have been: 'the best that I can wish you is that we shall never see each other again'. James was held up at Brest by bad weather but finally, after a smooth passage, reached Kinsale on March 12, the first English king to visit Ireland for nearly three centuries. His convoy encountered nothing more than an English merchant ship.[15] A feature of the period is the failure of both French and English to interfere seriously with one another's lines of communication. The effect of the revolution was to throw the English naval programme out of gear. Men were short, pay in arrears, refitting delayed. It was not till March 1689 that William appointed one of his active supporters, Arthur Herbert, as first lord of the admiralty and commander-in-chief of the fleet in the Channel and Irish waters. Belated instructions were sent to Herbert to cruise between Ushant and the Irish coast to prevent the French sending troops or arms to Ireland or Scotland. In case he took James's own ship, he was, by William's personal orders, to treat him with respect and take him to a Dutch port.[16]

[13] *Négociations de M. le comte d'Avaux en Irlande, 1689–90*, ed. J. Hogan (I.M.C.) (cited as d'Avaux).
[14] D'Avaux, pp. 1–6.   [15] Ibid., p. 23.
[16] J. Ehrman, *The navy in the war of William III*, pp. 255–61; *Finch MSS* (H.M.C.), ii. 194–5.

The French fleet consisted of twenty-two ships, which brought a number of James's Irish, Scots and English supporters as well as French officers, arms and ammunition. James was accompanied by his two natural sons – the Duke of Berwick and his younger brother, the grand prior. The English Jacobites included the duke of Powis, Lord Thomas Howard and Thomas Cartwright, bishop of Chester. John Drummond, earl of Melfort, was the most notable Scot; he was appointed secretary of state for Ireland, a post in which he made himself highly unpopular with both Irish and French. Among the Irish were Judge Rice and Colonels Patrick Sarsfield and Roger McElligott.[17]

From Kinsale James proceeded to Cork, where he got a great welcome and was met by Tyrconnell who presented his report and was rewarded for his services with a dukedom.[18] The bishop of Chester introduced his brother bishop of Cork and some of the Protestant clergy to James, who received them kindly. The Bandon Protestants prostrated themselves before James and were graciously pardoned. It was evident that he wished to conciliate his Protestant subjects. He gave himself credit for his clemency in a declaration he later addressed to the people of England: 'the calumnies of our enemies are now shown to be false, for since our arrival in Ireland we have made it our chief concern to satisfy our Protestant subjects. Their just complaints have been listened to, and even those who took up arms against us have been treated with lenity . . . let the people of England judge us by our conduct in Ireland what they may expect from us'. It was not long before the Cork Protestants were to receive tougher treatment from their French governor, Boisseleau.[19]

James's journey from Cork to Dublin was a triumphal progress: 'all along the road the country came to meet his majesty . . . as if he had been an angel from heaven'.[20] He reached Dublin on Palm Sunday, March 24, and was received with full honours by the city and garrison. D'Avaux described the cheer-

[17] *Jacobite narrative*, pp. 316–17.
[18] D'Avaux, p. 37; Williamites did not recognize the title, as it was conferred after the 'abdication'.
[19] Leslie, p. 111; *Cal. S.P. dom., 1689–90*, p. 95; King, pp. 130–1.
[20] *Jacobite narrative*, p. 46.

ing as overwhelming, and attributed it to Catholic expectations of deliverance from English bondage.[21] A curious account of the arrival is given in a Williamite pamphlet which describes the royal progress from St James's gate to the Castle along newly-gravelled streets. Outside the city was a stage with two harpers and below it a number of singing friars with a large cross, 'and about forty oyster-women, poultry- and herb-women in white, dancing'; at the city boundary the mayor and corporation presented James with the freedom of Dublin, while pipers played 'The king enjoys his own again'. Another account refers to a banner over the Castle, with the inscription:

> Now or never,
> Now and forever.

A Protestant observer noted that the king 'came with far less splendour than the lord deputy was used to do; he was very courteous to all as he passed and it is said he wept as he entered the Castle'.[22] On the following day James issued a proclamation declaring freedom of religion for all, provided that 'nothing be preached or taught which may tend to alienate the hearts of our people from us'. At the same time he called on all Irish residents who had gone to England or Scotland to return within forty days, assuring them that they and their property would be protected.[23]

D'Avaux's preliminary impressions of the situation were optimistic. The Protestants in the south had been disarmed, and it was expected that the troops dispatched to disarm the Protestants of the north would have little difficulty in doing so. The chief trouble was likely to be created by James's indecision: he often changed his mind and his final choice was not always the best; he spent much time on details and neglected essentials; he listened to everyone, and it took as long to wipe out the effects of bad advice as to get him to accept good advice. An inner cabinet was formed, consisting of Melfort, Tyrconnell and d'Avaux himself, which met every evening. Friction soon developed between Melfort and Tyrconnell. D'Avaux also was

---

[21] D'Avaux, p. 48.

[22] *Ireland's lamentation*, p. 26; *Apology for the Protestants*, p. 36; *Ormonde MSS*, n.s., viii. 362.

[23] Ibid., ii. 397.

critical of Melfort and thought he had a bad influence on James.[24]

Melfort encouraged James to oppose the demands of Irish Catholics and to make plans for an early landing in Scotland. This advice was in line with James's own inclinations; he was therefore much more ready to listen to Melfort than to Tyrconnell or d'Avaux. When they were still in Cork, James and Melfort were already talking optimistically of going to Scotland and from there to England. Melfort wrote from Cork to Louvois, hinting at an early move to Scotland, from which he said good news had been received.[25] Justin MacCarthy also wrote to Louvois, saying that Ireland was quite secure: William would not dare to come, and if he did it would cost him dear; the sole problem for James was to put his army in order as quickly as possible and find means to transport it to Scotland.[26] Louvois answered Melfort that if James made an ill-considered attempt on Scotland or England he was likely to lose all three kingdoms.[27] With the first report of James's landing that reached Tyrconnell in Dublin he seems to have been asked to write to some of the Scottish nobility. On March 15 he wrote to the duke of Hamilton, giving a glowing picture of the Irish scene: 'this good posture will, I hope, encourage your grace and the rest of the king's friends there to stick by him and yourselves. I hope before the end of July to have the honour to embrace you in Scotland'.[28] Soon after James got to Dublin he wrote to Dundee sending a lieutenant-general's commission and saying that he would, if possible, come himself to Scotland; in any case he proposed to send 5,000 men when he got Dundee's report. Rumour multiplied the figure: letters from Ireland to the continent gave the news that James intended to go to Scotland with 30,000 men.[29] Dundee wrote urging James to come to Scotland with an Irish force, but he stipulated that Melfort should not be employed in the Scottish administration.[30] Soon after reaching Dublin James

[24] D'Avaux, pp. 23, 36, 54.

[25] *Anal. Hib.*, xxi. 76.

[26] Min. guerre, A1, 895, no. 15.

[27] *Anal. Hib.*, xxi. 36.

[28] *Buccleuch MSS* (H.M.C.), ii. 36.

[29] *H.M.C. rep. 11*, app. vi. 160; *Coll. Hib.*, iii. 112, 160. James's letter was intercepted by the Williamites.

[30] Harris, *William III*, p. 185.

sent agents to the Highlands with a proclamation for general
Scottish consumption, promising liberty of conscience and the
maintenance of the Protestant religion as established by law.[31]
One of the clan MacLean came to Dublin offering Highland
support to James and asking for regular troops. D'Avaux was
opposed to troops being sent before Derry was brought under
control; he was still more opposed to James himself leaving
Ireland before it was completely under his authority.[32]

D'Avaux had qualified approval for Tyrconnell: he was well-
intentioned but lazy, and seemed to find work distasteful. He
thought that Tyrconnell's complaints of ill-health were to a
great extent caused by mortification and resentment of Melfort's influence over James. D'Avaux regarded Tyrconnell as an
ally: if he had been a Frenchman he could not have been more
zealous for the interests of France.[33] Tyrconnell's ill-health was
more specifically diagnosed by a French officer who wrote that
Tyrconnell was much troubled by palpitations and an open sore
on his leg.[34] While Melfort was in the ascendant, Tyrconnell
took little part in the conduct of affairs. There is no doubt that
he felt slighted and that he resented the confidence placed in
Melfort. Other Irish Catholics had a similar sense of disillusion.
D'Avaux told Louis that they were saying that, if James paid so
little attention to them, he could go by himself to Scotland; they
had no wish to follow him there.[35]

3. BANTRY BAY

James was not accompanied to Ireland by the infantry and
cavalry units formed from those of his subjects who had made
their way to France. They were ordered to wait at Brest until
the French ships had returned from Kinsale. French officers and
a further supply of money, arms and ammunition were to go
with them.[36] The convoy did not sail till April 26 (O.S.).
Gabaret, who had escorted James to Ireland, now sailed again,
but, to his mortification, was not in command of the expedition.
This was entrusted to Chateaurenault, who had no previous experience of high command and had been put in charge by court

[31] D'Avaux, pp. 60, 65–70. [32] Ibid., pp. 60–1.
[33] Ibid., pp. 138, 148. [34] Min. guerre, AI, 895, no. 28.
[35] D'Avaux, p. 57. [36] *Anal. Hib.*, xxi. 28.

influence against Seignelay's better judgement. The fleet consisted of twenty-four ships of the line, two frigates and six fire-
ships. On April 29 it was off Kinsale, when English men-of-war
were sighted. The wind was wrong for going into Kinsale, and in
any case disembarkation in sight of a hostile fleet would have
been hazardous; so Chateaurenault made for Bantry, some
forty miles westward.[37]

Admiral Herbert had been cruising off the Irish coast during
the earlier part of April, and had then put in to Milford Haven
to refit.[38] England was not yet formally at war with France, but
there was a *de facto* state of hostilities.[39] Herbert next intended
to make for Brest, where he knew that the French expedition was
ready to sail; but there was an east wind, so he made instead for
Kinsale, which he judged to be the French destination. When
his scouts sighted the French fleet his chief object was to keep it
from getting into Kinsale, with the result that he lost track of it,
looked in vain for it in Baltimore Bay, and on the evening of
April 30 found that it was in Bantry Bay. It had in fact been
there since that morning and had succeeded in disembarking
the men and stores without interference.[40] The number of
troops is variously estimated at 1,500 and 3,000. Among them
was John Stevens, an English Catholic, who had been in Ireland
as a gentleman of the bedchamber to Clarendon: his journal is
an excellent description of the war in Ireland.[41] In addition to
James's own subjects a number of French officers landed at
Bantry, including engineers who were soon dispatched to
Derry.[42]

Herbert's fleet was inferior in size. It consisted of 18 ships of
the line (as compared with Chateaurenault's 24), a frigate and
3 fire-ships. The inferiority is a reflection on the organization of
William's navy at the time: sufficient attention was not given
to having enough sea-going ships available to prevent the

[37] E. Sue, *Histoire de la marine française*, iv. 315, 318.

[38] *Finch MSS*, ii. 202.

[39] War was declared on 7 May (*London Gazette*, 13 May 1689).

[40] The account of the naval operations is based on Herbert's dispatch,
published in *London Gazette*, 9 May 1689, and on Chateaurenault's version,
in Sue, pp. 317–23.

[41] *Journal of John Stevens*, ed. R. H. Murray, p. 43 (hereafter cited as
Stevens); *Jacobite narr.*, p. 71.

[42] J. Macpherson, *Original papers*, i. 193–4.

French reinforcing the Jacobites in Ireland.[43] On the morning of May 1 Herbert put into Bantry Bay where the French ships were at anchor. The French got under sail and began the battle, firing fiercely at the English ships, which withdrew to seaward followed by the French. The fight went on from about 11 a.m. till 5 p.m. when the two fleets parted, the English withdrawing towards the Scillies, and the French after a short and ineffective pursuit putting back into Bantry Bay. Remarkably little harm was done to the ships of either side, though the English sails and rigging were badly damaged. The estimated casualties were: English, 96 killed, about 250 wounded; French, 40 killed, 93 wounded. It has been called a skirmish, but the number of ships involved and the length of the action makes it the most considerable engagement that has taken place off the Irish coast.

Both sides claimed the victory, but in fact the French had achieved their objective in safely landing their convoy and securing an uninterrupted return to France. The English fleet had failed to prevent men and arms from reaching James, and their victory celebrations had little relation to the reality of the situation. When the fleet reached Portsmouth, William himself came down to congratulate it, and was entertained to dinner on Herbert's flagship. Herbert was made earl of Torrington, two of his captains were knighted (one being Sir Cloudesley Shovell of later fame), and each seaman was promised ten shillings. The rewards seem to have been partly a recognition of Herbert's part in aiding William's expedition to England and partly an attempt to conciliate the navy, which was suffering from a sense of neglect. The house of commons passed a vote of thanks to Herbert 'for one of the bravest actions done in this last age'.[44] Herbert himself took a more modest view of his achievement, and wrote to Lord Nottingham: 'I am sorry I cannot tell you that fortune has favoured my endeavours further than by bringing off the fleet without loss of a ship, after an attempt upon all the disadvantage that ever men lay under.'[45]

The news reached Dublin that the French had won a victory and that the English fleet had fled. James dutifully ordered a *Te Deum*, but is said to have been mortified by the result. When

[43] Ehrman, pp. 246, 253–7.
[44] *London Gazette*, 20 May 1689; *Commons' jn.*, x. 142.
[45] *Finch MSS*, ii. 205.

he was told that the English had been defeated, the old sailor in him bridled and he retorted: 'it is the first time, then'. He comforted himself with the thought that it was out of loyalty to him that the behaviour of the English navy had been so much out of character.[46] Chateaurenault expressed his disappointment at the inconclusive result and blamed his subordinates for not showing the same enterprise as himself. The subordinates defended themselves by blaming Chateaurenault for not giving sufficiently definite orders.[47]

James was anxious to make full use of Chateaurenault's fleet. He wanted it to go to the north of Ireland to stop William helping Derry; to transport heavy guns for the siege; to clear the waters between Ireland and Scotland of English ships; and to convoy 10,000 troops to Scotland. If, as represented by d'Avaux, Chateaurenault's orders forbade such measures, James urged that he should return as soon as possible to assist a landing on Anglesey: James himself would meanwhile try to arrange for a Scottish expedition as best he could.[48] Chateaurenault had already left before this programme could be communicated to him. Seignelay later declared that it would have been hazardous for his small fleet to have entered St George's Channel: James's request for a larger fleet to visit Irish waters would depend on the general situation.[49] The French navy has been criticized for its lack of enterprise in failing to exploit the superiority it then enjoyed over the British navy. But it would have been very difficult for it to have maintained its position off the north coast of Ireland, so far from its base and with no suitable harbour for refitting. The sole assistance given by the French to any of James's maritime projects was that three frigates convoyed three hundred of Purcell's dragoons from Carrickfergus to Scotland where they joined Dundee just before the battle of Killiecrankie, in which they acquitted themselves well.[50]

4. ARMY PROBLEMS

Tyrconnell's new colonels had had a free hand in recruiting for their regiments, and the result was to produce formations which

---

[46] Dalrymple, i. 332.   [47] Sue, pp. 323–5.
[48] D'Avaux, p. 145, 150–2.   [49] Ibid., pp. 306–7.
[50] *Jacobite narr.*, p. 86; *James II*, ii. 352; *London Gazette*, 18 July 1689.

were extremely uneven in both quantity and quality. The standard infantry regiment was composed of 13 companies of 62 men each. D'Avaux reported that Tyrconnell's army had regiments with 35, 40, or even 44 companies, and that to find officers to staff these inflated units wholly unsuitable persons had been commissioned. There were colonels who had never served in an army; tailors, butchers and shoemakers had raised companies at their own expense and had been made captains. D'Avaux thought that this indiscriminate recruiting might well have saved Ireland, as reports of an army 50,000 strong deterred William from attacking; but weeding out unsuitable colonels and captains was extremely embarrassing.[51] We have no corroboration for d'Avaux's account of the civilian occupations of the captains, and it seems unlikely that craftsmen would have been able to maintain companies. But it is clear from other sources that there were many inflated units and that it was decided to reduce both the number of regiments and the number of companies in each.

James's secretariat estimated that 100,000 men had been raised, which seems a high figure; it was decided to reduce the army to 7 regiments of horse, 7 of dragoons, and 35 of foot with 13 companies in each, except for the guards which consisted of two battalions (26 companies). The *Jacobite narrative* estimated the reorganized army at 35,000 men, a figure which is generally in line with a French statement drawn up at the end of May. Tyrconnell was sent out to disband the surplus troops, which was most disagreeable to those who were dismissed, although he seems to have allowed some extra companies to remain and to have promised those who had to go that they would be taken back at the first opportunity.[52] The opportunity came after a few months, when Schomberg's invasion was imminent and the operations against Derry and Enniskillen had severely depleted the ranks of the army. The captains of the disbanded companies were invited to come to the king's assistance and

[51] D'Avaux, pp. 78, 182.

[52] Macpherson, i. 180; *Jacobite narr.*, p. 53; *Anal. Hib.*, xxi. 121. The French statement shows 35 new infantry regiments in addition to 7 of the old army. Tyrconnell's papers list the new colonels to be retained and to be disbanded, together with the number of companies in each regiment (N.L.I., MS 37).

promised pay if they did so.[53] But in the meanwhile the disbanded men were disorderly and efforts were made to control
them by the appointment of provosts-marshal. Friction in the
army was created by the distribution of French officers (each
being given a step up in rank) among the Irish regiments. One
French officer, Boisseleau, was allowed to raise a regiment of
two battalions; its officers were mostly from the Cork neighbourhood, and it seems likely that for the other ranks he drew on the
troops landed at Bantry.[54]

John Stevens, the English Catholic, formed a very poor first
impression of the Irish army: 'what our army either was or
might be made is very hard to give an account of. The common
computation was incredible; for most reckoned the whole
nation, every poor country fellow having armed himself with a
skeine, as they call it, or dagger, or a ropery like a half-pike.' He
thought the muster-rolls inflated, and that most of those who
enlisted did so with scant appreciation of the duties involved
and deserted as soon as they were ordered out of their own
locality. Want of discipline was a major defect: 'they will follow
none but their own leaders, many of them men as rude, as
ignorant, and as far from understanding any of the rules of
discipline as themselves'.[55] There is no doubt that much of this
criticism was deserved; the Irish army did not show up well in
the fighting that took place in the summer of 1689. It is remarkable that such an improvised army should have acquitted itself
as well as it did in some of the later engagements of the war.

The army was short of almost everything it needed: muskets,
artillery, clothing, medical stores. The muskets sent from France
with Chateaurenault's fleet were of bad quality. Those commandeered from the Protestants were said to be so old and un-
serviceable that not more than one in twenty was of any use.
One regiment was sent to Derry with seven muskets in all.
Almost all the armourers were Protestants and could not be
relied on; d'Avaux asked for armourers to be sent from France.
His correspondence is full of complaints about the shortage of
necessaries and the inefficiency of those whose duty it was to
supply them. James's secretariat estimated the field-artillery

[53] *Ormonde MSS*, ii. 408–9.
[54] Macpherson, i. 191, 193; D'Avaux, p. 118.
[55] Stevens, pp. 61–3.

available as twelve cannon and two little mortars (four others being out of order).[56]

Before James left France Louvois was already contemplating the dispatch of French troops to Ireland in return for Irish troops to be sent to France. He wrote on February 16/26 to Justin MacCarthy, saying that French troops would be able to come to Ireland in the following winter and inviting him to command the Irish troops sent to France – the first step in the negotiation that eventually led to the exchange. MacCarthy replied that he had always wished to return to the French service and would do his best to choose good officers and men. He gave no hint that they could ill be spared from the Irish army.[57] When the proposition was first put up to James, he seems to have been opposed to it, but it was not long before d'Avaux brought him round to the idea that it would be to his advantage to have troops that were better disciplined than his own. D'Avaux himself told Louvois that French regiments were essential: the sooner they came the better, and he undertook to see that the best Irish troops were sent to France in their place.[58] This policy, which the French throughout insisted on, was a peculiar method of strengthening James's army, which suffered from an acute shortage of trained soldiers.

Louvois made it clear that no troops could be sent to Ireland until the end of December, as the French army was fully engaged on the German and Flemish borders and would be until the end of the campaigning season. He suggested sending four or five thousand French infantry and getting six or seven thousand in exchange. D'Avaux was to make sure that James did not send inferior officers of the type who had raised the new levies. Louis wanted men of birth, some of whom should have had military experience.[59] James was not satisfied with these demands and bargained in a way that d'Avaux thought unbecoming in a king, or even in a gentleman. He wanted parity in the numbers exchanged, though the quality of the officers and men would be much inferior. According to d'Avaux, the colonels whom James wanted to send were pitiful creatures, not fit to be ensigns. By this time Justin MacCarthy (now Lord

[56] D'Avaux, pp. 140, 323, 334; *James II*, ii. 328; Macpherson, i. 179.
[57] *Anal. Hib.*, xxi. 27; Min. guerre, A1, 894, no. 15.
[58] D'Avaux, pp. 77–8.   [59] Ibid., pp. 274–5.

Mountcashel) had been captured at the battle of Newtown-butler. When d'Avaux asked for Sarsfield instead, James refused and stamped three times round the room in a rage. D'Avaux thought the best plan would be for Louis to brief Mary of Modena and see what she could do with her husband.[60]

[60] Ibid., pp. 517–21. For the dispatch of the Irish troops to France see pp. 138–9 below.

V

THE 'PATRIOT PARLIAMENT'

ON MARCH 25, the day after he reached Dublin, James issued a proclamation summoning a parliament for May 7.[1] This move was welcomed by most of his supporters. They looked forward to the repeal of the land-settlement and of the anti-Catholic laws, and also to measures that would reduce the dependence of Ireland upon England and strengthen the Irish economy. The parliament was to be the culmination of the Catholic revival and set the seal on all that Catholics had been working for since 1685. Legislation acceptable to Irish Catholics was certain to be unacceptable to English opinion, but James had no alternative. His financial situation was desperate: revenue was far below the normal, military expenses were heavy, and the money he had received from France was inadequate for his requirements. Additional taxes were needed, and to get them he would have to meet at least some of the Irish demands.

Everything was ready for a parliament; the corporations had been remodelled, the county sheriffs were men of Tyrconnell's choice. According to William King, the election writs were accompanied by letters from Tyrconnell to the mayors and sheriffs recommending particular persons, and that in most cases those persons were elected.[2] The only mention we have of any opposition was in Dublin city, where King says that Gerard Dillon, 'a most furious papist', failed to be elected because he

---

[1] *Ormonde MSS*, ii. 398.   [2] King, p. 151.

had purchased an estate under the act of settlement and was therefore presumed likely to oppose the repeal of the act.[3] A contemporary Williamite pamphlet shows that 230 members were returned out of the full quota of 300. There were no county representatives for Donegal, Fermanagh or Londonderry; and a number of boroughs, mainly in Ulster, failed to make returns, being 'in the Protestants' hands'.[4]

King says that there were six Protestants in the commons. The two of whom he approved were the representatives of the University of Dublin, Sir John Meade and Joseph Coghlan, who had been with difficulty prevailed upon to stand: 'the university must choose and it could not stand with their honour to choose papists' – a reflection which suggests that Tyrconnell allowed the university some liberty of election.[5] King does not mention Arthur Brownlow, who was returned for Armagh county. His family background was an unusual combination of Ulster planter, 'old English' and Gaelic Irish. His father's name was Chamberlain, of an 'old English' family from County Louth; but he inherited the estate and took the name of his mother's father, Sir William Brownlow of Lurgan, who had married an O'Doherty lady from Inishowen. Arthur Brownlow had a good knowledge of Irish and was a great collector of manuscripts, his chief treasure being the Book of Armagh. He had been one of the few sheriffs approved by Tyrconnell out of those selected by Clarendon. Tyrconnell seems to have taken the opportunity of allowing the Protestant freeholders of County Armagh to elect one of their number. Brownlow attended the parliament, but apparently offended some Catholic members and had to make his escape, disguised in a Quaker cloak and hat.[6] As Meade, Coghlan and Brownlow were all elected to the Williamite parliament of 1692, they were evidently not regarded as having betrayed the Protestant cause by sitting in

---

[3] Ibid., p. 152.

[4] *An exact list of the lords spiritual and temporal . . .*, which also contains the names of the commons. As the proceedings of this parliament were destroyed by order of the Irish parliament of 1695 it is necessary to rely on Williamite sources for much of our information about it.

[5] King, p. 152.

[6] *Clarendon corr.*, i. 287; *Seasonable advice to the electors of County Armagh*, 1753; E. O Tuathail, 'Arthur Brownlow and his MSS' in *Irish Booklover*, xxiv. 26–8 (1936).

James's parliament. The other Protestant members were committed Jacobites and incurred the displeasure of the Williamite authorities.[7]

Of the Catholic members more than two-thirds bore names of English origin, and the house of commons was much more representative of the 'old English' than of the Gaelic Irish. The Gaelic members included Justin MacCarthy, who sat for County Cork until his elevation to the lords as Viscount Mountcashel, and Charles O'Kelly, author of *The destruction of Cyprus*, who sat for County Roscommon. The best known of the 'old English' representatives was Patrick Sarsfield, who sat for County Dublin. There were also Fitzgeralds, Nugents and members of other long-established families. Dr Alexius Stafford, who sat for a Wexford borough, was a remarkable priest whom James made dean of Christ Church and a master in chancery; he died on the field of Aughrim.[8] Sir Richard Nagle, the attorney-general, was elected speaker.

The membership of the house of lords is variously estimated by contemporary accounts, some of which include peers who were summoned but did not attend. 'An exact list', published in the autumn of 1689, gives the names of thirty-one lay lords and four bishops. Most of the lay lords belonged to 'old English' families, but the Gaelic Irish were represented by Lords Iveagh, Clanmaliere, Clancarty and others. There were five Protestants: Granard, Longford, Barrymore, Howth and Rosse; the last of these was married to Lady Tyrconnell's daughter. A remarkable feature was that the bishops summoned were those of the Church of Ireland, and not the Catholic bishops. This was severely criticized by O'Kelly, who attributed the decision to James's determination to do nothing for the restoration of the Catholic church that would offend English Protestant opinion.[9] The four bishops who attended were Meath, Ossory, Limerick and Cork. Three others, including the archbishop of Armagh, were excused for age or infirmity; the rest had fled to England. The ablest of those who sat was Anthony Dopping,

[7] They were Sir Thomas Crosby, Jeremy Donovan and Sir William Ellis; for an account of them see Simms, *The Jacobite parliament of 1689*, p. 6.

[8] O'Kelly, p. 453.

[9] Ibid., pp. 35–6.

bishop of Meath, who in effect acted as leader of the opposition.

By the time that parliament met on May 7 it was known that James's forces were faced with strong resistance from Protestants in Derry and Enniskillen. Both Catholics and Protestants commented on the imprudence of allowing parliamentary debates to divert attention from the pressing need to gain control of these intransigent Ulster towns. O'Kelly complained that the whole summer was wasted in vain consultations, when it might have been better spent in devoting more energy to the siege of Derry.[10] John Stevens's comment was even blunter: 'nothing could be more pernicious or a greater obstruction to the king's service than was this parliament'.[11] King made the same point: James 'had not all Ireland under his control, and the time spent on parliamentary affairs lessened the prospects of taking Derry and Enniskillen'.[12]

The session was held in the King's Inns, a former Dominican convent on the north side of the Liffey, near the present Four Courts. James opened it in person, wearing his robes and a crown newly made in Dublin. The chief theme of his speech was liberty of conscience, which he declared himself determined to establish by law. His programme also included the good of the nation, the improvement of trade and 'the relieving of such as have been injured by the late acts of settlement, as far as may be consistent with reason, justice and the public good of my people'.[13] The speech in general, and in particular the failure to promise actual repeal of the act of settlement, must have disappointed his hearers, though there was no note of criticism in their reply.[14]

2. CONSTITUTIONAL QUESTIONS

The legality of the parliament has been disputed. The Williamites called it the 'pretended parliament', and denied its authority on the ground that James was no longer king of England and consequently no longer king of Ireland, the latter being 'inseparably annexed, united and belonging to the

---

[10] O'Kelly, p. 34.   [11] Stevens, pp. 69–70.   [12] King, pp. 147–8.
[13] *The speech of King James II, 7 May 1689.*
[14] Leslie, app., p. 3.

imperial crown of England'.[15] The Jacobite view was that William was a usurper and that James continued to be king of both England and Ireland. The parliament has also been criticized on the ground that it did not comply with the provisions of Poynings' law, which required the legislation to be first certified into England and returned under the great seal. James's English seal was said to have gone to the bottom of the Thames and to have been recovered in the following summer by a fisherman. While in France James had got a fresh seal made, which he brought to Ireland, but naturally the bills for his Dublin parliament were not 'certified into England' and then sent back in strict compliance with the terms of Poynings' law.[16] This objection may be regarded as technical. Poynings' law was not designed for a situation in which the king was in Ireland and could give his personal sanction to the holding of an Irish parliament. The parliament that James summoned in Dublin had a better claim to be considered legitimate than had the Williamite parliament in Westminster. Which was the pretended parliament and who were the rebels would depend on the outcome of the war.

Since the reign of Charles I Irish constitutional lawyers had objected both to Poynings' law and to the claim of the English parliament to legislate for Ireland. Both objections had been raised in the negotiations between Charles I and the confederate Catholics. The Ormond peace of 1649 promised that a parliament should be called which should be free to consider the repeal or suspension of Poynings' law: 'concerning the independency of the parliament of Ireland of the parliament of England, his majesty will leave both houses of parliament in this kingdom [i.e. Ireland] to make such declaration therein as shall be agreeable to the law of the kingdom of Ireland'.[17] Legislation for Ireland in the English parliaments of Charles II

[15] The words are used in the Irish act, 7 Will. III, c. 3, which annulled the proceedings of the 1689 parliament.

[16] G. Burnet, *History of his own time*, iii. 326; H.M.C., *Stuart MSS*, i. 77. For doubts about the Thames story see H. Jenkinson, 'What happened to the great seal of James II?' in *Antiquaries' Jn.*, xxiii (1943), 1–13. Jenkinson shows that the Williamite authorities recovered James's seal and converted it to serve William and Mary, but he has his reservations about the fisherman.

[17] P. Walsh, *History of the remonstrance*, ii. app., p. 46.

revived the argument against English parliamentary authority over Ireland.

Before the session began the legislative programme was scrutinized by James and his council, which was in effect a compliance with the spirit of Poynings' law. D'Avaux, who was himself a member of the council, describes this scrutiny in terms that suggest that James was at first persuaded to agree to the modification of Poynings' law: . . . 'the Irish parliament will be made independent of England. Previously the practice, when an act was to be passed in the Irish parliament, was to send it to England; the king had it examined by the council and the Irish parliament was obliged to conform to it. There was much discussion whether such acts should in future be examined and approved by the viceroy only or, in accordance with Scottish practice, by parliamentary commissioners chosen for the purpose of joint discussion with the viceroy. The Irish thought it would be preferable for the matter to go before the viceroy alone, and the king agreed.'[18] On May 15 a bill was introduced into the commons for the repeal of Poynings' law, but its progress was held up. Writing on May 26, d'Avaux attributed this to the pressure of other parliamentary business; he gave no hint of James's opposition.[19] But when discussion was resumed on June 21 a spokesman is said to have conveyed James's wish that 'he and his heirs should have the bill[s] first agreed to by him and his council before they should go before the commons' – which would amount to a complete rejection of the proposed measure. The account goes on to say that the bill was ordered to be recommitted, and the house inclined to be as free as the parliament in England'.[20] King says that the bill was dropped as a result of James's opposition, 'though the Irish had talked much and earnestly desired the repeal of Poynings' law, it being the greatest sign and means of their subjection to England'.[21] There was some Irish condemnation of the failure to repeal Poynings' law. Bishop O'Moloney of Killaloe is mentioned as one of those who cursed 'the parliament as a company of easy men for not sticking to their demands . . . in the

[18] D'Avaux, pp. 89–90.
[19] *A journal of the pretended parliament*; d'Avaux, p. 193.
[20] *A true account*, pp. 6–7.
[21] King, p. 153.

next they will have other things done, especially the overturning of Poynings' laws'.[22] The demand to be free of a medieval restriction was natural for Irish politicians, who were stimulated by the success of the English parliament in modifying the constitution to its own advantage. A similar attitude was to be adopted after the war by the Irish parliament of William. Parliamentary privilege rather than a sense of Irish nationality seems to have been the primary motive. It says much for James's obstinacy and the importance he attached to English opinion that he succeeded in keeping Poynings' law intact.[23]

With some reluctance James agreed to an act declaring that the English parliament had no right to pass laws for Ireland. The act declared that Ireland had always been a kingdom distinct from that of England; its people had never sent representatives to a parliament held in England, but had their laws made in their own parliament: 'yet of late times (especially in times of distraction) some have pretended that acts of parliament passed in England, mentioning Ireland, were binding in Ireland'.[24] Such a claim was declared to be against justice and natural equity, oppressive to the people and destructive of the constitution. The act also prohibited the practice of preferring appeals from the court of king's bench in Ireland to the corresponding court in England and substituted an Irish appellate court. Appeals from the high court of chancery in Ireland to the English house of lords were also prohibited. The declaratory act of 1689 was a forerunner of the long argument conducted by Molyneux, Swift and Grattan for the right of Ireland to be independent of English laws and courts. Molyneux and Swift ignored the expression that the parliament of 1689 had given to this claim. Grattan did not overlook it, though he put his own interpretation on it: the Irish Catholics, he said, should not be reproached for fighting under King James's banner 'when we recollect that before they entered the field they

[22] Macpherson, *Original papers*, i. 339.

[23] Several historians have, mistakenly, stated that Poynings' law was repealed, e.g. Froude, *English in Ireland* (1887 ed.), i. 212; Lecky, *History of Ireland in the eighteenth century*, i. 118; G. N. Clark, *Later Stuarts*, p. 305.

[24] The text of the act is given in Thomas Davis, *The patriot parliament of 1689*, pp. 43–8.

extorted from him a Magna Carta, a British constitution'.[25] The act was singled out for particular praise by Thomas Davis: 'the idea of 1782 is to be found full grown in 1689, the pedigree of our freedom is a century older than we thought, and Ireland has another parliament to be proud of'.[26] The act seems to have suggested to Gavan Duffy the emotive title he gave to Davis's articles: *The patriot parliament of 1689*. Here again James betrayed his English outlook: he regarded the provisions of the act as 'such diminutions of his prerogative as nothing but his unwillingness to disgust those who were otherwise affectionate subjects could have extorted from him'.[27]

3. THE REPEAL OF THE SETTLEMENT

To many of James's supporters the repeal of the restoration land-settlement was the primary object of the parliament. But it proved to be a highly controversial piece of legislation, and much of the session was taken up in acrimonious wrangling about it. James's English advisers were strongly opposed to the repeal of the settlement, which was regarded as an essential security for English control of Ireland. They were supported by the 'new interest', Catholics who had bought lands, the title to which was based on the settlement. Several of James's judges were in this position, and they formed an active pressure group against the repeal. An attempt was made to put forward a compromise bill in the house of lords, which is said to have provided for the restoration of only half the lands of dispossessed proprietors.[28] This was defeated, and the opposition was confined to obstructing the repeal bill. The latter was introduced in the commons on May 10 and received with a huzza and supplementary motions that nothing could be more advantageous to the king and the country than to destroy the horrid and barbarous act of settlement, which should be burned by the common hangman.[29] When the bill reached the lords, it was opposed by two of the 'new interest' judges who asserted that they had a legitimate right to the lands they had

[25] *Grattan's speeches* (1811), i. lxxiv.
[26] Davis, p. xciii.   [27] *James II*, ii. 361.
[28] *A journal of the proceedings . . . from the 7th to the 20th of this instant May.*
[29] Ibid.

bought and objected to being dispossessed. James took their side, and threatened to dissolve parliament if the 'new interest' purchasers were not left in possession. Several members of the commons said that in that case they would not join in the war.[30] D'Avaux urged James to hold a conference, as a result of which James's objections to total repeal were withdrawn for the time being: the 'new interest' was to be compensated from forfeited estates. But James continued to support the obstructive judges, and the commons retorted by postponing the initial date for the payment of the subsidy.[31] In the lords the chief opposition speaker was the bishop of Meath, who condemned the bill as unjust and inopportune: 'is it now a time for men to seek for vineyards and olive yards, when a civil war is raging in the nation and we are under apprehensions . . . of invasions from abroad?' He warned the house not 'to dispose of the skin before we catch the beast'.[32] His eloquence was unavailing, and the bill with some amendment was approved by the lords. The bishops and four of the Protestant lay lords wished to register their protest, but James objected to the term on the ground that it had rebellious overtones: they might register their dissent without specifying their reasons.[33] However he seems to have been pleased that they had shown their disapproval of the bill. Charles Leslie, the non-juror, says that it was well known that James encouraged the Protestant lords to oppose the bill, and that he had complained to Lord Granard that 'he was fallen into the hands of a people who rammed many hard things down his throat'.[34] Further delay was caused by a series of conferences between the two houses, which sorely tried the patience of the commons. Tyrconnell's nephew, Sir William Talbot, was sent to implore the lords to pass the bill as quickly as possible 'because the heart and courage of the whole nation are bound up in it'.[35] Eventually agreement between the two houses was reached and James gave his reluctant assent to the bill.

The act repealed the acts of settlement and explanation, and annulled all titles derived from them (with the exception of

---

[30] D'Avaux, pp. 190–2.
[31] Ibid., p. 215.   [32] King, p. 396.
[33] *A true account.*   [34] Leslie, p. 51.
[35] *Journal of the proceedings of the parliament.*

a few specific items).[36] The landholders of 1641 or their heirs were authorized to take steps for the recovery of their property and all outlawries arising from the insurrection of 1641 were cancelled. A court of claims, consisting of three or more commissioners, was to be set up to determine the rights of individuals to recoverable property. The act went beyond mere repeal of the settlement, and included provision for the forfeiture of lands belonging to those who had rebelled against James, or had gone to live in rebel areas, or had even corresponded with rebels; King observed that it would apply to almost every Protestant who could write.[37] Such forfeited lands were to be vested in the crown for the purpose of compensating the 'new interest' purchasers. James himself was to be compensated for the loss of his Irish estate by a grant of Lord Kingston's lands in Cork and Roscommon. He was also to keep the Phoenix Park and the royal lands at Chapelizod near Dublin. By a special clause the London companies' lands in Ulster were vested in the crown, to be used for compensating the 'new interest'. Those who had been dispossessed before 1641, notably the Ulster Gaels, were not specifically provided for.

For the 'old English', in particular, the act gave the prospect of a large-scale recovery of the lands that Cromwell had taken and that Charles II had failed to restore. As the bishop of Meath had foretold, army officers left their posts and hastened to inspect their ancestral property. James made this his justification for holding up the procedure provided by the act. Soon after parliament had been prorogued a proclamation announced that 'because some may neglect the public safety of the kingdom upon pretence of attending their private concerns, especially that of their estates' there would be no court of claims for the present.[38] No such court seems to have been set up later. Temporary or unauthorized possession of land was taken in many cases, but there was no general transfer of ownership. The Jacobite defeat made the repeal a dead letter. But the

---

[36] The text of the act is given by Davis, pp. 79–124. Section 18 (pp. 98–9) provided that the quit-rents payable to the crown under the acts of settlement and explanation should continue to be paid, notwithstanding the repeal.

[37] King, p. 155.

[38] *Ormonde MSS*, ii. 407.

act confirmed Protestants in their determination to guard against any further attempt by Catholics to reverse the land-settlement.

Protestant propaganda made the most of the repeal, but it was not the cause of the Williamite confiscations that later took place. The ownership of the land was a major issue in the war, and William had already announced that he would forfeit the lands of his opponents for the benefit of his supporters.[39] The real argument against the act of repeal was that it distracted attention from the military effort at a critical stage of the war. Prolonged and acrimonious debates should not have been allowed to coincide with the siege of Derry. The provisions of the act involved complicated investigations into title, which threatened to conflict with the energetic prosecution of the war.

4. THE ACT OF ATTAINDER

A measure that aroused even more Protestant indignation was the act of attainder, directed against those who were said to have joined William's side either in England or in the north of Ireland. King described it as without parallel since the days of ancient Rome, and as a deliberate design to bring about the extirpation of the Protestants.[40] In fact, religion was not the criterion, but refusal to acknowledge James. The act referred to the 'most horrid invasion of the king's unnatural enemy, the prince of Orange, assisted by many of his majesty's rebellious and traitorous subjects'. It contained the names of over two thousand individuals, divided into different categories. The first category consisted of those who had notoriously joined in the rebellion and contained 1,340 names, headed by the second duke of Ormond and the archbishop of Dublin. They were to be declared traitors and liable to the usual penalties of death and confiscation, unless by August 10 they surrendered to a judge and then, after due trial, were acquitted. Other categories were those who had left Ireland and were given till September 1

[39] In his declaration of 22 Feb. 1689, see p. 56 above.
[40] King, pp. 155, 182. An appendix gives the act in full as an authentic copy of the document found in the Jacobite rolls office after the battle of the Boyne.

or October 1 to return and make their submission to James. The final category consisted of those whose absence was caused by age or infirmity. They were not to be attainted; but, as it would impoverish the country to send them their rents, their lands were meanwhile to be vested in the crown. The time allowed for repentance was very short, and we do not hear of any persons returning to the Jacobite allegiance. According to King the names were deliberately kept secret, so as to deny any opportunity to those who might have been inclined to return.[41] He was particularly critical of the clause that invalidated any royal pardon that was not enrolled by 30 November 1689; he says that it made James so angry that it made his nose bleed.[42] The memoirs of James's life refer ruefully to this restriction as a case in which he sacrificed his own interest to the wishes of his subjects. The Protestant parliament of 1697 put a similar restriction on William's prerogative of mercy. Each parliament was suspicious of the excessive leniency of its sovereign.[43]

The act of attainder has been criticized as the great mistake of the parliament.[44] But the overwhelming majority of those named were clearly supporters of William and in favour of the overthrow of James. It is difficult to take the view that the act was any more outrageous than the very summary judicial proceedings for treason which took place after the rising of 1641 and which were to be repeated by the Williamite authorities after the Boyne. To Catholics who had a lively recollection of the 'adventurers' act' and of Cromwell's proceedings, the attainder of Protestant rebels was an obvious piece of retributive justice.

The act of attainder was an essential complement of the part of the act of repeal that reserved the lands of rebels for compensating loyal Jacobites whose lands were restored to the old proprietors. Commissioners were appointed, who seized the lands of absentee Williamites and leased them out. These proceedings also helped to divert officers from their military duties, and in April 1690 James forbade the further leasing of forfeited estates.[45]

[41] King, p. 183.   [42] Ibid., pp. 37, 155.
[43] *James II*, ii. 361; 9 Will. III, c. 5.
[44] Davis, p. 141; Lecky, i. 130.
[45] *Ormonde MSS*, ii. 436.

5. MATTERS OF RELIGION

Catholics naturally hoped for legislation that would restore their church to the position it held before the reformation. After the Boyne Williamites claimed to have found copies in Dublin of an address presented to James by the Catholic bishops which asked for the repeal of the act of uniformity and other penal laws, and for the restoration of the Catholic clergy to their livings, churches and authority. The address urged that there was no need to humour English Protestants, who were more likely to be upset by James's secular measures than by the restoration of the catholic Church in Ireland.[46]

But James was determined that the established church should not be formally deprived of its position. When the parliamentary programme was drawn up disestablishment was not proposed; it was decided to maintain the existing policy of leaving vacancies unfilled, and using the money to subsidize the Catholic clergy, and also to provide that Protestants and Catholics respectively should support their own clergy.[47] In his opening speech to parliament James made no reference to either church; his theme was liberty of conscience. D'Avaux had reported that the act for liberty of conscience was to repeal all anti-Catholic laws; and the bill as first sent up by the commons appears to have included provision for the repeal of the acts of supremacy and uniformity. A contemporary pamphlet says it was for 'taking away the king's supremacy in ecclesiastics and abrogating all laws against papists'.[48] Another pamphlet says that James told the bishop of Meath that he did not like the commons' bill, that it diminished his prerogative and was designed to make him break his word to the established church; he did not intend to do away with the act of uniformity nor to destroy the Protestant religion, but only to take away penalties that were against liberty. James's stand is said to have been made on the advice of an English Protestant, Chief Justice Herbert, who warned him that the commons' proposal would lose the king all his Protestant friends. The pamphlet continues: 'but the work is effectively done by other bills, and

---

[46] *An address given in to the late King James by the titular archbishop of Dublin.*
[47] D'Avaux, p. 111.
[48] *Journal of . . . the pretended parliament.*

the act of uniformity will stand like the edict of Nantes, till there be no occasion for it'.[49] The version given in this pamphlet is corroborated from the Jacobite side by O'Kelly, who says that James could not be persuaded to rescind the impious laws enacted by Queen Elizabeth against the Roman church and restore the jurisdiction of the pope, lest it might alienate from him the hearts of his Protestant subjects, whom he always courted.[50]

The act for liberty of conscience declared that persecuting people for their religion in no way advanced Christian faith, but on the contrary raised divisions among the king's subjects and discouraged strangers from settling. All varieties of Christians were therefore to be permitted to meet in worship, both in public and in private, and their 'pastors, teachers, preachers, ministers or other instructors' were to be allowed to function freely, provided they did nothing that conflicted with allegiance to the king. Curiously enough, priests are not specifically mentioned, and the act reads like a charter for Protestant dissenters, though its terms would be equally applicable to Catholics. The oath of supremacy and the 'new oath of allegiance' (prescribed by an English act of James I) were no longer required, and any statutory restrictions that were inconsistent with religious liberty were declared void.[51] The act certainly undermined the act of uniformity, but it left it on the statute book and did not substitute a Catholic for a Protestant establishment. The *Life of James* says that

he gave his royal assent with a good will to the act for liberty of conscience which granted a free exercise of religion to all that professed Christianity, without any penalty, loss or molestation whatever: which from the provocation he then had from the generality of Protestants in Ireland . . . and the superiority of his Catholic subjects in that kingdom was a demonstration that his so much continuing for that liberty proceeded from a settled judgement of its being most conformable to reason, justice and true Christian moderation.[52]

[49] *True account of the whole proceedings.*
[50] O'Kelly, p. 34.
[51] The act is included in a collection of acts of the 1689 parliament, apparently printed at the time in Dublin (B.M., G 6022/122 – title-page missing). This was kindly pointed out to me by Miss M. Pollard, Rare Books Librarian, Trinity College, Dublin.
[52] *James II*, ii. 361.

Later in the year, James made the act for liberty of conscience the basis of a proclamation forbidding the seizure by Catholics of Protestant churches, including those which had been abandoned by their clergy.[53] In the period between the English revolution and the battle of the Boyne there were many instances of Protestant churches being seized. James's efforts to prevent such seizures were often unsuccessful. In September 1689, while he was out of Dublin, Christ Church was taken and consecrated to Catholic use, apparently on the ground that it was traditionally the chapel royal. When the bishop of Meath asked for its return, James is said to have replied: 'had he been in town, it should not have been taken away, but, since it was, he could not restore it without disobliging the Irish, whose interest was all he had to trust to; and indeed they could not abide any but their own nation'. James incurred some Protestant criticism when, in spite of these sentiments, he himself attended mass in Christ Church.[54] St Patrick's Cathedral and a number of Dublin churches were also seized, but in February 1690 it was reported that the Dublin Protestants had got back all their churches except for Christ Church.[55] In the country there seems to have been widespread seizure of churches, and James's proclamation was disregarded. King prints James's order directing the return in proper condition of a Wexford church which had been seized and the pews and altar broken; but he says that the church was never restored while the Jacobite régime lasted.[56]

An act that had the object of removing a major Catholic grievance related to tithes. It stated that Catholics had been maintaining their own clergy and, in addition, were burdened by the payment of tithes to the Protestant clergy who performed no spiritual duties for them. It was therefore provided that Catholics should in future pay tithes to their own clergy and to no others. An act regulating tithes in Ulster cancelled the special, and higher, scale in force for that province and thus lightened the dues payable by Protestants in an area where most of them were Presbyterians.[57] King, from the standpoint of a clergyman, claimed that the apparent equity of the tithes act

[53] *Ormonde MSS*, ii. 418–19.   [54] Ibid., n.s. viii. 372–3.
[55] *The present state of affairs in Ireland.*   [56] King, pp. 213, 395–6.
[57] These acts are in the collection referred to in note 51, above.

was mere hypocrisy; Protestants had been so harried that few had anything titheable left, and the priests would be sure to take possession of the glebes without being given them by parliament.[58] The act did not cover the case of 'appropriate tithes', payable to bishops and other dignitaries. 'Impropriate tithes', in the possession of the laity, were excepted from the provisions of the act. They were dealt with in another act, which declared that Catholics should pay such tithes to the bishops and dignitaries of their own Church, and that those only were to be considered Catholic bishops and deans who were named such by the king – a marked step towards the official recognition of the Catholic church.[59] But this measure fell short of what Catholics wanted. One commentator called it irreligious on the ground that it left Protestant bishops in possession of church lands: 'they mended the matter in parochial priests, for they gave possession unto them of all the tithes of Catholic people, leaving to ministers the tithes of their own'.[60] D'Avaux told Louis that two members of the commons had complained to him that James was unwilling to remove the Protestant bishops and clergy and put Catholics in their place, or to restore church property.[61]

James's policy in the field of religion satisfied neither side. Protestants were aggrieved that their previous monopoly had been broken; Catholics were not satisfied by changes that fell far short of restoring the pre-reformation position.

6. FINANCE AND ECONOMICS

In return for unpalatable concessions James could hope for additional revenue from the parliament, and this was badly needed. According to d'Avaux's calculations the peace-time receipts from customs and excise amounted to £270,000 a year, but this had slumped to about £162,500 because of the decline in trade.[62] Under war conditions the decline was likely to become even steeper. At the same time military expenditure had risen enormously. In the circumstances, James's request for an additional £15,000 a month for thirteen months was very modest. The commons showed their good will by raising the

[58] King, p. 201.   [59] Ibid., pp. 198–9.   [60] *Jacobite narrative*, p. 69.
[61] D'Avaux, p. 199.   [62] Ibid., p. 185.

monthly quota to £20,000.[63] The subsidy was to be levied on real estate, and was earmarked for the army. The act stated that it had been necessary to raise a far greater army than the king's revenue could maintain in spite of French assistance.[64] It apportioned the monthly quota for £20,000 among the different counties and cities throughout Ireland, including the areas held by the Williamites. Commissioners for each area were nominated to arrange for the levy; in most areas they included a few Protestants. They were to choose 'honest and able inhabitants' in every locality to survey each estate and fix the amount to be paid in respect of it. The sum could be taken from the tenant who could then deduct it from his rent, unless he was paying his landlord as little as half the yearly value. This clause must have been unwelcome to tenants who were enjoying rent-free occupation as a result of the flight of the landlords. Tyrconnell had proposed that the subsidy should be paid in corn and meat to feed the troops, but this was rejected in favour of cash.[65]

Collection must have been very difficult, even outside Ulster, and it is evident that the amount raised fell far short of the quota. This was officially admitted in February 1690 in a proclamation which stated that the subsidy could not be levied in areas 'infested with rebels' nor out of lands which were waste. As circumstances did not then permit of another parliamentary session, a monthly subsidy of £20,000 for three months was levied by executive order on personal property.[66] Stevens, the English Jacobite, says bluntly that the parliamentary subsidy was never turned to any account.[67] Even if it had been realized in full, it would not have gone far to meet the expenditure which, in the autumn of 1689, Tyrconnell estimated at £100,000 a month.[68]

While the supply bill was going through parliament, James's advisers were examining other methods of raising finance. The most promising appeared to be the issue of brass and copper money; this 'money of necessity', which included coins of other

---

[63] D'Avaux, p. 191.

[64] Copies of the act, published in Dublin in 1689, are in the King's Inns Library, Dublin, and the B.M.

[65] D'Avaux, p. 218. [66] *Ormonde MSS*, ii. 427.

[67] Stevens, p. 68. [68] *Anal. Hib.*, iv. 107.

metals, was the mainstay of Jacobite finances for the next year. It was estimated that coins to the face value of about £1,000,000 in sixpences, shillings, half-crowns and crowns, were minted during this period.[69] This experiment in managed currency was controversial, but more successful than might have been expected in an age accustomed to valuing coinage by the metal of which it was composed. Its value fluctuated with the fortunes of the Jacobite cause, holding up after the failure of Schomberg's expedition in the autumn of 1689, and sinking with the build-up of William's strength in the spring of 1690, when it was common to give forty to fifty shillings of brass money for a guinea.[70] In October 1689 Tyrconnell urged Mary of Modena to get more copper sent from France: 'for it is our meat and drink and clothes and we have none left, for we are forced to coin our brass guns for want of it'.[71] We hear of guns of 4,300 lbs and 7,321 lbs being melted down for coinage.[72] After the battle of the Boyne William's government treated brass money with contempt, offering no more than a penny for a brass half-crown.[73] The coinage was constantly derided in anti-Jacobite propaganda, and memories of it were kept alive in Protestant toasts that coupled it with popery and wooden shoes as one of the evils from which William had delivered Ireland. King complained that Protestant traders were the chief victims of the devaluation.[74] James's memoirs claimed that to begin with the combination of brass money and price control had 'no ill effect upon commerce and was a great relief to the king's necessity; but this proving too easy a resource . . . occasioned the coining twice as much as was the usual current cash of the kingdom, which made it such a drug that things were soon sold for treble the rate they had formerly been at'.[75]

The parliament showed a zealous, but not immediately relevant, concern for the economic progress of the country. An act prohibiting the import of English, Scottish or Welsh coal foreshadowed the protectionist attitude of the saying quoted by

[69] Story, p. 93. For recent accounts see A. E. J. Went, 'James II's money of necessity, often called gun-money' in *Dublin Hist. Rec.*, xvi. 16–21 (1960) and D. Stevenson, 'The Irish emergency coinages of James II' in *British Numismatic Jn.*, xxxvi. 169–75 (1968).

[70] *Ormonde MSS*, n.s. viii. 374; *Finch MSS*, ii. 274.

[71] *Anal. Hib.*, iv. 103.   [72] *Ormonde MSS*, n.s. viii. 371–2.

[73] Ibid., ii. 441–2.   [74] King, pp. 151–6.   [75] *James II*, ii. 369–70.

Swift: 'burn everything English except their people and their coal.' Coal imports were condemned as causing local unemployment and loss of currency. To prevent the act being exploited by the mineowners of Kilkenny and other Irish collieries, the price at the pithead was fixed at ninepence a barrel.[76] In fact, cargoes from England were no longer arriving, and Irish coal was inadequate for Dublin's needs. A report of February 1690 mentions that fuel was very scarce, that most of the hedges round Dublin had been cut, and that posts and railings in the city had been taken for firewood.[77]

An elaborate act for the advance and improvement of trade and for the encouragement of shipping and navigation set aside the restrictions imposed by the navigation laws and permitted direct trading with the colonies. There was a significant proviso binding the masters of Irish ships to bring back colonial cargoes to England, Ireland, Wales or Berwick-on-Tweed and to no other destination. This and other clauses assumed the continuance of a close economic relationship between Ireland and England. Shipbuilding was encouraged by a rebate of part of the duty on cargoes for the first three or four voyages of ships built in Ireland. Tax exemptions and other privileges were offered to seamen, shipwrights and similar experts. There was an interesting provision for the establishment of free schools in Dublin, Belfast, Waterford, Cork, Limerick and Galway to teach mathematics and navigation.[78]

The French were anxious for legislation that would give France the favoured economic position in relation to Ireland that was previously enjoyed by England. In particular, they wanted the export of raw wool, hitherto confined to England, to become a French monopoly. D'Avaux says that the commons passed bills banning the export of wool to England and facilitating the export of wool and other articles to France.[79] Neither of these passed the house of lords, and d'Avaux put this down to James's opposition: 'he has a heart too English to take any step that could vex the English, and that holds up the woollen business'.[80] There seems in fact to have been a considerable export of wool to France, and this, together with the trade in

---

[76] Davis, pp. 52–4.
[77] *An account of the present state Ireland is in.*
[78] Davis, pp. 55–62.   [79] D'Avaux, p. 226.   [80] Ibid., p. 255.

hides and tallow, was a major factor in financing essential imports from France.[81]

A bill for the naturalization of French subjects also passed the commons, but was blocked in the lords by James's intervention. After a month of dispute it was redrafted to apply to all countries, as James did not wish there to be a special relationship between the French and the Irish.[82] This is evidently the 'act for the encouragement of strangers and others to inhabit and plant in Ireland', of which we have only the title.

The parliamentary session did much to disillusion James's Irish supporters. It was made clear to them that he regarded Ireland as a stepping-stone to the recovery of England and was reluctant to do anything that would alienate English opinion. His refusal to agree to the repeal of Poynings' law kept the Irish parliament under English control. His stand against the replacement of English commercial privileges by French showed that a Jacobite victory was unlikely to have removed English regulation of the Irish economy. The legislation and proceedings of the parliament are significant as demonstrations of what Catholics wanted, and of the limits to which they could press an unwilling king. The repeal of the act of settlement was clearly the primary object of most members; but self-government and the status of the church were also important objects, and the acts relating to them fell far short of Catholic aspirations.

Had James won the war, the legislation of the parliament would have produced significant changes in Ireland. But these changes would not have undone the English conquest or restored Gaelic rule; and they would in some ways have restricted the freedom of the Catholic church. The parliament in the main represented the 'old English' landlord interest. Its measures would have replaced a Protestant by a Catholic oligarchy, whose privileged position would have been based on crown grants and on a legal and constitutional system derived from that of England. The Irish parliament would have been able to assert its independence of the English parliament, but Poynings' law would still ensure its subordination to the crown. Such

[81] *Anal. Hib.*, iv. 115, 121; O'Kelly, p. 406.
[82] D'Avaux, pp. 341–2.

legislation as conflicted with the economic interests of England would not have been likely to last long. In Ireland, no less than in continental Europe, a Catholic dynasty would certainly have sought to influence the policy and personnel of the Catholic church, which would thus be deprived of that freedom which was an unintended benefit of the penal laws.

VI

DERRY AND ENNISKILLEN

~~~~~~

I. KING JAMES DEFIED

IT WAS clearly of importance to James to bring Ulster under
control as soon as possible. It would be most imprudent for him
to cross to Scotland while a Protestant resistance movement held
a considerable part of the province round Derry and Enniskillen.
Richard Hamilton's small force had been checked at Coleraine
and had little prospect of taking the walled city of Derry. There
was disconcerting news of a Williamite relief force getting ready
to sail from Liverpool. D'Avaux urged that all the French
generals and a strong Irish army should be sent north without
delay. James was reluctant to supersede Hamilton and began
by sending the French Major-General Pusignan to support him
with a small force. Eventually he agreed that Rosen and
Maumont, his highest-ranking French officers, should also be
sent. He insisted, in spite of d'Avaux's protests, that he himself
should go with them for at least part of the way.[1] The reluctant
d'Avaux accompanied James through a devastated and deserted
countryside, over terrible roads and unbridged rivers. When
they got to Omagh in County Tyrone, d'Avaux persuaded
James to turn back and leave his generals to deal with Derry.
His arguments were reinforced by news that thirteen English
ships were coming into Derry, and there seems to have been an
element of panic in James's decision to retreat.[2]

[1] D'Avaux, pp. 53–4, 59, 73.
[2] Ibid., pp. 96–7.

Meanwhile Hamilton had resumed his advance and cleared the country between Coleraine and Lough Foyle. He marched down the eastern side of the Foyle to a point opposite Derry, where the river presented a formidable obstacle. The nearest bridges were some fifteen miles upstream at Strabane and Clady. Hamilton made for Strabane, where he joined Rosen's force which had pushed ahead from Omagh.[3]

Derry was now crowded with refugees. It was estimated that there were 30,000 of them within the narrow confines of the walls, an oblong enclave about 500 yards long by 300 yards wide.[4] The garrison consisted of Protestant soldiers of Mountjoy's regiment, who had been sent back by Tyrconnell after Derry had closed its gates in December 1688 against Lord Antrim's Catholic regiment. The commander was Lt-Col Robert Lundy, a Scottish Protestant who was married to the daughter of a Church of Ireland dean.[5] Lundy had a good reputation as a soldier, but he was evidently unhappy about Derry's change of allegiance and had with reluctance accepted William's commission. The bishop, Ezekiel Hopkins, held the traditional Anglican doctrine of non-resistance to the Lord's anointed; finding that his preaching had no effect on defiant Derrymen, he had left the city.[6] Others, who were less doctrinaire, thought that resistance to James was rash and dangerous. But the conservative and timid were overborne by the stronger spirits who took the view that only by defiance of James and reliance on William could the safety of the colony be assured. They remembered 1641, when the Ulster Gaels had risen. Many of the colonists had then been killed or driven from their homes. Derry had been a city of refuge and had withstood Sir Phelim O'Neill. The subsequent war linked Catholicism with Gaelic resurgence. The same link associated the Catholic policies of James and Tyrconnell with a renewed attempt by the older inhabitants to recover their position. O'Neills were raising

---

[3] *Anal. Hib.*, xxi. 87.

[4] G. Walker, *A true account of the siege of Londonderry*, p. 21. Walker's figures (p. 9) of 300 yards and 180 yards are an underestimate. See map on p. 102.

[5] Rowland Davies, successively dean of Cloyne and Cork; his diary, edited by R. Caulfield, is an interesting account of the war.

[6] *Reflections on a paper*; J. Mackenzie, *A narrative of the siege of Londonderry*, p. 5.

regiments, and there were Os and Macs in the Jacobite corporation of Derry.

Derry could hope for strong support from England. The city and county had been granted to the city of London eighty years previously and, after an uncertain start, the property (in particular the fisheries of the Foyle and Bann) was proving a profitable investment. The Irish Society in London helped the Derry emissary, David Cairnes, to get an interview with William, who promised to send supplies and men.[7] Captain James Hamilton (Richard's Protestant nephew) was dispatched with a small quantity of arms and ammunition, £1,000, and a commission for Lundy. His arrival on March 21 had encouraged the citizens to proclaim William and Mary.[8] Meanwhile two regiments were ordered to embark at Liverpool for the defence of Derry. Cairnes came back on April 10 with a letter from William to Lundy calling on him and his fellow Protestants to discharge their duty to their country, their religion and their posterity, and to keep out the 'deluge of popery and slavery'. They were assured that the two regiments about to sail would be followed by further forces sufficient to 'rescue the whole kingdom and resettle the Protestant interest there'.[9]

When the Jacobite troops passed by on their way to Strabane a council of war was held in Derry, in which it was decided to hold the river crossings and defend the Donegal side of the water. All males between sixteen and sixty in the Lagan – the part of Donegal that lies in the valleys of the Foyle and the Swilly – were ordered to report on April 15 at appointed centres 'there to draw up in battalia to be ready to fight the enemy and to preserve our lives and all that is dear to us'.[10] Lundy and a number of others moved out of Derry to positions at strategic points on the river-bank as far upstream as Castlefin, twenty miles away.

Sharp fighting took place on April 15 at Clady on the Finn, where troops commanded by Richard Hamilton forced the crossing. The Jacobites – 600 horse and 350 infantry – found the bridge broken and a large enemy contingent (one estimate is 7,000) entrenched on the far side. The Jacobite cavalry plunged

[7] Ibid., p. 55. [8] Ibid., p. 19.
[9] Ibid., p. 55. [10] Ibid., pp. 22–3; Walker, p. 48.

into the river and reached the other side with only two or three casualties. Meanwhile the infantry used planks to cross the broken bridge. These combined feats put the Protestants in such panic, according to a Jacobite account, that they took to their heels crying 'to Derry, to Derry'.[11] Three miles downstream another crossing was made at Lifford, where the Mourne and Finn join to make the Foyle. Rosen was in command here, and described the action in a dispatch. There was no bridge, and rain had made the river higher than usual. The 'rebels' were posted in a small fort on the far bank, with some artillery. Rosen at first thought it would be impossible to cross, but he could see the disorderly retreat from Clady and judged that his opponents would be too demoralized to offer much resistance. He swam his own horse across the river followed by his men, which so astonished the enemy that they fired one round and then retreated.[12]

The Jacobites had shown courage and initiative in these actions. The Protestants had offered negligible resistance, and their retreat to Derry was little better than a disorderly flight. They blamed Lundy for the disaster and ascribed it to his treachery. But it was hardly surprising that an organized Jacobite force with experienced commanders should have been too much for a hastily assembled collection of amateurs, poorly armed and with no experience of active service. These successes gave the Jacobites control of the rich Lagan countryside, with plenty of fodder for their cavalry. They raised their morale and their hopes of taking Derry without much trouble.

They had a correspondingly depressing effect on the Protestants. Lundy insisted that the city could not be defended, and he found many to agree with him. The two regiments from England arrived in Lough Foyle on April 15, the day of the Clady engagement; unfavourable winds had delayed them by a week. A council of war was held which decided that provisions were short and that Derry was not tenable against a well-appointed army. The conclusion was that the two regiments should go back to England. They did so, taking the leading officers in Derry with them, and leaving the inhabitants to make what terms they could.[13] Pessimistic reports were sent

[11] Berwick, *Memoirs*, i. 44–5; *Jacobite narrative*, p. 45.
[12] *Anal. Hib.*, xxi. 87–9.   [13] Walker, p. 17.

back to England, which led to a decision to stop further supplies for Derry, as there was reason to fear that the Jacobites were already in possession of it.[14]

James was meanwhile on his way back to Dublin and had reached Charlemont, County Armagh, when he got a letter from his son Berwick, who had taken part in the successful action at Clady. Berwick wrote that there was no word of an English fleet, and that the general opinion was that if James appeared in person Derry would open its gates to him.[15] This was enough for James, and in spite of d'Avaux's protests he turned again towards Derry. His journey was an example of the physical energy he combined with mental lethargy. On April 17 he rode from Charlemont forty-two miles to Newtownstewart, and by next morning had reached the outskirts of Derry, more than twenty miles farther on. He arrived to find that negotiations had been started between Derry representatives and the Jacobite commanders, in which a prominent part was taken by an archdeacon of the Church of Ireland.[16] Hamilton and Rosen assured the citizens that, if they submitted and handed over their arms and horses, they would be allowed to live peaceably. They were given till noon on April 18 to reply; meanwhile the Jacobite army would not come within four miles of the town. James appears not to have realized this stipulation, and advanced towards the city with part of his army. There was firing from the wall and several of James's men were killed. The Jacobites beat a hasty and disorderly retreat, and James himself was evidently disconcerted.[17]

The incident brought to a head the difference of opinion within the city. The more conservative were shocked that the king should have been fired on, and sent emissaries to beg his pardon. A number took the opportunity to leave for England with the returning fleet.[18] The resistance movement was also strengthened. The approach of the Jacobite troops was regarded as a breach of faith; it also revealed to the citizens the poor condition and morale of the Jacobite army, which, faced with a

---

[14] *Finch MSS*, ii. 203.   [15] D'Avaux, p. 102.

[16] *James* II, ii. 332–3. The archdeacon was James Hamilton, archdeacon of Raphoe. He seems to have been a brother of Andrew Hamilton, author of *A true relation of the actions of the Inniskilling men.*

[17] Walker, pp. 17–18; Mackenzie, pp. 27–8.   [18] Walker, p. 18.

walled town, signally failed to maintain the spirit it had shown at the Finn crossings. James made further efforts to induce the city to surrender, offering the inhabitants a free pardon. The final reply was that his envoy would be fired on if he came again.[19]

2. THE SIEGE BEGINS

The Jacobite headquarters was established at St Johnston, five miles off, where a council of war was held. It was decided that James should go back to Dublin, taking Rosen with him, and that Maumont, the French lieutenant-general, should be left in charge of the Derry operation, with Hamilton as second-in-command.[20]

Within the city preparations were made to stand a siege. Seven regiments of foot and one of horse were mobilized, in all 7,020 men and 341 officers. Lundy refused to take part in these preparations and in his place two governors were jointly appointed: Major Henry Baker, a professional soldier from County Louth who had previously been stationed in Derry, and the Reverend George Walker, rector of Donoughmore, County Tyrone.[21] The *Life of James* refers to Walker as a 'fierce minister of the gospel, being of the true Cromwellian or Cameronian stamp', and attributes to his influence the decision of Derry to refuse the proffered terms.[22]

Walker's diary of the siege is the most celebrated of the contemporary accounts, and gives full credit to his own share in the defence of the city. Scots Presbyterians felt that justice had not been done them by Walker. Their contribution was given greater weight in the *Narrative* of the Reverend John Mackenzie, a Presbyterian minister who played down Walker's contribution and maintained that he was only nominally joint-governor. Mackenzie's hero was Adam Murray, a Scots settler from County Derry who showed much dash as a cavalry leader. The rival accounts set going an unpleasant post-siege controversy,

---

[19] D'Avaux, p. 109.   [20] *James II*, ii. 334–5.

[21] Walker, p. 20; C. Dalton, *Irish army lists, 1661–85*, p. 34.

[22] *James II*, ii. 334. Macaulay describes Walker as an 'aged clergyman', confusing him with his father. He was about 43 (W. S. Kerr, *Walker of Derry*, p. 14).

which makes clear the ill-feeling between Scots and English colonists in seventeenth-century Ulster. During the siege there was an interdenominational truce to the extent that the cathedral was used by Presbyterians on Sunday afternoons, after Episcopalian services in the morning.[23]

The discredited Lundy made his escape, disguised as a private soldier with a load of match on his back. In the annual celebrations of the shutting of the gates the Apprentice Boys' Clubs still burn a gigantic effigy with the inscription 'Lundy the traitor': he is the Guy Fawkes of Ulster, and his name is part of the vocabulary of present-day political abuse. But he seems to have been a defeatist rather than a traitor. He did not join James, but went to Scotland, where he was arrested and taken to the Tower of London. Later he was rehabilitated, was sent on English pay to be adjutant-general in Portugal, and helped to defend Gibraltar against the French.[24]

The siege of Derry is celebrated in Ulster tradition and has been given a wider fame in Macaulay's magnificent, and frankly partisan, account. Macaulay's theme is of desperate and courageous amateurs, deserted and betrayed by the professionals, short of food and scarcely protected by weak and neglected ramparts, but sustained by racial and religious pride. It was challenged by Hilaire Belloc, who made effective use of the French dispatches to argue that the Jacobite army had neither the men nor the equipment to conduct a siege and that the defenders of Derry, so far from being endowed with superhuman endurance, showed a lack of initiative in remaining within their walls until they were almost starved.[25] There is some truth in both versions. There were formidable problems in improvising the defence of Derry with new regiments of inexperienced men, short of food, afflicted by disease and enemy bombardment, and with thousands of refugees to care for. On the other hand, the problems of the attacking force were no less serious. To begin with there were too few troops and, though they were supplemented by a series of spasmodic reinforcements, the men were

---

[23] Mackenzie, p. 32.
[24] C. Milligan, *Siege of Londonderry*, pp. 145-9.
[25] Macaulay, *History of England*, ch. xii; H. Belloc, *James II*, pp. 235-50.

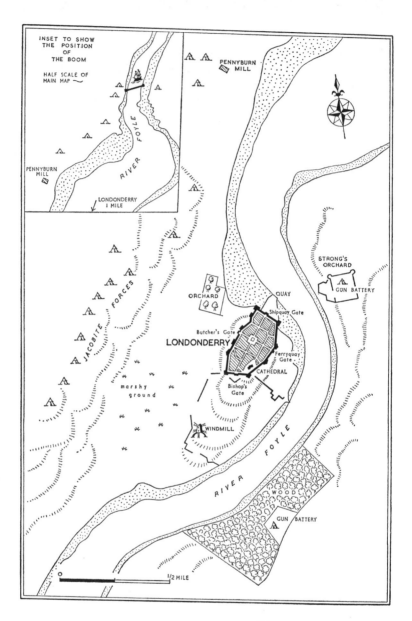

INSET TO SHOW
THE POSITION
OF
THE BOOM

HALF SCALE OF
MAIN MAP

PENNYBURN
MILL

RIVER FOYLE

PENNYBURN
MILL

LONDONDERRY
1 MILE

PENNYBURN
MILL

STRONG'S
ORCHARD

GUN BATTERY

JACOBITE FORCES

ORCHARD

QUAY

Shipquay Gate

Butcher's Gate

LONDONDERRY

Ferryquay
Gate

CATHEDRAL

Bishop's
Gate

marshy
ground

WINDMILL

RIVER FOYLE

WOODS

GUN BATTERY

1/2 MILE

SIEGE OF DERRY, 1689

ill-trained and ill-equipped; sickness and desertion constantly reduced their strength. The Jacobites were deplorably weak in artillery and siege equipment.

The geographical position of Derry had points for and against each side. The town was protected by the river, which came much nearer than it does today. On the north-east the high tide lapped against the wall at two bastions separated by the ship quay; on the west and south-west there was a large swamp, which at spring tides turned Derry into an island. If the Foyle remained open, the town could hope for relief by sea. But there was high ground on both sides of the river from which Derry could be bombarded.[26] The houses rose above the wall and offered an easy target. The river and marsh were a protection, but they also restricted freedom of manœuvre and left little forage for the defenders' horses, which had to be killed off during the siege. The fortifications were designed to keep out a hostile Irish mob; they were not capable of standing up to regular siege operations. The wall was about a mile round and about twenty feet high with two feet thickness of stone supported by an inner embankment of earth. There were four gates with towers – Shipquay, Ferryquay, Bishop's and Butcher's; a single outwork had been constructed to the south-west in front of Bishop's Gate. There were twenty guns, many of them given by London city companies fifty years before. Most of them were on the walls, but during the siege two were mounted on the cathedral tower. On the other hand, the besiegers started without siege guns or engineering equipment. A single 24-pounder which was sent later was the only gun large enough to have much effect on the walls. Mortars which fired high-trajectory bombs were the Jacobites' most effective weapons, but they did more damage to houses than to the fortifications.

Maumont, the French commander, began vigorously, though he had only 4,000 men. Culmore, a fort five miles downstream, surrendered to him without a fight, and this gave him command of the entrance to the river from Lough Foyle. But very soon Maumont was killed in a clash with the defenders. Four days later Major-General Pusignan was fatally wounded in another

---

[26] The topography and the Jacobite lines are well shown in a map made shortly after the siege by Captain Francis Nevill (copy in N.L.I.).

clash. James could only protest that generals were too valuable to be wasted in this way.[27]

Hamilton, who took charge after Maumont's death, had had little experience of higher command or of siege warfare, and was severely handicapped by lack of artillery and other equipment. The plan to bring guns from Charlemont fort had been abandoned for lack of gun-carriages.[28] In any case, the transport of a battery of heavy guns over Irish roads would be very troublesome, though the Williamites were later to show that it was not impossible. Efforts were made to send two guns from Carrickfergus, but one sank into a ditch and the carriage of the other broke.[29] A 24-pounder and an 18-pounder came from Dublin, but little use was made of them against the walls.[30] If Hamilton was to take Derry it would have to be by blockade or by sapper and miner work, for which he might call on French engineers. To begin with, he stationed his main forces at a considerable distance to the west and south-west of the city, which allowed the defenders to graze their cattle and horses on the near-by ground outside the wall. Two Jacobite battalions were stationed in an orchard on the other side of the Foyle, together with some mortars which lobbed bombs over the river and did considerable damage to the houses.[31] Hamilton's first determined approach was made a fortnight later – on the night of May 5 – when he occupied a strategic point called Windmill Hill about five hundred yards south-west of the wall. This success was short-lived, as on the following morning the defenders sallied and drove their opponents back with heavy losses.[32]

During the rest of May there was little fighting. The main development was a closing in of the Jacobite forces, which occupied the high ground to the west and north-west of the city. Derry was now hemmed in by a blockading army. But the blockade was less effective than it might have been, as a number of non-combatants had been allowed to leave the city. James was anxious to preserve the image of a monarch impartially benevolent to Protestants as well as Catholics, provided they

---

[27] *Anal. Hib.*, xxi. 90–2; R. Clark, *Anthony Hamilton*, pp. 285–6.
[28] D'Avaux, p. 81.   [29] Min. guerre, A1 895, no. 135.
[30] Ibid., A1 895, nos 135, 137.
[31] Walker, pp. 24, 28; T. Witherow, *Two diaries of Derry in 1689*, p. 285.
[32] Walker, p. 25.

would accept his authority. While he was himself near Derry a thousand people were allowed to leave, mostly old people and women and children.[33] At the beginning of May James authorized Hamilton to grant pardon to 'such persons as are now in actual arms and rebellion against us in our city of Londonderry', and a considerable number seem to have been allowed to come out of the city. Walker estimated that upwards of 10,000 accepted the protection of the Jacobites.[34] James got alarmed and wrote to Hamilton: 'I think it absolutely necessary you should not let any more men come out of Derry ... for they may want food and be glad to rid themselves of useless mouths'.[35]

On May 27 a dispatch to Paris from the French supply officer in Dublin reported disappointingly slow progress: 'the siege of Derry continues. Now that the purchasing of rations is finished and we can give our men bread and the arms for those without them have arrived and the French engineers here are going to Derry, we are going to send additional troops to make a regular siege. Work is going ahead on tools and other things that the engineers have asked for, but very slowly. Most of the soldiers in front of Derry have still only pointed sticks, without iron tips.'[36] It was not an encouraging report to make more than a month after the siege had nominally begun.

An alarming development for the Jacobites was the news that a force was being dispatched from England to relieve Derry, consisting of four regiments under Major-General Kirk. Kirk was a rough soldier whose brutal suppression of Monmouth's rebellion had earned James's favour. James regarded his defection to William as gross ingratitude.[37] His handling of the Derry operation raised doubts about the reliability of his new allegiance. If his force was to be kept out the Jacobites would have to block the river. The construction of a boom was entrusted to Pointis, the naval gunnery officer whom Seignelay had sent to Ireland in January 1689. According to Pointis's

[33] Mackenzie, p. 30.

[34] James to Hamilton, 1 May 1689 (R.I.A., MS 24. G. 1); Walker, p. 21.

[35] James to Hamilton, 10 May 1689 (T.C.D., MS E. 2. 19).

[36] *Anal. Hib.*, xxi. 114–15.

[37] *James II*, ii. 367. Only three regiments were actually sent (Story, *Continuation*, p. 5).

own account it was made of beams studded with iron clamps through which a thick rope ran to hold the beams together. He was sure that in a sheltered place like Lough Foyle no ship could get up enough way to force the boom, but to put everyone's mind at rest he was going to make a second one. He was already quite confident and would be happy to see the English try their luck, if they were foolish enough to do so.[38] But it appears that the first boom was a failure. Walker says that it was made of oak, which would not float and was broken up by the tide; a second boom of fir was more successful. It stretched across the deep-water channel about two miles below the city.[39]

Early in June James decided to send Rosen back to Derry; but it appears that he was not to supersede Hamilton in the actual conduct of the siege so much as to support him, and in particular to prevent the English reinforcements from reaching Derry.[40] Pointis reported that Hamilton had refused to serve under Rosen, as he did not wish to get involved in a dispute with him.[41] James continued to correspond with Hamilton about the siege, and Rosen evidently resented the position. He had been made marshal of the Jacobite forces in Ireland, yet Hamilton, in such close proximity to him, was treated as having an independent command. Rosen's dispatches give a gloomy picture of mismanagement and muddle. Some allowance must be made for his temperament and for the ill-feeling between him and Hamilton. But the impression we get from the other French officers is much the same: shortage of equipment, discouraged troops continually eroded by sickness and desertion, unenterprising commanders.[42]

Walker gives picturesque expression to Rosen's disappointment at the slow progress of the siege: 'he swore by the belly of God he would demolish our town and bury us in its ashes, putting all to the sword without consideration of age or sex'.[43] Although Rosen disclaimed responsibility for the siege operations, the pace of Jacobite activity was quickened after his

[38] B. M., Add. MS 32, 499.

[39] Walker, p. 29; the position of the boom is shown in Nevill's map.

[40] *Anal. Hib.*, xxi. 139.   [41] Min. guerre, A1, 963, no. 16.

[42] The French dispatches are in the ministère de la guerre archives in the Bibliothèque Nationale, Paris; a number of them have been published in *Anal. Hib.*, xxi.

[43] Walker, pp. 32–3.

arrival. Guns were moved nearer the walls, and a trench was made across the marsh towards Butcher's Gate. From the French reports it appears that trenching was difficult, as the trenches filled with water every high tide and there was continual rain. The shovels and picks broke, and promised supplies of fresh tools failed to arrive.[44] The guns were too small to be effective, and for most of the time the two largest were kept down at the boom to prevent the English ships from coming up the river. Apart from other troubles, the language difficulty was a great handicap, particularly in action: 'such occasions do not allow one to manage with an interpreter, particularly with the people of this nation whose understanding is heavy and laborious'.[45]

On June 28 the regiment of the young earl of Clancarty (Justin MacCarthy's nephew) assaulted the wall near Butcher's Gate and succeeded in lodging miners in a cellar under one of the bastions. But the defenders' fire was so hot that Clancarty was driven back and forced to leave his miners and a hundred of his best men dead on the spot.[46] From this point on, the Jacobites concentrated on a blockade and on keeping reinforcements from reaching the city. Rosen wrote to James that he took the liberty of saying that his majesty would long ago have been master of Derry if Rosen's advice had been followed, no protections given and no one allowed out of the city.[47] He followed this up with his notorious proclamation of June 30 that if the city had not surrendered by the next day he would drive all the Protestants in the surrounding area under the walls. He carried out his threat and a large number of Protestants, men, women and children, were herded in front of the wall, the idea being that the garrison would take pity on them, let them in and thus be shorter of food than ever. The garrison's retort was to erect a gallows on the wall, on which they threatened to hang their prisoners; the latter were allowed to send out a letter to Hamilton with news of the fate in store for them. Hamilton intervened and gave orders that the Protestants should be allowed to go home; which did not improve his relations with Rosen. Walker says that the chance was taken to smuggle out

[44] *Anal. Hib.*, xxi. 140–1, 180.   [45] Ibid., 144–6.
[46] Walker, p. 33. Walker mistakenly gives the date as June 30.
[47] *Anal. Hib.*, xxi. 181–2.

five hundred weaklings from the city and take in some able-bodied fighters in their place.[48] When James heard of the incident he was furious, called Rosen a barbarous Muscovite (he came from Lithuania) and supported Hamilton's intervention.[49] It is extraordinary that Rosen should have taken a step that went back so flagrantly on the protections given in the king's name to the Protestants of the Ulster countryside. From the time his order was countermanded Rosen became more and more disgruntled. His correspondence with James and Melfort often bordered on insolence and he constantly complained of ill-health and asked to be recalled.

It was now a question whether Derry would be starved out before relief came from Kirk's force. For the Jacobites it was a great advantage that Kirk proved to be extraordinarily unenterprising. Several pilots had assured him that they were willing to try and get a ship through the boom, but Kirk held a council of war at which it was suggested that there might also be sunken boats loaded with stones, and that Derry could not be in much difficulty because the citizens had sent no message to the fleet. The decision was therefore taken not to risk the attempt by water but to wait for further reinforcements and try to land on shore. A message from the fleet was brought to the city by a volunteer, Captain Roch, who swam past enemy fire, but was unable to get back to the fleet. The citizens were tantalized by the sight of the relief ships lying idly in Lough Foyle until they disappeared from view; it was not for some time that the news was received that the fleet had gone into Lough Swilly and had made a landing on Inch Island.[50]

By the end of June Derry was hard pressed. Nerves were getting frayed. There was friction between the leaders, and Walker's steadfastness came under suspicion. Food and ammunition were both short. Dogs, cats, tallow and hides were being eaten. Iron cannon-balls had run out, and substitutes were improvised from bricks covered with lead.[51] The enemy bombardment had done much damage to the houses and many people had to sleep outside during a wet and chilly summer.

[48] Mackenzie, pp. 41–2; Walker, pp. 35–6.
[49] Leslie, p. 100.
[50] Witherow, pp. 15–16; Mackenzie, pp. 40, 43.
[51] Walker, pp. 32, 34, 37.

This brought on fever and dysentery, especially among women and children. One of the victims was Governor Baker, who died at the end of June. His place was taken by John Mitchelburne, another professional soldier, who gave expression to the city's defiance by planting a red flag on one of the bastions in full sight of the enemy. It was later given an even more conspicuous position on the cathedral tower, and Mitchelburne's 'bloody flag' is part of the Derry tradition.[52]

3. THE RELIEF OF DERRY

The Jacobites were well aware of the state of affairs inside the walls, and had grounds for hoping that generous terms would induce Derry to surrender. Early in July James sent Hamilton a *carte blanche* authority to bargain with the city. If necessary he could promise the inhabitants a full pardon and guarantees of their property and the practice of their religion.[53] Hamilton sent his offer into the city in a hollow shell, which is still preserved in the cathedral porch. It led to negotiations which gave some prospect of a settlement. The defenders were near the end of their strength; starvation was imminent and the English fleet had disappeared from Lough Foyle. Negotiations seemed worth while, if only to gain time. Commissioners were sent out to bargain with the Jacobites. The terms proposed were an indemnity for the defenders, free exercise of the Protestant religion, permission for all who wanted to leave for England or Scotland. All these were agreed to; the argument was on the timing. The Jacobites wanted immediate capitulation. The defenders bargained for ten or twelve days' delay.[54] In the meantime the long-awaited message was received: a small boy made his way into the city with a letter tied in his garter to say that Kirk had landed a force on Inch Island in Lough Swilly. Heartened by this news the defenders stipulated for time; the besiegers refused, and negotiations were broken off.[55]

It was a bold move to continue resistance. Provisions were desperately short. Walker's grim price-list of dogs and cats, rats

---

[52] *Account of the transactions in the north of Ireland,* introd., p. 6.
[53] T.C.D., MS E. 2. 19.
[54] Mackenzie, pp. 43–4, 61–2.   [55] Ibid., p. 44.

and mice, is famous. So is his 'fat gentleman', who hid himself from what he fancied were the greedy eyes of his neighbours.[56] Fever was raging and the enemy kept up a fierce bombardment. Thousands died of famine and disease, and conditions within the walls were appalling: houses in ruins, backyards filled with graves hastily made and often disturbed by enemy fire, bodies thrown into cellars. There was great unrest among the garrison and signs that a section was still in favour of making terms.[57]

At the same time the morale of the Jacobite army was low. Officers neglected their duties and left their posts without leave, the excuse being that they were recruiting. Their bad example encouraged their men to desert. James threatened the officers and offered pardon to repentant deserters.[58] A French officer wrote: 'the troops are tired and many of them are ill; they have been out in the open for several months without tents in a country where it rains almost every day and the nights are extremely cold'.[59] Rosen took a serious view of Kirk's force on Inch Island. He was afraid that the besieging army would be attacked in a pincers movement, by Kirk from the north and by the Enniskilleners coming up from the south. Towards the end of July there are more and more references to plans for withdrawal. On July 20 James wrote to Hamilton to press the siege as actively as he could: if he found Derry could not be taken by force he should continue the blockade as long as he safely could; Derry would be very short of food after July 26. But meanwhile he should devastate the country round in case an English attack left him no time to do so. To make a withdrawal easier he should send off the sick and wounded; and if, which God forbid, he had to lose a place that had cost so many men, he should guard the river crossings as well as he could.[60] In the meantime the Jacobite generals at Derry had held a council of war, in which they were unanimous that Derry could not be taken by assault and that starvation was the only hope. Rosen told d'Avaux that Vauban and all the best engineers in France could not take Derry with the equipment available.[61] When

---

[56] Walker, pp. 39–40.
[57] W. Hamill, *A view of the danger and folly of being public-spirited*, pp. 10–13; Witherow, pp. 94–5.
[58] *Ormonde MSS*, ii. 406. [59] *Anal. Hib.*, xxi. 141.
[60] R.I.A., MS 24. G. 1. [61] D'Avaux, supp., p. 37.

James got the council's decision he wrote on July 22 that Hamilton should prepare to raise the siege and should actually do so unless he saw a prospect of the town surrendering for lack of food. Melfort wrote the same day: 'I confess it is hard to leave a town so near starved and of so much consequence for the king to have; but if it be so, that mortification must be swallowed.'[62]

Kirk's inactivity was disapproved of by William and his principal commander, Marshal Schomberg. Neither was satisfied with Kirk's reluctance to attempt the boom. He was told that his views about the boom appeared to be 'no otherways grounded than upon supposition'. He was to consult his sea officers and decide whether the boom could not be broken. Schomberg later remarked that Kirk was 'a capricious fellow'.[63] These orders, and Walker's appeals, seem to have decided Kirk to make the attempt. He returned to Lough Foyle with part of his fleet and with three merchant ships, laden with provisions. The attempt on the boom was made on July 28, led by the *Mountjoy* of Derry. There was an incoming tide but, at the critical moment, the wind dropped. The boom resisted the *Mountjoy*, which recoiled on to the shore, while the Jacobites blazed away at her with cannon and muskets. The captain was killed, but the rising tide and the firing of her own guns lifted the ship, and she got clear without much damage. The actual breaking of the boom was mainly the work of the crew of H.M.S. *Swallow*, which sent out a long-boat to cut the fastenings. Another of the merchant ships, the *Phoenix* of Coleraine, then broke through, and she and the *Mountjoy* went up the river unscathed by continuous enemy fire. There was so little wind that the *Mountjoy* was towed by the *Swallow*'s long-boat.[64] It was an astonishing feat on an evening of dead calm, within point-blank range of the enemy's guns.

The boom proved useless after all, and Kirk's fears of sunken boats were not realized. An Irish critic asserted that there had been barges in the Foyle, that Hamilton had been advised to block the channel by sinking them, but that he had refused to do

[62] *H.M.C., rep. 8*, app. part i, p. 497.

[63] Schomberg to Kirk, 3 July 1689 (Bodl., Carte MSS, clxxxi, f. 238); *Cal. S.P. dom., 1689–90*, p. 199.

[64] *London Gazette*, 12 Aug. 1689; S. Martin-Leake, *Life of Sir John Leake*, i. 27–9. Macaulay, following Walker, mistakenly gives the date as July 30.

so for fear of spoiling Derry's future trade.[65] The same critic blamed the Jacobite gunners:

the king's soldiers answer that the gunners were drunk with brandy. But the question remains whether these officers became inebriated without any evil design, or whether they were made to drink on purpose to render them incapable to perform their duty, and whether the English money on board the fleet was not working on them for this effect. In any case, these gunners lost Ireland through their neglect of duty.[66]

A contributory cause may have been the heavy loss of French gunners. Rosen reported in the middle of July that of the thirty-six at Derry only five were fit for service; the rest were dead or ill.[67]

The breaking of the boom was decisive. The *Phoenix* had a cargo of meal, the *Mountjoy* carried beef, peas, flour and biscuit.[68] There was no more prospect of starving Derry, and the siege was raised soon after. On the night of July 31 the Jacobites burned their tents and huts and set off on the road to Lifford.[69] The failure of the siege was disastrous for James's cause and secured a firm base in Ulster for William. But it had been a near-run thing. With greater determination and more efficiency on the part of the Jacobites the result might have been different. But a siege was alien to the Irish tradition of warfare, and for most of the Jacobite army Derry was too far from home. Melfort was a poor organizer and Hamilton showed little initiative. Too much attention was paid to the parliamentary session and too little to the equipment and reinforcement of the besieging army. Rosen was not the man to ease a difficult situation, and ill-feeling between French and Irish officers hampered operations. D'Avaux was very critical of Hamilton and accused him of forming a cabal against the French.[70] The shortage of heavy guns made starvation the most likely method of taking Derry, and failure to close the river effectively was a

---

[65] *Jacobite narrative*, p. 66.   [66] Ibid., p. 84.
[67] D'Avaux, p. 339.   [68] Mackenzie, p. 46; Witherow, p. 100.
[69] Mackenzie, p. 46.

[70] D'Avaux, p. 159. Relations between Hamilton and the French were prejudiced from the start by the fact that he was known to be out of favour with Louis XIV, to whose daughter he had presumed to pay attention (d'Avaux, supp., pp. xiv, xv).

cardinal error. The blockade was also weakened by James's policy of allowing numbers to leave the city and live under royal protection in the countryside.

For William the relief of Derry was an unexpected mercy; he had given up hope of saving it.[71] For the defenders it was a triumph of persistence and faith. They attributed their deliverance to God and themselves and thought poorly of Kirk's procrastination. They had suffered greatly: thousands had died; the city was a stinking ruin; all over the countryside farms were smouldering and crops destroyed. It was long before Derry recovered, and the citizens felt that they should have had more help from the English government.[72] They kept their walls and fostered with unforgiving pride the traditions of their ordeal.

4. THE DEFENCE OF ENNISKILLEN

Enniskillen, the second centre of Protestant resistance, was at first sight of much less importance than Derry. It was not a walled town; but there was a castle, which had figured prominently in the Ulster warfare at the end of the sixteenth century, and the site was one of great natural strength. It was on an island at the junction of Upper and Lower Lough Erne, protected by the lake on one side and by river and marsh on the other. Two stone bridges linked it with the mainland to the north and south. The town itself was a Protestant settlement, a creation of James I's plantation. But it was small and unimpressive: eighty houses with thatched roofs. Its importance was as a centre of resistance for Protestants drawn from a wide area, including north Connacht as well as southern Ulster. The fact that Ballyshannon at the mouth of the Erne was also in Protestant control gave communication with the outside world, and made the Erne valley a formidable barrier against a Jacobite attack. The defenders of Enniskillen were never cooped up as were the Derry men. They were rough-riding countrymen and used their horses to make troublesome raids over a wide area. They were a continual threat to the long line of Jacobite communications that straggled from Dublin to Derry past Charlemont, Dungannon and Omagh.

[71] *Finch MSS*, ii. 237.
[72] *The Derry complaint*, 1699.

To begin with, Enniskillen was not taken very seriously by the Jacobites. Tyrconnell had sent two companies to occupy it in December 1688, but when they were refused admission by the local Protestants he paid little attention to the rebuff and posted the troops elsewhere.[73] The Protestants prepared for resistance, organizing their forces and strengthening the defences of the town; they then declared openly for William and Mary. In March 1689 Tyrconnell dispatched Pierce Butler, Viscount Galmoy, with a force to bring southern Ulster under control. He found a formidable obstacle in Crom, a 'planter's castle' on the shores of Upper Lough Erne which the Protestants had turned into a frontier garrison. Galmoy, having no artillery, improvised two guns from tin bound with buckram, but failed to impress the garrison. His ultimatum to Enniskillen was equally ineffective. After a successful sally by the defenders of Crom, Galmoy withdrew to the south. The Enniskilleners were encouraged by their success and enraged by what they regarded as gross perfidy on Galmoy's part. There was to have been an exchange of a Jacobite prisoner for the dean of Kilmore's son who had been seized by Galmoy. The Jacobite was handed over, but the dean's son was hanged on the charge of having accepted William's commission.[74]

Galmoy's retreat left the Enniskilleners in a position to threaten the Jacobite communications, and they conducted a number of successful raids. Their numbers were swollen by a band of Sligo Protestants who had attempted to join Lundy in Derry but had been cut off by the Jacobite advance. The Enniskilleners found an effective commander in Thomas Lloyd, a Roscommon settler who developed a talent for guerrilla warfare and proved an abler leader than the governor, Gustavus Hamilton. James's memoirs refer to Lloyd and say that his men called him their 'little Cromwell'.[75] One of his most notable feats took place on May 7 at Belleek on the River Erne. Lloyd had been sent to relieve Ballyshannon, which was under attack

[73] A. Hamilton, *A true relation of the actions of the Inniskilling men*, p. 4. Hamilton was a Church of Ireland clergyman; his account is supplemented by that of the Presbyterian William McCarmick, *A farther impartial account of the actions of the Inniskilling men*; but Enniskillen generated less rancour than Derry did.

[74] Hamilton, pp. 9–13; McCarmick, pp. 30–3.

[75] *James II*, ii. 383.

from the Connacht side. He routed a Jacobite force of horse and foot and captured a number of prisoners.[76] The Enniskilleners followed up this success by seizing Jacobite posts in County Cavan and extending their raids as far as Kells, forty miles from Dublin. This stirred James to detail Rosen, his senior French commander, to move against Enniskillen. He was to take four infantry battalions together with cavalry and dragoons and four pieces of artillery. This would have been a formidable expedition, but the plans were never put into effect. When Rosen reached the rendezvous at Trim there were no dragoons; part only of the cavalry, and that without proper arms, most of them without saddles and bridles; only two of the four infantry regiments, one of them indifferently armed and the other extremely badly; most of the ammunition for the guns was the wrong size. In spite of these shortcomings, Rosen was prepared to march on Enniskillen, but the orders were countermanded and he was sent to Derry instead.[77]

Meanwhile the Enniskilleners claimed a further success, this time against Sarsfield, who commanded a cavalry force in County Leitrim and was trying to prevent boats being taken up the Erne from Ballyshannon to Enniskillen. A Williamite broadsheet describes the fight as a resounding victory: 'Sarsfield and five or six more narrowly escaping, the rest being most killed and about two hundred taken, the best of which they kept and the rest they stripped and sent away to carry the news to their friends.'[78] A Jacobite informant reported that the Enniskilleners were 'much puffed up with their success against Sarsfield'.[79] But an effort to relieve the pressure on Derry by attacking the Jacobite garrison in Omagh was not so successful and the Enniskilleners were repulsed.[80]

About the end of June James ordered Berwick, who was at Derry, to join Sarsfield, who was south of the Erne, in a combined operation against the Enniskilleners.[81] Berwick established his force of cavalry and dragoons at Trillick, twelve miles north-east of Enniskillen. He advanced towards the town and routed the force that came out to meet him. But he was unable

---

[76] Hamilton, pp. 19–20.   [77] D'Avaux, pp. 220–1.
[78] *An exact relation of the glorious victory* . . .
[79] *H.M.C., rep. 8,* app. p. 494.
[80] McCarmick, pp. 46–7.   [81] D'Avaux, p. 376.

to exploit his success, as Rosen recalled him to deal with the threat from Kirk's force in Lough Swilly.[82] This was a setback to James's plan for subduing Enniskillen. Later he tried to revive it and Berwick was quite ready to fall in with his father's scheme. A curious letter that Berwick wrote to Sarsfield at the end of July shows that he still had hopes – never to be fulfilled – of breaking the line of the Erne and making a joint attack on the Protestant rebels who held it. The letter addresses Sarsfield as 'dear Notorious', a nickname that implies an already high reputation in the field, though his operations against the Enniskilleners did little to enhance it.[83]

5. THE BATTLE OF NEWTOWNBUTLER

James's final attempt to solve the problem of Enniskillen was to entrust it to Justin MacCarthy, Viscount Mountcashel, who was sent north with three regiments of foot, sixteen troops of cavalry and dragoons and eight field-guns. He was to be joined by dragoons under Major-General Anthony Hamilton (Richard's brother), and by Ulster Gaels under Cuconnacht Mor Maguire. James had thoughts of going himself to Enniskillen, but was warned off by the prudent d'Avaux.[84]

If MacCarthy's force could join up with those commanded by Berwick and Sarsfield, Enniskillen would be under heavy pressure. But the Enniskilleners had themselves been strengthened by supplies of arms and ammunition sent to them by Kirk round the coast from Lough Swilly.[85] Kirk also sent them some good officers, notably Colonel William Wolseley, a tough, forceful Englishman. Wolseley was able to make effective use of the Enniskilleners' knowledge of the countryside, which is a bewildering network of lakes and marshes, separated by small hills or 'drumlins'.

The fighting began on July 30 with an assault by MacCarthy against Crom Castle on Upper Lough Erne.[86] James, probably

[82] *Anal. Hib.*, xxi. 197.   [83] *Irish Sword*, ii. 109.
[84] D'Avaux, pp. 374, 384; Harris, *William III*, p. 221.
[85] *A letter from Liverpool.*
[86] Hamilton, pp. 34–8, and McCarmick, pp. 60–1, give accounts of the fighting at Crom and Newtownbutler.

unwisely, had specifically ordered him to take Crom before beginning the joint attack on Enniskillen.[87] The castle had a strong position on the lake shore, some fifteen miles south of Enniskillen by water. The approach was protected by outworks, which MacCarthy's troops captured without much difficulty. Against orders the men rushed forward to the castle walls, where they were received with heavy musket fire and driven back with considerable loss. David Creichton, the defender of Crom, sent to Enniskillen with an urgent appeal for help; and in response a strong force marched down the Dublin road under the command of Lt-Col Berry, one of the officers who had come with Wolseley. MacCarthy ordered Anthony Hamilton and his dragoons to drive back Berry's force and occupy a position 'where a hundred men could stop ten thousand'.[88] On the morning of July 31 Hamilton engaged Berry's force but, instead of obeying orders, followed the retreating Enniskilleners for five miles through Lisnaskea towards Enniskillen. At this point the road formed a narrow causeway between marshes till it crossed the Colebrooke river. Hamilton made his dragoons dismount and was leading them along the causeway when they came under heavy firing from either side, where the Enniskilleners had ambushed the road. Hamilton was wounded and handed over to his second-in-command, who ordered a retreat which soon became a disorderly rout as the Enniskilleners pursued the flying Jacobites. The dragoons stopped when they reached MacCarthy and the main army, but Hamilton continued his flight till he reached Navan in County Meath. He was later court-martialled, but acquitted; his subordinate was convicted and executed – a verdict that did not meet with general approval. D'Avaux said that Hamilton did not deserve to be an officer and had been made a major-general only to please Tyrconnell.[89]

Soon after his victory over Hamilton, Berry was joined by Wolseley. A democratic council of war was held in which the

[87] D'Avaux, p. 384.

[88] Ibid., p. 385.

[89] *Jacobite narrative*, p. 82; d'Avaux to Louis, 4/14 Aug. 1689, quoted in d'Avaux, supp., p. xvi. Anthony and Richard Hamilton were brothers of Lady Tyrconnell's first husband and on very friendly terms with Tyrconnell. For Anthony's career see R. Clark, *Life of Anthony Hamilton*.

troops were consulted whether to retire to Enniskillen or to attack MacCarthy, who was at Newtownbutler. The Enniskilleners were all for attack; the word was 'no popery', which they found 'very acceptable'. MacCarthy withdrew to a strong position to the south of Newtownbutler, traditionally at the hamlet of Kilgarret. The narrow road ran up a hill at this point, with marshy ground on either side. He posted cannon across the road and marshalled his men on the hillside. The Enniskillen horse, who tried to advance along the road, were effectively barred by the Jacobite cannon-fire. But the foot and dragoons made their way through the bog on either side of the road, seized the cannon and killed the gunners. This allowed the Enniskillen horse to ride up the hill. The Jacobite cavalry, instead of facing them, wheeled about and took the road southwards. The infantry at first stood their ground, but then followed the example of the cavalry and ran for it, throwing away their arms. MacCarthy's Munstermen did not know the lie of the land and, instead of making for the open country to the east, turned south-west through the lakes and marshes that lay between Newtownbutler and Lough Erne. The Enniskillen cavalry quickly seized Wattle Bridge, over a tributary of the Erne, which was the only way of escape southwards. The Enniskillen foot pursued the fugitives, beating the bushes for them and ruthlessly putting to death all they found. Many of the Jacobites in desperation plunged into the lake and were drowned. MacCarthy and half a dozen of his officers stood their ground. For a time they sheltered in a small wood. Then MacCarthy came out on horseback and fired his pistol at the Enniskilleners who were on guard over the captured cannon. They fired back, and MacCarthy was wounded in several places; one shot would have been fatal if it had not been intercepted by his watch. An Enniskillener was about to dispatch him with his clubbed musket when a Jacobite officer called out that he was their general, and he was given quarter. His personal bravery was evidently an attempt to atone for the poor showing of his army. The *Life of James* gives a brief account of the battle: 'though the foot fought with great obstinacy and the general did all that could be expected from a brave and experienced officer, yet the king's horse soon giving way the rest were totally routed and my lord Montcassel very ill

wounded and taken prisoner'.[90] James showed his concern for
MacCarthy by sending a doctor and a surgeon to attend him in
Enniskillen.[91]

Wolseley had won a striking victory. He reported that there
were over 2,000 dead and that nearly 500 prisoners and all the
enemy's baggage and cannon had been taken. He put his own
strength at 2,200 and that of the enemy at 5,500. He attributed
his success to the excellence of his officers and the marksmanship
of his men.[92] MacCarthy had a good reputation as a soldier, but
his men had shown all the weaknesses of a raw and undisciplined
army – impetuous in advance and headlong in retreat. The
battle was a severe blow to the morale of the Jacobites, already
lowered by the long and useless siege of Derry. It enhanced
still further the reputation of the Enniskilleners, and encouraged
William and Schomberg to give them a prominent place in
subsequent campaigns.

[90] *James II*, ii. 368–9.
[91] McCarmick, p. 65.
[92] *Great news of a bloody fight in Newton in Ireland.*

VII

THE FAILURE OF SCHOMBERG

~~~~~~~~~~~~~~~~~~~~~~~~~~~~~~~~~~~~~

I. THE IRISH EXPEDITION

WILLIAM'S HOPES of getting the Irish Jacobites to surrender had soon faded. Sending Richard Hamilton to Tyrconnell in January 1689 had proved a deplorable fiasco. A month later William had published a declaration promising religious toleration and security of property if the Jacobites surrendered, and threatening confiscation of estates if they did not; but it met with no response.[1] It became clear that military force would be needed to establish William's authority in Ireland. There was much delay in mustering and equipping the expedition. William, with some justification, was suspicious of the English regular army and was not then prepared to make use of it in Ireland. He sent Marlborough with 8,000 men to Holland to take the place of the Dutch troops he had brought to England. The commander of the Irish expedition was to be Schomberg, a celebrated veteran of Louis XIV's army, who had left the French service at the time of the revocation of the edict of Nantes. He had then joined the elector of Brandenburg, who had put his services at William's disposal. Schomberg's father was German, but his mother was English. He was now seventy-four, but still active; he was, however, of a professional cast of mind, cautious, fond of elaborate planning, and opposed to improvisation.

A committee of the privy council was appointed to deal with

[1] *H.M.C., rep. 12*, app., pp. 164–5 (see p. 56, above).

Irish affairs. It included Schomberg as well as leading English politicians. The plan adopted was to raise new regiments, to be commanded in the main by Irish Protestant nobles and gentlemen exiled in England.[2] In the latter part of March the house of commons voted funds sufficient to equip a force of 20,000 and maintain it for six months, with a promise of further finance if the war in Ireland were to last longer.[3] The slow progress made in organizing the expedition aroused criticism, one of the critics being John Evelyn: 'the new king much blamed for neglecting Ireland, now like to be ruined by the Lord Tyrconnell and his popish party, too strong for the Protestants'.[4] The failure to relieve Derry was also criticized, and the house of commons voted that those who had caused delay in sending relief were enemies of the king and the kingdom.[5] Schomberg was not formally appointed to command the Irish expedition till the middle of July, and was then held up for several weeks at Chester, waiting for troops, equipment and shipping. Meanwhile he made a number of complaints, which were particularly directed against Shales, the supply officer: Shales was a muddler and unreliable; he had not sent enough provisions and was particularly short on beer; the muskets he supplied were so bad that he must have been bribed to pass them; it was strongly suspected that he had till lately been a papist.[6]

It had been expected that Schomberg would reach Ireland while Derry was still under siege, but he was so much delayed that the siege had been raised before he left England. He sailed on August 12 from Hoylake, near Chester, with twelve regiments of infantry, leaving his horse and the rest of the foot to follow as soon as they were ready. The wind was favourable, so instead of waiting off the Isle of Man for the rest of his forces he made straight for Belfast Lough and anchored in Bangor Bay on August 13.[7] William had local command of the sea, and the

---

[2] *H.M.C., rep. 12*, app. pp. 167–9.   [3] *Parl. hist.*, v. 195–6.
[4] J. Evelyn, *Diary*, iii, 76.   [5] *Commons' jn.*, x. 260–3.
[6] *Cal. S.P. dom., 1689–90*, pp. 188–220.
[7] Ibid., p. 193; Story, pp. 6–7; *Great news from the army*; *More good news from Ireland*. The latter pamphlet's statement that Schomberg's horse had still to come conflicts with Story, but is corroborated by particulars of later sailings in the *London Gazette*, etc. Groomsport is sometimes named as the landing-place, but contemporary references are all to Bangor. Groomsport seems to be first mentioned in Smith and Harris,

French navy made no attempt then or later to interfere with Schomberg's communications. Nor was any attempt made to attack the Williamites as they landed. There was a Jacobite force in the neighbourhood commanded by the Scottish brigadier Maxwell, which was estimated at 500 horse and dragoons. Schomberg is said to have been apprehensive that his infantry would be attacked and to have made his men work far into the night making an entrenchment: 'for (said he) if they have one dram of courage or wit they will attack us this night, since they will never expect the like opportunity'.[8] Maxwell made no attack, but hastily retreated without even burning Belfast; the only Jacobite force that remained in the neighbourhood was two regiments in the great Norman fortress of Carrickfergus. According to d'Avaux, Maxwell's conduct was loudly complained of by the Irish, who had no faith in Scotsmen.[9] Schomberg's men were greeted with joy by the local Protestants 'falling on their knees with tears in their eyes and thanking God and the English for their deliverance, telling the soldiers never were people more welcome, kissing them for joy'.[10]

By the end of August four cavalry regiments, one regiment of dragoons and six more infantry regiments had arrived from England. Of the total of eighteen infantry regiments, two were Dutch, three Huguenots, and the rest levies newly raised in England.[11] The chaplain of one of these regiments was George Story whose 'impartial history' is a remarkably objective account of the war, though his Williamite sympathies are plainly discernible. Two more cavalry regiments and an infantry regiment were sent from England early in September. With the forces from Derry and Enniskillen the Williamite strength in Ireland was by then over 20,000, though not all of them were brought into the field against the main Jacobite army.[12]

Schomberg made it his first business to take Carrickfergus,

[8] *More good news from Ireland.*   [9] D'Avaux, p. 443.
[10] *Great news from the army.*   [11] Story, p. 11.
[12] *London Gazette,* 12 Sept. 1689; the figure of 30,000 there given seems to be an over-estimate.

Ancient and present state of the county of Down (1744), p. 129. According to a diary in Schomberg's *Life* only part of the convoy arrived on 13 Aug., between 5,000 and 6,000, the rest waiting off the Isle of Man for four days (Kazner, *Leben Schombergs,* ii. 288).

which was held for James by Munster and Ulster troops, commanded respectively by MacCarthy More and Cormac O'Neill. He invested the place with twelve regiments (about 9,000 men), supported by cannon and mortars, and made a full-scale attack with trench works and heavy artillery. Later he complained that most of his cannon were of bad metal and burst. A naval bombardment supported the military attack. The garrison, though greatly outnumbered, put up a gallant defence. It was to be a feature of the war that the Jacobites fought better from behind walls. They stripped lead off the castle roof to make bullets and worked hard at the repair of breaches in the walls. They held out for a week before surrendering on honourable terms that allowed them to join the nearest Jacobite garrison. Story described them as 'lusty, strong fellows, but ill-clad'; he added that 'to give them their due they did not behave themselves ill in that siege'.[13] The Jacobites claimed that the terms were 'barbarously violated by the soldiers, who without regard to age, sex or quality disarmed and stripped the townspeople, forcing even women to run the gauntlet stark naked'.[14] There is corroboration from the non-juror Charles Leslie of Glaslough for the rough treatment of those who surrendered at Carrickfergus, and one of Schomberg's officers admitted that the terms were 'not too strictly observed by us'.[15] Story blamed the 'Irish Scots' and says that Schomberg himself had to ride in among them, pistol in hand, to keep the Irish from being murdered.[16]

2. JACOBITE REACTION

Their failure at Derry and their defeat at Newtownbutler were heavy blows to the Jacobites, who were already dissatisfied with their experience of James and of some of the advisers he had brought with him. Melfort in particular was severely criticized for mismanagement. According to d'Avaux, Tyrconnell openly declared that Melfort would be the ruin of the country, and the general opinion was that he was either a traitor or extremely

[13] *James II*, ii. 372; Story, pp. 7–10; J. Dalrymple, *Memoirs of Great Britain and Ireland*, iii (ii). 88; *London Gazette*, 29 Aug.–2 Sept. 1689.
[14] Macpherson, i. 222. A Williamite broadsheet, *Great news from the duke of Schomberg's army* describes a woman being stripped by other women.
[15] Leslie, p. 161; B.M., Add. MS 5540.   [16] Story, p. 10.

incompetent. His influence over James was such that prominent members of the administration were regretting that the king had ever come to Ireland. James's confessor told Melfort that if he did not leave he would be assassinated. At the end of August James granted Melfort's request to withdraw to France, and he left soon afterwards.[17] James himself was in despair at the situation and thought of going back to France. He changed his mind when Melfort told him that it was just what Tyrconnell wanted.[18]

There was consternation in Jacobite Ireland when the news was received of Schomberg's landing in Ulster with a substantial army. There seemed little prospect of offering resistance to a commander of his experience and reputation. The Jacobite army was very much below strength. At a review taken about the time of Schomberg's landing there were several regiments only two hundred strong, and no regiment came near its full complement.[19] Rosen estimated that James could not put more than six or seven thousand men in the field and that a third of them were unarmed. For those that had muskets there were not more than four rounds apiece.[20] Gun-money, so far from solving the financial problem, had produced rocketing prices and a general shortage of goods. There was panic in official Dublin and ill-concealed satisfaction on the faces of Protestants. They found means of corresponding with Schomberg and were ready to form a fifth column for him.[21] As a precautionary measure Protestants were ordered to hand in their arms and horses; a number of them, including William King, dean of St Patrick's, were detained; churches and meeting-houses were searched. Proclamations were issued which specifically referred to Protestants as disaffected to the Jacobite government. Those Protestants who had recently come to Dublin from the country were ordered to return; residents were restricted to their own parishes.[22]

To repel the invader all Catholics between the ages of sixteen and sixty were ordered to arm themselves as best they could, and to be ready to obey the orders of the appropriate officials. Those living in coastal districts were to take their horses, cattle and

[17] D'Avaux, pp. 313, 344, 434, 509.   [18] Ibid., pp. 379, 390.

[19] Ibid., pp. 451–4. The full complement was 806 privates.

[20] *Anal. Hib.*, iv. 201; d'Avaux, supp., p. 31.

[21] D'Avaux, p. 472; Leslie, p. 54.

[22] *Ormonde MSS*, ii. 403–5; n.s., viii. 369.

cash at least ten miles inland.[23] The emergency measures were evidently abused, and further orders forbade the unauthorized commandeering of horses and forcible recruiting; the new militias were warned to plunder the enemy and not the faithful subjects of the king.[24] Offers were made to Schomberg's soldiers to transfer their allegiance; every man who came over, irrespective of religion or nationality, would be given forty shillings; officers would be given equivalent commands.[25] In Dublin orders were given to form a militia of the inhabitants without reference to religion. In the words of a pamphlet 'King James arms his dejected Protestants again, and we are all summoned out into St Stephen's fields'. But the French objected to the move and orders were issued to Protestants to lay down their arms.[26] Trinity College was seized and converted into a prison for Protestants. Six of the fellows and masters were ordered to be arrested, but the bishop of Meath got James to withdraw the order. Soldiers quartered in the college did much damage, but the library was saved by Father Teigue Mac-Carthy, one of James's chaplains.[27]

The French generals took the view that James's forces were too weak to defend Dublin against Schomberg, and that his best plan would be to retire to Athlone and try to hold the line of the Shannon till winter, when French reinforcements might be expected. James refused to accept this advice: 'he was resolved not to be tamely walked out of Ireland, but to have one blow for it at least'.[28] It was alleged that the French advised him to burn Dublin, and that only James's intervention prevented this.[29] Tyrconnell, who now came forward again, supported the policy of standing firm. The emergency had an excellent effect on his health, which improved rapidly.[30] James showed courage and initiative in setting out for Drogheda with a small force of two hundred, his own guards and some gentlemen volunteers. He reached it on August 26, while Schomberg was still besieging Carrickfergus.[31] A council of war was held in Drogheda at

[23] Ibid., ii. 407.   [24] Ibid., pp. 412–14.   [25] Ibid., p. 411.

[26] *Great news from the port of Kingsale in Ireland.*

[27] College register, quoted in J. W. Stubbs, *History of the University of Dublin*, pp. 130–4. Credit for saving the library is also given to Michael Moore, the scholarly priest whom James appointed provost.

[28] D'Avaux, p. 443; *James II*, ii. 373.

[29] *Great news.*   [30] D'Avaux, p. 380.   [31] Macpherson, i. 222.

which the French strongly urged James to go back to Dublin. James said he wanted Irish advice, as the matter was one of national security, and dispatched Sir Richard Nagle to consult Tyrconnell and others. They recommended that the re-organization of the army should be speeded up in the hope that it could be got ready in time to meet Schomberg at Drogheda, if his advance was sufficiently leisurely.[32] James ordered Berwick to conduct a delaying action based on Newry: this took the form of breaking up causeways and burning the countryside. Mean-while Tyrconnell joined James at Drogheda, bringing with him substantial reinforcements.[33]

3. CONFRONTATION AT DUNDALK

Schomberg's plan was to march south through Newry to Dundalk. When he sailed for Ireland most of his provisions and transport were not ready. He gave orders for them to be shipped to Carlingford Lough so that he could pick them up there; some heavy guns were also sent by sea from Carrick-fergus. He left Belfast on September 2 and reached Newry three days later, to find that it had been burned by Berwick, who had retreated to the south beyond Dundalk.[34] The Jacobites made no attempt to hold Schomberg up in the difficult Moyry Pass between Newry and Dundalk. Lack of a supply train soon put Schomberg's troops in difficulties, as the retreating Jacobites had laid waste the countryside. Story himself was a sufferer: 'I was forced to go and dig potatoes, which made the greatest part of a dinner to better men than myself; and if it was so with us it may easily be supposed the poor soldiers had harder times of it'.[35] When they reached Dundalk, the ships had not arrived and the soldiers, deprived of bread and beer, lived on local mutton which, eaten freely 'without bread and nothing to drink but water, cast a great many into fluxes'. Storms had delayed the ships, and it was a week before bread could be brought overland from Belfast.[36] On the march Schomberg was joined by three regiments of Enniskillen horse and dragoons. As they were without uniforms and had brought a number of camp-followers

[32] D'Avaux, pp. 459–60.   [33] Macpherson, i. 223.
[34] Story, pp. 11–13.   [35] Ibid., p. 42.
[36] — to John Cary, 23 Sept. 1689 (B.M., Add. MS 5540); Story, p. 18.

riding on 'garrons', their arrival caused some astonishment. A diary kept by one of Schomberg's entourage records:

the arrival of the so-called Inniskilling dragoons increased the number of the army, but not its mutual harmony. The sight of their thin little nags and the wretched dress of their riders, half-naked with sabre and pistols hanging from their belts, looked like a horde of Tartars . . . These brave people offered themselves as volunteers for the advance guard. Only they could not bear to be given orders, but kept saying that they were no good if they were not allowed to act as they pleased. This was such a contrast to Schomberg's strict discipline that he decided to make an exception and let them go according to their own genius.[37]

Schomberg thought the Enniskilleners would be more dependable than the newly-raised English levies, and that when they got their uniforms they would look smarter. However, in action they preferred their shirt sleeves, according to a Williamite broadsheet.[38]

On September 7 Schomberg's army camped in low marshy ground about a mile north of Dundalk, and was to remain there for the next two months. The site, in a hollow at the foot of the hills, was subject to heavy rainfall, and it was later noted that James's army had the advantage of drier weather and more solid ground.[39] During this time the Jacobite army was at Drogheda; reports reached Schomberg that it was still assembling and was unlikely to muster more than 20,000 effective troops. It should have been to Schomberg's advantage to have continued to march south, where he would have found better ground and had the opportunity of bringing to battle a raw army led by commanders of less experience and ability than himself. Story says that the local Protestants of County Louth had collected provisions in the expectation of Schomberg's arrival.[40] Such an advance could have been timed to co-ordinate with an enterprising naval move on the part of Captain George Rooke, who brought his squadron of twelve ships along the coast of County Dublin, threatening to cut communications between Dublin and the Jacobite army. The Dublin commander, Simon Luttrell, used the militia to such good purpose that no landing was made; he was afraid that if a Williamite

[37] Kazner, ii. 305–6.   [38] *True and impartial account.*
[39] Story, p. 39.   [40] Ibid., pp. 16–17.

force landed it would be joined by local Protestants and that, in the absence of the Jacobite army, Dublin would be taken.[41]

But in fact Schomberg stopped at Dundalk, which was an encouragement to the Jacobites. Rosen deduced that Schomberg's army 'wanted something necessary for their going forwards'. A deserter told James that Schomberg's troops were sick and already in want of provisions. The Jacobites therefore decided that it would be safe for their own forces to advance.[42] On September 14 James led his army to Ardee, halfway between Drogheda and Dundalk. Two days later he moved forward to the river Fane, five miles south of Dundalk. Deserters came in to say that Schomberg was fortifying Dundalk and seemed to be preparing for a siege rather than a battle.[43] This is borne out by Schomberg's own dispatch of September 20, which has a markedly defensive tone: 'I do not see why we should risk anything on our side. We have one little river before us and they another.' He had a regular series of trenches made to protect his position.[44]

Encouraged by Schomberg's inertia James moved his forces within cannon-shot (half a mile) of the enemy and arrayed them in battle order. The Jacobite secretary made the most of the occasion and recorded that the soldiers 'transported with courage by the presence and great example of their king at the head of them could not forbear by shouting and other demonstrations of joy to dare and challenge the invaders, who nevertheless could not be provoked nor invited by any means out of their fortifications'.[45] On the Williamite side Story says that Schomberg's subordinates urged him to attack, to which his answer was: 'let them alone and we will see what they will do'.[46] A curious Jacobite broadsheet described the scene and noted that the gleaming scythes, with which most of the infantry were armed, seemed to strike terror into the enemy. The same source says that James's headquarters were in 'some very mean cottages . . . where his bedchamber was a poor Irish cabin (hard to creep into) without either door, window or chimney: the French ambassador and the duke of Tyrconnell had suitable

---

[41] Macpherson, i. 223; d'Avaux, p. 476.
[42] Ibid.; Story, *Continuation*, p. 9.　　[43] Macpherson, i. 22.
[44] Dalrymple, iii (ii). 31; Story, p. 19.
[45] Macpherson, i. 222.　　[46] Story, p. 22.

apartments in his majesty's quarters'.[47] Schomberg's inactivity was incomprehensible to d'Avaux: he must be much
weaker than the Jacobites had thought, or else he must be
planning to provoke a rising in Dublin and trying to lure the
Jacobite army as far as possible from the capital.[48] D'Avaux
reported to Louis that James had no intention of attacking
Schomberg's trenches but wished to gain a moral advantage
and encourage his troops, who seemed eager for battle although
most of them were without effective weapons. D'Avaux was
amazed at the change that had taken place in James's army; he
had thought it would have been inconceivable for it to face
Schomberg. He gave the credit to Tyrconnell and the Irish
officers, who had redoubled their efforts after the departure of
Melfort. On d'Avaux's advice several Irish officers had been
made brigadiers, which had given general satisfaction.[49]

The nearness of the two armies made it easy for the Jacobites
to distribute literature inviting Schomberg's men to desert; it
was printed in French as well as in English and had some effect
on the so-called Huguenot regiments. One of their number was
found to have a letter addressed to d'Avaux; another had
written to both James and d'Avaux, promising to bring over a
number of men from the French regiments. Schomberg's inquiries
showed that these regiments contained a number of Catholics
who had deserted from the French army and made their way
through Holland to England, where recruiting for Ireland was
taking place without much security clearance. Nearly two
hundred Catholics were combed out and sent back to England.[50]
A French officer, who was taken prisoner by the Jacobites, told
them that if Schomberg could have relied on his French regiments he would have attacked James.[51]

William wrote more than once urging Schomberg to attack
the enemy. Schomberg countered with criticisms of his officers
and complaints about the men's weapons and shoes and about
the badness of the roads. He had a poor opinion of the newly
raised regiments: 'the Irish lords thought of nothing but to have

[47] *A relation of what most remarkably happened during the last campaign.*
[48] D'Avaux, p. 474.
[49] Ibid., p. 479.
[50] Dalrymple, iii (ii). 34; Story, pp. 24–5. *Jacobite narrative*, pp. 251–3.
[51] D'Avaux, p. 616.

boys at a cheap rate'. He had ideas of marching west to the Shannon and asked for an additional landing to be made elsewhere on the coast. He made much of the strength of James's army: 'at least double the number of ours, of which a part is disciplined and pretty well armed, and hitherto better nourished'.[52] His chief enemies were in fact the weather and disease. The tents had been pitched in marshy ground and provided wretched accommodation, so that orders were given to build huts instead.[53] Fever and flux spread rapidly, and the condition of the huts became appalling: 'the living occupants seemed very sorry when the others were to be buried . . . whilst they had them in their huts they either served to lay between them and the cold wind or at least were serviceable to sit or lie on'.[54] There was an acute shortage of medicines, the surgeons' chests having no specifics for flux or fever. Some of the sick were removed by sea, but conditions on the ships were so bad that some arrived with no living cargo. Those for whom the ships had no room were sent in wagons and suffered tortures on the rough roads. Their destination was the 'great hospital' in Belfast, in which several thousand died that winter. Altogether some seven thousand of those in the Dundalk camp died.[55] The *London Gazette* carried encouragingly misleading reports that the health of the troops was good and that they were well provided for.[56] Much of the sickness was due to carelessness and insanitary habits. Story contrasted the English quarters with those of a Dutch regiment that was so well hutted that it lost only eleven men.[57]

The two armies remained at close quarters for over a fortnight till, on October 6, James fell back on Ardee, which was converted into a defended frontier position by the time James went back to Dublin at the beginning of November.[58] October weather had taken its toll of James's army also. Rainstorms soaked the tents and huts and caused a shortage of turf. Many fell sick from damp quarters and half-cooked meat.[59] Jacobite medical arrangements were no better than Schomberg's. A French officer found two hundred sick in an old church, most of them on the bare ground. In another 'hospital' there were three

---

[52] Dalrymple, iii (ii). 38–51. [53] Story, p. 27. [54] Ibid., p. 30.
[55] Ibid., pp. 35, 39. [56] *London Gazette*, 21 Oct. 1689.
[57] Story, p. 38. [58] *James II*, ii. 383. [59] Stevens, pp. 86–7.

hundred without surgeon, medicine or attendants.[60] Soon after James went back to Dublin, Schomberg withdrew his forces northwards and made his winter headquarters at Lisburn.

4. SLIGO CHANGES HANDS

Connacht was the scene of much more activity in the autumn of 1689. Colonel Thomas Lloyd, the 'little Cromwell' who had distinguished himself in the defence of Enniskillen, commanded the Williamite forces in Sligo, and for some time kept the initiative in the surrounding countryside. At the end of September he gained a notable success in a surprise attack on Boyle, County Roscommon, where he routed a Jacobite force commanded by Colonel Charles O'Kelly, the veteran who was to write the history of the Irish war as 'the destruction of Cyprus'. Lloyd sent a jubilant dispatch to Schomberg and told him that he had captured O'Kelly's portmanteau with the Jacobite reports on the state of their forces in Connacht.[61]

But this success was only temporary, and Lloyd was soon under pressure from Sarsfield who had collected a large force for the recapture of Sligo: '5,000 choice men out of the Irish army joined with 2,000 of the Connacht forces'. The Williamites were forced back on Sligo, a small town guarded by two indifferent forts. One of the forts was soon abandoned by Lloyd, but the other was vigorously defended by a Huguenot captain, named St Sauveur. There is a stirring account of the Irish assault on this fort: 'one remarkable stratagem made use of by the Irish for the storming of the fort was, they built a box of timber as high as the wall with stairs through which they might ascend to the top of the wall without danger'. The defenders countered this move by throwing out a bundle of shavings to the base of the device and sending down a man in a basket to set the shavings alight. He fulfilled his mission but when he was being pulled up the rope was cut by a shot and 'let the poor adventurer fall'. However, another rope was let down and pulled him up to safety. St Sauveur put up a gallant fight for some time, but his provisions ran out and he was short of water. He surrendered to

[60] D'Avaux, p. 547.

[61] *An exact account of the royal army under the duke of Schomberg with particulars of the defeat of the Irish army near Boyle.*

Sarsfield on honourable terms that allowed the garrison to march out with their arms and baggage. A Williamite account pays a tribute to Sarsfield, saying that he was punctilious in keeping the bargain and that when the terms had been signed he entertained the officers of the garrison.[62]

According to Story, as the garrison marched out Sarsfield stood at the bridge with a purse of guineas and offered to anyone who would fight for King James a horse and arms and five guineas advance pay. But they all answered 'that they would never fight for the papishes (as they called them)', except for one man who took horse and arms and guineas, and deserted next day.[63]

5. WINTER QUARTERS

James was well pleased with the results of the campaign, such as it was. He had braved Schomberg, and a challenge declined could be taken as a moral victory. The spirits of the Irish had risen remarkably; the danger now was unjustified optimism. Some of James's supporters thought he could have successfully forced Schomberg's trenches at Dundalk, or at any rate could have fallen on his disease-ridden army as it marched northwards.[64] This bold confidence did not take account of the real weakness of the Irish army – its lack of training and equipment. John Stevens made a better estimate: the troops 'expressed a great alacrity and readiness to march towards the enemy, though most of them were very raw and undisciplined and the generality almost naked, or at least very ragged and ill-shod'. He thought the only creditable part of the army was the cavalry, though their numbers were small.[65] Harrying Schomberg's retreat might have been easier than storming his trenches; but the Enniskilleners, who had routed a Connacht force in September, would probably have been a match for the Jacobites in guerrilla fighting.

False optimism resulted in the Jacobites wasting the winter

---

[62] *A full and impartial relation of the brave and great actions that happened between the Iniskilling men and the French Protestants on the one hand and the Irish rebels commanded by Sarsfield on the other.* The siege-engine in question was known as a sow.

[63] Story, p. 34.   [64] *Jacobite narrative*, p. 89.   [65] Stevens, p. 79.

and failing to take the opportunity to train and equip the army. O'Kelly censured the 'revels, gaming and other debauches' that characterized James's court in Dublin. Stevens, whose regiment was quartered in Trinity College, was of the same opinion. He was disgusted by the drunkenness and loose living that he saw in Dublin: he called it 'a seminary of vice . . . and living emblem of Sodom'.[66] There were frequent quarrels between French and Irish officers. D'Avaux thought that the French were wasting their time and were given no responsibility or promotion.[67] Tyrconnell hoped to get essentials from France and wrote repeatedly to Mary of Modena to enlist her support. He asked for tents, shirts, uniform cloth and '40,000 coarse hats'. Copper for debased Jacobite currency was another requirement: 'it is our meat, drink and clothes'. He also asked Mary to have ten tons of steel sent: 'for we begin now to make fire-arms here'.[68] John Browne of Westport was the contractor, and had 150 men, mostly Protestants, making musket-barrels in Dublin: as match was short, the muskets were 'firelocks', the latest type of weapon. Gunsmiths were also at work in Kilkenny, making use of the local coal.[69] The correspondence of a Jacobite colonel gives the impression that Tyrconnell, Nagle and their subordinates were busily engaged in pushing on the equipment and clothing of the army.[70] Dublin was put in a state of defence, with trench works and palisades, and gates on the bridges. Dundalk was strengthened as an advanced post and two battalions were stationed there.[71]

After his bout of energy James had relapsed into passivity and took little part in the administration. For much of the winter he retired to Kilkenny, so as to avoid infection from his fever-stricken soldiers. He appeared to be plunged in deep melancholy, which raised much speculation.[72] One result of his stay in Kilkenny seems to have been the conversion of Kilkenny College (whose Protestant headmaster had fled) into a university under the style of the Royal College of St Canice, with a rector, eight

[66] Stevens, p. 93; O'Kelly, p. 41. [67] D'Avaux, p. 694.

[68] *Anal. Hib.*, iv. 103, 107, 110–11.

[69] *An account of the present state Ireland is in.*

[70] Simms, 'A Jacobite colonel: Lord Sarsfield of Kilmallock', in *Irish Sword*, ii. 205–10.

[71] *The present state of affairs in Ireland*; d'Avaux, p. 631.

[72] *Great news from Dublin.*

professors and two scholars and an elaborate charter; the scheme seems to have existed only on paper.[73] In Dublin his interests were mostly religious, which produced some Protestant sarcasm: 'he only delights to hear Fr Hall preach, who persuades him that all the miracles of St Patrick, St Brigid and St Columba fall short of what his miracles will be in future years, having performed so many works of supererogation; and that Ireland will be truly *insula sanctorum*, which it was of old'.[74] A more secular aspect was reported to Schomberg's army, that James was 'amusing himself with balls and operas'.[75]

Schomberg spent the winter at Lisburn, while his troops were dispersed to various parts of Ulster. Nearly all of the province was in Williamite control, though the Jacobites still held Charlemont. Much of the country was devastated, the colonists were resentful and many of the Catholic population had fled. The troops were ill-housed and ill-fed, and it was said that more of them died during the winter than in the Dundalk camp.[76] There was some skirmishing on the frontier during the winter, notably round Belturbet, County Cavan; but there was no real attempt to disturb the *status quo*.

In England there were loud complaints of the mismanagement of the Irish expedition. The commons demanded a commission of inquiry (which William astutely parried), and resolved to have commissary Shales arrested and his papers seized.[77] Schomberg's reputation had fallen, and William came to the reluctant conclusion that he himself would have to take command in Ireland. The conclusion was looked on with disfavour both by English politicians and by Bentinck, William's trusted Dutch adviser. There were obvious objections to it. Going to Ireland would separate him by two seas from Holland. The English political situation required close personal attention; whigs and tories were at loggerheads, and Jacobites were active. William's correspondence with Bentinck makes it clear that he had come to the decision only because he thought that the Irish expedition had been mishandled and that, unless he went to Ireland himself, 'nothing worth while would be

---

[73] Harris, *William III*, app., pp. lvi–lix.
[74] *An account of the present state of Ireland.*
[75] *Danish force*, p. 32.
[76] Story, p. 38.   [77] *Parl. hist.*, v. 454–7.

done'.[78] The most serious consequence would be that he could take no part during the summer of 1690 in the continental war against Louis XIV, which for William was always a major preoccupation. He wrote to his ally, the elector of Bavaria, that it was 'a terrible mortification' to him to be able to do so little for the common cause and to have to go to Ireland where he would be 'as it were out of knowledge of the world'.[79]

[78] N. Japikse, ed., *Correspondentie van Willem en Bentinck*, iii. 70, 86 (hereafter cited as Japikse).
[79] Ibid., p. 158.

VIII

THE BOYNE

I. BUILD-UP OF FORCES

DURING THE spring and early summer of 1690 there was a continuous reinforcement of the Williamite army in Ireland, both in men and in material. A major addition to its strength was a force of 6,000 infantry and 1,000 cavalry hired from the king of Denmark. Steps to obtain these men had been taken in the previous year, when Derry seemed about to fall and there appeared no prospect of overcoming Jacobite resistance without additional troops. Robert Molesworth, a Dublin-born envoy, had been sent to Copenhagen to negotiate a treaty, which specified that Denmark should provide seasoned troops, fully equipped. Their commander was a German aristocrat, the duke of Würtemberg-Neustadt, who reached Ireland in March 1690.[1] The arrival of the Danish force awakened memories of the Norse invasions of Ireland. Jacobite propaganda deplored William's conduct in calling in 'the old invaders of our country'. Williamites noted with satisfaction that the Irish seemed to be terrified and dejected at the landing of the Danes.[2]

In April and May, English, German and Dutch troops were sent to Ireland, and the supply position was also built up. In

[1] The correspondence of Würtemberg and other officers of the Danish force is a valuable source for the war in Ireland: see K. Danaher and J. G. Simms, ed., *The Danish force in Ireland, 1690–1* (I.M.C.).

[2] *Jacobite narrative*, p. 253; *Cal. S.P. dom., 1689–90*, p. 572; *Great news from Ireland*.

place of Shales two commissaries-general had been appointed – William Robinson, the architect of the Royal Hospital, Kilmainham, and Bartholomew van Homrigh, a Dutch merchant settled in Dublin, who had left to join William.[3] Two Amsterdam Jews, the brothers Pereira, were given the contract for supplying bread. Letters written by Robinson from Lisburn in the spring show that he, van Homrigh and the Pereiras were already at work; sites for the ovens were being chosen and cheese was anxiously awaited.[4] Money was short and the pay of the troops was badly in arrears, but some cash was sent over in April.[5] William's convoys regularly crossed the Irish Sea without interference. Tyrconnell lamented the lack of a few French frigates to cut off the enemy's supplies.[6] The Williamite naval commander, Sir Cloudesley Shovell, thought that twenty French ships would be able to do incalculable damage to William's transports.[7] Shovell was an enterprising commander who made several raids on Jacobite harbours, including a sensational attack on Dublin, in which his ships crossed the bar, entered the Salmon Pool and took away a twenty-gun frigate, one of the best ships in the small Jacobite navy. The exploit created great excitement in Dublin. James himself came down to shore with all his available troops; Protestants saw a chance of escaping, and two of them succeeded in getting away to the strains of Lilliburlero.[8]

All through the winter of 1689–90 Charlemont, on the Armagh–Tyrone border, was held as a Jacobite enclave in spite of a rather half-hearted investment by Schomberg's forces. The commander of the fort was Teague O'Regan, a veteran from County Cork, who had seen service in France during Charles II's reign. His colourful language and eccentric appearance made a great impression on the Williamites. By the second week

[3] For van Homrigh see p. 35 above.

[4] Robinson to [?W. Blathwayt], 24 March and 8 May 1690 (N.L.I. MS 13654).

[5] Schomberg to William, 22 March 1690 (Dalrymple, iii (2). 88); *Danish force*, p. 36.

[6] Tyrconnell to Mary of Modena, 30 April and 20 May 1690 (*Anal. Hib.*, iv. 121, 127).

[7] *Finch MSS*, ii. 273.

[8] *Ormonde MSS*, n.s., viii. 380–1; *London Gazette*, 28 April 1690; J. de la Brune, *Histoire de la révolution d'Irlande*, p. 98.

in May he was almost starved out and accepted Schomberg's terms which allowed the garrison to march out, drums beating and colours flying, and join the Jacobite army at Dundalk. James was delighted at O'Regan's tenacious defence, knighted him and sent him to defend Sligo, which he did with notable success.[9]

For the Jacobites an important development was the long-planned exchange by which French troops were to be sent to Ireland and Irish troops to France.[10] The difficulty created by the capture of Justin MacCarthy at Newtownbutler was removed by MacCarthy's sensational, and controversial, escape from Enniskillen; he had been on parole, but when he let it be known to the Williamite officers that he proposed to escape the parole was withdrawn, and he was thus able to escape without dishonour.[11]

The formation of MacCarthy's force raised many problems for d'Avaux. James was obstructive and turned down many of d'Avaux's requests. Men and officers of the required standard were hard to find. Finally five regiments of very unequal size were dispatched, making a total of 5,387. D'Avaux complained to Louvois that he had had all the trouble in the world to collect them. A final inspection on board had weeded out unsuitable men, but he could not say the same of the officers, 'two-thirds of whom were very bad'.[12] When they arrived at Brest the French official was horrified at their condition; he described them as 'without shirts, without shoes, most of them without hats, shockingly dirty and, generally speaking, devoured by vermin'. Some of them were rejected and the force was reconstituted into three regiments, Mountcashel's (MacCarthy's), O'Brien's and Dillon's. They formed part of the French army and took an oath to serve the French king 'against all the world with no exception, save against the king of Great Britain'. Equipped and directed by the French, they proved first-class soldiers and soon won honours in Savoy and Catalonia. Louis XIV got far more value from the Irish than James did from the French soldiers who took their place. Their conduct

[9] Story, pp. 60–2; Simms, 'Sligo in the Jacobite war' in *Ir. Sword*, vii. 130–5.
[10] See p. 72 above.
[11] J. A. Murphy, *Justin MacCarthy*, pp. 24–5.
[12] D'Avaux, p. 701.

encouraged the French to ask for more, and MacCarthy's men were the forerunners of the large numbers of Irish who served in France after the surrender of Limerick in 1691.[13]

Tyrconnell did not look forward to the new commander who was to come with the troops from France. This was Lauzun, who had failed to obtain the Irish command at the beginning of 1689 but had been specially asked for by James to take the place of Rosen. Lauzun was an unfortunate choice. He was vain and ambitious, and his military experience was negligible. Tyrconnell was very forthright on the subject in writing to Mary of Modena, whose gratitude to Lauzun as her escort from England was primarily responsible for James's request. Tyrconnell pointed out that Lauzun was on bad terms with Louvois, who would be unlikely to co-operate with him, particularly as he had not been consulted about the appointment. Louvois's attitude was all-important: 'could M. de Louvois be gained, or at least softened, I would have no doubt of our being soon masters of this kingdom; whereas if he be against us I apprehend what may follow'. Tyrconnell added that the French officers in Ireland were upset by Lauzun's appointment and talked of him as untrustworthy and a mischief-maker. D'Avaux, who was now ordered back to France, told Louvois that Tyrconnell was convinced that Lauzun's intrigues would be the ruin of Ireland and was talking of retiring; in that case many of the Irish would come to terms with Schomberg.[14] James was glad to be rid of d'Avaux, who had done little but argue and reproach since he had come to Ireland: his manner was not respectful enough for James's taste.[15] It was arranged that d'Avaux should leave with the ships that brought Lauzun and the French troops and were to take the Irish troops to France on the return voyage. D'Avaux professed himself glad to be recalled; he had no wish to be associated with someone so incompatible as Lauzun.[16] His career was not damaged, and he later served as ambassador in Sweden and Holland.

It had been proposed to send the troops from France in December 1689, but they were delayed to take advantage of the fact that the English fleet would be preoccupied with escorting

[13] Min. guerre, A1 960, no. 23; Murphy, pp. 30–6.
[14] *Anal. Hib.*, iv. 101; d'Avaux, p. 521.
[15] Berwick, *Memoirs*, i. 59.   [16] D'Avaux, pp. 609, 618.

a new queen from the Netherlands to Spain.[17] The French ships arrived in Cork on 12 March 1690, exactly a year after James's landing at Kinsale. They brought about 6,000 officers and men, together with arms, ammunition and other supplies.[18] Some Irish troops were subsequently drafted in to fill gaps in their numbers. There were five regiments, but only three of them were French: one consisted of Walloons; the largest (two battalions) was Zurlauben's regiment of Germans, some of whom had been taken prisoner in the previous year's campaign and others picked up from a captured ship. Many of them were Protestants, which was not to James's taste. Reports came from Dublin that five hundred of them went to the Protestant churches 'to the great dissatisfaction of the Irish', and that James had asked his queen to tell Louis that in future he should send only 'thorough-paced Roman Catholics'.[19] After the Boyne a number of them changed over to William's side.

The arms and supplies from France were deficient in both quantity and quality and did not compare with those which William was pouring into Ireland.[20] There was much friction between the French and James's officers. Lauzun complained bitterly about the transport arrangements at Cork; they appear to have been highly unsatisfactory, but the French changes of plan had not made things easy. They were first to come to Limerick, then to Kinsale; Cork was a last-minute choice.[21] When they reached Dublin the French appear to have taken charge of the city in a way that offended Irish susceptibilities. A Dublin Protestant recorded in his diary that Lauzun had boxed the ears of Simon Luttrell, the city governor.[22] Refugees who made their way to Schomberg's camp reported that Lauzun had taken possession of the town and the castle and that the French orders were to act on the defensive. The plan was to be delaying actions from Newry southwards to the

[17] D'Avaux, p. 654; Story, p. 57. Maria Anna of Neuberg was the second wife of Charles II of Spain.

[18] Min. guerre, A1 894, no. 89.

[19] Ibid., nos 60, 89; 960, no. 146; *James II*, ii. 387; *Great news from Ireland*; *Danish force*, p. 34.

[20] *James II*, ii. 387; *Ir. Sword*, ii. 208.

[21] Min. guerre, A1 894, nos 157, 167.

[22] *An account of the late action*; *Ormonde MSS*, n.s., viii. 380.

Boyne, in hopes that a rising in England or the intervention of the French navy would save the situation.[23]

James was still intent on going to England, and reports of Jacobite activity there raised his hopes. Tyrconnell, unexpectedly, encouraged this idea and urged Mary of Modena to persuade Louis to send a fleet to escort James to England. He argued that if William came to Ireland the best counter-move would be for a French fleet to take the French troops and the best of the Irish to England and trust Tyrconnell to do what he could to resist William with what was left: 'I am sure I could keep up the bustle here.'[24] Not surprisingly, Louis was completely opposed to the scheme; he could see no prospect of such a move succeeding as James was not assured of any substantial body of support in England. The French navy had previously shown itself unwilling to enter the Irish Sea for fear of being cut off.[25] It is hard to believe that James would have been welcomed in England if he had arrived with a force of French and Irish. The xenophobia that had made William unpopular would have been transferred to James, intensified by religious opposition. Louis's advice was that James should remain on the defensive in the hope that William's forces would fall sick, as had Schomberg's. Before Lauzun had left France Louvois had warned him to restrain his martial ardour and play for time.[26]

2. WILLIAM IN IRELAND

William's journey to Ireland was held up by parliamentary business till towards the end of May, when he announced that he could wait no longer and adjourned parliament. His friend Bishop Burnet thought that William was glad to get away from politics and was confident of success in Ireland: his chief worry was what to do with James; he toyed with a plan to lure James on to a boat and send him to the continent.[27] William sailed on June 11 from Hoylake with a fleet of about three hundred vessels escorted by Sir Cloudesley Shovell's squadron of war-

[23] Story, pp. 65–6.
[24] Tyrconnell to Mary of Modena, 20 May 1690 (*Anal. Hib.*, iv. 127).
[25] Louvois to Lauzun, 10 June 1690 (Min. guerre., A1, 960).
[26] Lauzun to Louvois, 26 June 1690 (Ranke, *Hist. of England*, vi. 109).
[27] Burnet, iv. 82.

ships. Fog patches and calm delayed his voyage and it was not till June 14 that he landed near Carrickfergus. He brought with him 15,000 troops, a train of artillery from Holland and, most eagerly awaited, £200,000 in cash.[28] He was accompanied by a number of notables: Prince George of Denmark, the duke of Ormond, Bentinck and others. Sir Robert Southwell, Petty's friend and correspondent, came as secretary of state for Ireland; George Clarke, a fellow of All Soul's, Oxford, was secretary at war.[29] William got a great welcome in Belfast, though it was mixed with northern caution. Story describes the crowd as doing 'nothing but stare, never having seen a king before in that part of the world; but after a while some of them beginning to huzza the rest all took it (as hounds do a scent)'.[30]

William pleased the Presbyterians by receiving a deputation of their ministers, who were proud to salute him as a fellow-Calvinist; they pointed out that they formed the majority of the Ulster Protestants and drew attention to the services performed by the Presbyterians in the siege of Derry. This was too much for Dr George Walker (now bishop-designate of Derry), who 'could not contain himself and contradicted what they said with great warmth. though not loud enough for the King to hear'. William responded by increasing the *regium donum*, the annual payment of £600 to Presbyterian ministers granted by Charles II and withheld by James II. His first thought was to make the amount £800, but on the persuasion of the Scottish Lieutenant-General Douglas he increased it to £1,200, which would give each minister £15: 'as King James works by his priests, so these men will do like service to his majesty [William] by uniting the people unto him and making a good report of things in Scotland'.[31] A warrant was signed at Hillsborough making the sum a charge on the Belfast customs, but technicalities, and perhaps episcopalian obstruction, held up the payment for over a year.[32]

[28] *London Gazette*, 19 June 1690; *Danish force*, p. 40.

[29] A large collection of letters received by Clarke during the Irish campaign was left behind and came into the possession of Trinity College, Dublin (T.C.D., MSS K. 5. 1–13). It is cited as Clarke corr.

[30] Story, p. 66.

[31] *Leyborne-Popham MSS* (H.M.C.), p. 271.

[32] *Cal. S.P. dom., 1690–1*, p. 481; a pillar at Hillsborough commemorates the grant.

William had the bearing of a vigorous and efficient leader, and everything about his arrival created confidence. Belfast Lough was like a wood with hundreds of ships laden with provisions and ammunition: 'so that now we fear no more Dundalk wants'.[33] In William's own words he had not come to let grass grow under his feet, and his close attention to detail pleased his soldiers. He had brought a portable wooden house (said to have been designed by Sir Christopher Wren), and throughout the campaign he slept among his troops.[34] Schomberg had planned an advance in two columns, one to the west via Belturbet, County Cavan, to Kells or Trim, the other to Dundalk via Armagh. William discarded the former route with little regard for Schomberg's feelings. The new plan was for William himself to make straight for Dundalk via Newry and the difficult Moyry Pass; the rest of the army under Douglas was to take the longer way to Dundalk via Armagh.[35]

On June 16 James set out for Dundalk to meet William. The Jacobites were in good heart and unexpectedly optimistic:

they triumphed and rejoiced as if they had got King William in a pound and the day were their own. They were assured either that the French fleet would cut off King William from England or that an insurrection would be made there . . . Some were so open as to tell their Protestant friends very lately that they would be glad to go to mass within this twelve months.[36]

At the same time security precautions were taken. Gatherings of more than five Protestants were forbidden in Dublin; those Protestants who had been released after Schomberg's failure were again imprisoned, Dean King among them. Protestants were forbidden to be out of their houses at night; many were arrested.[37]

Lauzun expressed no confidence in the situation. He was afraid that James was going too far from Dublin and ran the risk of being cut off by William. Supplies were short and the Irish troops were badly armed. James was full of physical energy – eighteen or twenty hours a day in the saddle – but it

[33] *An exact account of his majesty's progress.*

[34] Story, pp. 68–9.

[35] *Cal. S.P. dom., 1689–90*, p. 543; *Danish force*, p. 40; *Leyland–Popham MSS*, p. 271.

[36] *True and perfect journal.*　　　　　　[37] *Ormonde MSS*, n.s., viii. 385.

was hard to get him to put right what was wrong. James's idea in going north was to eat up the grass and leave the country stripped before William's advance.[38] Some thought he should have held the Moyry Pass between Newry and Dundalk, but this would have risked an outflanking movement by the Williamite forces coming round from Armagh. Discretion was the better part of valour, and James retreated from Dundalk. He was followed at a day's interval by William till the two armies faced one another on either side of the River Boyne.[39]

3. THE BOYNE WATER

The Boyne is the most famous of Irish battles. It is still celebrated each year by the Ulster Protestants as the charter of their religious and political liberties. In the Europe of the day it represented a signal success for the Grand Alliance against Louis XIV. Catholic Austria and Spain rejoiced at their ally's victory in Ireland; illustrated broadsheets of the battle were circulated in many parts of Europe. There appears to be no evidence for the common belief that the battle was celebrated by *Te Deums* in Rome. Alexander VIII was less hostile to France than his predecessor, Innocent XI, had been. According to Melfort the pope was surprised and scandalized by the *Te Deums* sung in Austrian cathedrals for 'Orange's victory'.[40] Jacobite critics have minimized the importance of the battle and referred to it as a mere skirmish of little significance.[41] The Jacobite losses were comparatively small, their army got away, and within a short time it was able to rally successfully on the Shannon. The war continued for over a year after the Boyne, and from the Jacobite point of view Aughrim, with its heavy death-roll, was the decisive battle of the war. But for contemporaries it was the Boyne that stole the headlines. The drama of two kings fighting at an Irish river for an English throne was in itself sensational. The fact that they represented the major power-groups in Europe and were supported by international

[38] Lauzun to Louvois, 1 July 1690 (Ranke, vi. 113).
[39] *Jacobite narrative*, pp. 95–7.
[40] H. Ellis, *Original letters*, 2nd series, iv. 205.
[41] For a vigorous statement of the Jacobite view, see H. Belloc, *James II*, pp. 253–68.

armies gave the Boyne a wider significance. James's flight and William's triumphal entry into Dublin had all the marks of an overwhelming victory.

The Boyne is the only considerable river between Dundalk and Dublin, and was the most defensible position if James were to make a stand anywhere in eastern Ireland. There was much debate whether he should do so. As in the previous year the French were for abandoning Dublin and withdrawing to the west. The French plan involved burning Dublin, which James rejected as 'too cruel'.[42] Tyrconnell realized the weakness of the Jacobite position and had some difficulty in making up his mind. On June 16 he wrote to Mary of Modena that rather than lose Dublin they must risk a battle: 'for if we be driven from it and this province lost, there will be little hope of keeping the rest long'.[43] A week later he had changed his mind and wrote that it was better not to fight: 'I am not for venturing the loss of all to preserve a place which you must lose as soon as the battle is lost'.[44] These uncertainties did not help James's prospects. No defensive positions had been made in advance along the river, and there were signs of half-heartedness about the decision to stand there. An agent is said to have been sent to Waterford the day before the battle to arrange for James's passage to France. That night his baggage was packed and some of the guns sent towards Dublin.[45]

On June 29 James's army, about 25,000 strong, crossed the Boyne in two columns, one over the bridge at Drogheda and the other three miles upstream at Oldbridge, where the river was easily fordable at ebb-tide. A force of about 1,300 was left to hold Drogheda and the rest of the army drawn up on the hillside above Oldbridge.[46] Lauzun thought the position indefensible. He reconnoitred the river upstream for six miles as far as Slane, where there was a bridge, and found that there were fords everywhere.[47] The French Lieutenant-General Lery took a more favourable view and thought there were good prospects of

[42] Lauzun to Seignelay 16/26 July 1690 (Ranke, vi.117).
[43] *Anal. Hib.*, iv. 129–30.   [44] Ibid., p. 133.
[45] Southwell to Nottingham, 6 July 1690 (*Finch MSS*, ii. 344); *James II*, ii. 395.
[46] Stevens, pp. 119–20; Story, p. 90. See map on p. 146.
[47] Ranke, vi. 117.

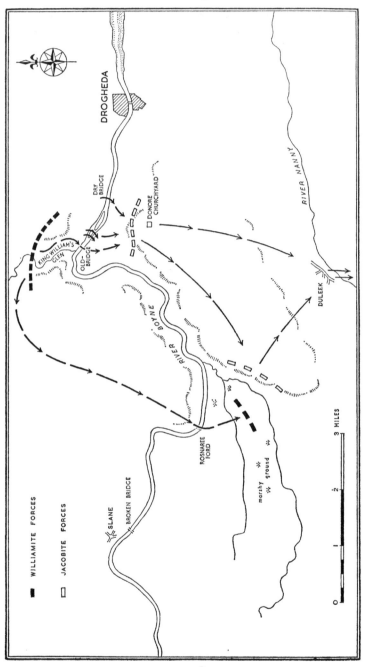

DROGHEDA

DRY BRIDGE

DONORE CHURCHYARD

KING WILLIAM'S GLEN

OLD-BRIDGE

RIVER BOYNE

RIVER NANNY

DULEEK

ROSNAREE FORD

marshy ground

SLANE

BROKEN BRIDGE

■ WILLIAMITE FORCES

□ JACOBITE FORCES

0   1   2   3 MILES

BATTLE OF THE BOYNE, 1690

success.[48] James himself thought 'that post an indifferent good one, and indeed the country afforded no better'.[49] Some attempt was made to throw up earthworks along the river bank and to block the crossings at the fords; it appears also that the bridge at Slane was broken.[50]

There was little time for preparation as William's army appeared next day, June 30, on the northern heights above the river. It was about 36,000 strong – half as large again as James's army and better equipped, particularly in artillery, which began a heavy bombardment in the latter part of the day.[51] From the Williamite side the river appeared to be a formidable obstacle. William's first impression was that fording it in the face of the enemy was not only difficult but almost impracticable.[52] According to one account he was urged to let some regiments try the crossing that day, but refused to do so as he was determined never to undertake anything on a Monday.[53] During his reconnaissance he was wounded by a ricochet shot from a Jacobite cannon. His thick leather jerkin blunted the impact of the shot, which only grazed his right shoulder. With the phlegmatic remark 'it's well it came no nearer' he got the wound dressed and resumed his inspection.[54] The enemy could see that he was hit and assumed that he was killed. A great shout rose from the Irish ranks. The report of William's death later reached Paris, where it was celebrated with drums and trumpets and the burning of William and Mary in effigy.[55] William's death would have removed Louis's most formidable opponent and the only serious rival to James.

William held a council of war that evening, which is described in a letter from the Danish envoy to King Christian V. He says that there was a difference of opinion. Schomberg, supported by some of the English generals, was in favour of a sham attack at Oldbridge to hold the enemy's attention while the main army marched upstream during the night, crossed at a ford and attacked the enemy on the flank. The Dutch general

---

[48] Min. guerre, A1, 961, no. 178.   [49] *James II*, ii. 393.

[50] Min. guerre, A1, 961, no. 176; *Jacobite narrative*, p. 99.

[51] Story, p. 70; *Danish force*, p. 62.

[52] Portland's narrative (R.I.A., MS 24. G. 1., no. 38).

[53] *Danish force*, p. 62. The belief that Monday was an unlucky day was widespread.

[54] Story, p. 75; *Danish force*, p. 62.   [55] *Present state of Europe*, p. 15.

Solms advocated a frontal attack to force the crossing at Old-bridge. William compromised by sending Schomberg's son, followed by a supporting force under Douglas, early on July 1 to cross the river upstream and make contact with the enemy. This diversionary move was made by about a third of the army, leaving the rest to fight the main engagement in the Oldbridge area. The first crossing at Oldbridge was to be made about 10 a.m. when the tide would be at the ebb.[56]

There are many accounts of the battle, and they are often contradictory on points of detail.[57] It appears, however, that the Williamite right wing, under Schomberg's son, was originally making for Slane bridge but hearing that the bridge was broken made the crossing two miles below Slane at the ford of Rosnaree. They were bravely opposed by Sir Neal O'Neill of Killyleagh, County Antrim, with eight hundred dragoons. O'Neill held up a greatly superior force for half an hour before being driven back, mortally wounded. Count Schomberg's men crossed the river and drew up on the other side, where they were joined by Douglas's supporting force. The Jacobites could see their opponents marching upstream and moved to the left to meet an attack from that direction which threatened to hem them in and cut off their line of retreat to Dublin. The French under Lauzun were the first to move and took up a position facing Count Schomberg, with broken ground separating the two forces. James, who had stationed himself at Donore church on the skyline behind Oldbridge, seems to have formed the opinion that the rest of William's army was going to follow its right wing up the river. He ordered the remainder of his own army to move to the left and himself joined Lauzun. The result was that two-thirds of the Jacobite army, including Sarsfield and a number of Irish troops as well as the French, faced the Williamite right wing to the south-east of Rosnaree. Tyrconnell, however, declined to move and covered the Oldbridge sector with part of the Jacobite cavalry and two brigades of infantry; about a third of James's army thus faced two-thirds of William's larger force.

[56] J. Payen de la Fouleresse to Christian V, 2 July 1690 (*N. & Q.*, 5th series, viii. 21–3); Story, pp. 77–8; *Danish force*, p. 42.

[57] For these accounts see Simms, 'Eyewitnesses of the Boyne' in *Ir. Sword*, vi. 16–27.

So far William's tactics had proved successful. The Jacobites had fatally weakened their position at Oldbridge, and the greater part of their army had taken up a position in which the nature of the ground forced them to remain inactive. James proposed that an attack should be launched, but Sarsfield, who had inspected the ground, replied that two bottomless ditches made an impossible barrier between the Jacobites and the Williamite right wing that faced them.[58]

The actual battle took place in the Oldbridge sector. It was a hot, bright day: 'as if the sun itself had a mind to see what would happen'.[59] Shortly after 10 a.m. the Dutch Blue Guards, who had marched down from the ridge under cover of the ravine now known as King William's glen, plunged into the river. Marching eight or ten abreast, their bodies held back the current, which made the water rise and they were soon up to their waists. When they were halfway across they were met by heavy fire from the Irish troops who lined the opposite shore. They reached the farther bank and were soon followed by two Huguenot regiments who crossed a little lower down. In the early stages the Williamite cavalry played little part. The Williamite infantry were charged again and again by Tyrconnell's cavalry who showed great dash and courage. Story says that for over three-quarters of an hour the fighting was so hot that many old soldiers said they never saw brisker work. Schomberg himself went to the support of the Huguenots and was killed in the mêlée. Another victim was George Walker, whose martial spirit brought him into the thick of the fighting; he was at once stripped by the Scotch–Irish who followed William's camp and had little respect for a bishop-designate.[60] William was full of anxiety for his Dutch troops. George Clarke, the secretary at war, later remembered standing near William and hearing him say softly to himself

'My poor guards, my poor guards, my poor guards'; but when he saw them stand their ground and fire by platoons, so that the horse were forced to run away in great disorder, he breathed out as people used to after holding their breath upon a fright or suspense, and said he had seen his guards do that which he had never seen foot do in his life.[61]

[58] *James II*, ii. 397; Min. guerre, A1, 961, no. 179.
[59] Story, p. 78.   [60] Ibid., p. 82.   [61] *Leyborne-Popham MSS*, p. 27.

The Danish troops crossed lower down when the tide was coming in. Some of them missed the line of the ford and were up to their shoulders and necks; they had to hold their muskets and powder above their heads. Würtemberg, their commander, was carried over on the shoulder of his grenadiers – the tallest of his men.

All the accounts show that crossing the river under fire was no easy feat. Würtemberg reported that the Irish cavalry behaved extremely well, though their infantry behaved badly. According to Story most of the Irish horsemen 'that charged so desperately were drunk with brandy, each man that morning having received half a pint to his share; but it seems the foot had not so large a portion, or at least they did not deserve it so well'. The Jacobite Stevens corroborates the issue of brandy – which was standard military practice – but thought it did more harm than good, as the men made a rush for the barrels and helped themselves too freely.[62] Story thought that if, instead of Irish infantry, the French had defended the river 'we had found warmer work of it'.[63]

The decisive movement took place about midday on the Williamite left. William, who got useful guidance from local Protestants, was told of a difficult but passable ford a mile below Oldbridge. He himself crossed there with Inniskilling, Dutch and Danish cavalry. His horse was bogged down on the far side, and he had to dismount and struggle through the mud 'so as to be near out of breath' – an ordeal for a sufferer from asthma. A contemporary broadsheet tells us that William 'was pleased to tell the Inniskilling men that he had heard a great character of them and therefore would do them the honour to head them himself, which accordingly he performed; for after they had passed the ford he charged at the head of them and they fought like tigers'.[64] The well-known picture by the Dutch painter Maas shows William galloping up the southern slopes at the head of the cavalry, while nearer Oldbridge columns of infantry are struggling through the water. William led his party up to the old village of Donore on the top of the hill, where they

[62] *Danish force*, p. 43; Story, p. 85; Stevens, p. 128.
[63] Story, p. 89.
[64] *Finch MSS*, ii. 329; *Account of King William's royal heading of the men of Inniskillin.*

were engaged in a rough-and-tumble with the Irish. Foes and friends were hard to distinguish, for both wore the same kind of uniform. The Inniskillings indiscriminately charged Dutchmen and Danes. In the dust and smoke of battle it was easy to miss the sprig of green that Williamites wore in their hats; the Jacobites wore white paper for France. Donore was gained, Richard Hamilton captured, and the Jacobites were in danger of being trapped in the bend of the river, which turns sharply to the south just above Oldbridge. A disorderly retreat began in the direction of Duleek, four miles to the south of Oldbridge, where there was a bridge over the Nanny water.

News of the retreat reached James and Lauzun, who were now threatened by the Williamites on two sides. They also made for the river-crossing at Duleek. There was much anxiety for James's safety. Lauzun kept up a refrain of 'faster, faster' to the cavalry; when it was represented that this would endanger the infantry, Lauzun replied that nothing was to be thought of except saving the king's person. Sarsfield's regiment was detailed to act as James's escort.

Great confusion was caused by both wings of the Jacobite army converging on Duleek. Stevens, who was with his regiment coming from the Rosnaree side, describes how the Irish cavalry from Donore collided with them at Duleek; the situation was saved by Zurlauben ordering his German regiment to fire on the Irish. Stevens says that the Irish infantry ran like sheep before the wolf, throwing away their muskets and their shoes.[65] The French retreated in good order, and the pursuit was not carried far beyond Duleek. The losses were comparatively light, about 1,000 on the Jacobite side and 500 on the Williamite.[66] There were few prisoners and the greater part of the Irish army got away. The Jacobites lost the few guns they had and all their baggage, including gold watches, silver dinner services and a

[65] Stevens, pp. 122–4.

[66] Story's estimate was between 1,000 and 1,500 Jacobites killed and 'nigh 400' Williamites (p. 85); Parker's (*Memoirs*, p. 23) was Jacobites 'not quite 800 killed', Williamites 'not above 500 killed'; the account in *Villare Hibernicum* put the deaths on both sides together at 'not above 1,600'. According to *Jacobite narrative*, pp. 102–3, 500 Jacobites and 1,000 Williamites were killed. But the Williamites were in a better position to estimate the number of deaths.

great mass of official papers. The Danish envoy remarked that the Williamite soldiers camping at Duleek without tents or baggage kept themselves warm on a chilly night with bonfires of the muskets and pikes that the Irish had thrown away. Drogheda surrendered on the following day and William's way to Dublin was clear. The terms granted to Drogheda were liberal: the garrison could go to Athlone, but without their arms; the Catholic clergy and anyone else who wished could accompany them; the inhabitants were assured that they would not be deprived of their possessions. The English regiment that occupied Drogheda 'took great care to preserve the town from the violence of the soldiers'.[67]

The Williamites had undoubtedly won the day, but in the military sense it was not an overwhelming victory. There are indications that the original plan was to cut off the Jacobite retreat by a pincers movement. This did not come off, because the Williamite right was immobilized after crossing the river at Rosnaree. It would have been more effective to have moved down the road from Slane towards Dublin, and according to James's memoirs the Williamites were beginning to move in that direction when he decided to retreat. The Danish envoy remarked that Count Schomberg had no orders to cut off the enemy retreat and that William himself did not pursue the enemy as closely as he might have done, 'perhaps wishing to put into practice Caesar's maxim and leave his enemy a golden bridge' so that he was able to escape.[68] The reference is to Caesar and Pompey at Pharsalia, and the implication is that William did not wish to cut off James's retreat and saddle himself with an embarrassing prisoner.

4. THE FLIGHT OF JAMES

James reached Dublin on the night of July 1. The story was told that Lady Tyrconnell asked him what he would have to eat; he replied that after the breakfast he had been given he had little

[67] Capitulation agreed between Brigadier William Tuite and Col de la Mellonière, 3 July 1690—copy enclosed with Fouleresse's letter to Christian V, 8 July 1690 (Copenhagen, Rigsarkivet, England B diplomatic reports, vol. 70); Story, p. 90.

[68] Fouleresse to Christian V, 2 July 1690 (*N. & Q.*, loc. cit.).

stomach for his supper.[69] Another account describes him as entering Dublin in a very silent and dejected condition and 'in a manner stunned'.[70] A Dublin Protestant recorded in his diary the speech that James is said to have made that night to his privy council, a bitter criticism of the Irish army:

when it came to a trial they basely fled the field and left the spoil to the enemies, nor could they be prevailed upon to rally, though the loss in the whole defeat was but inconsiderable: so that henceforth I never more determined to head an Irish army and do now resolve to shift for myself and so, gentlemen, must you.[71]

It was an ungracious speech, with the exception of his charge to them not to allow Dublin to be plundered or burned. He left next morning for Duncannon on Waterford Harbour, where he got a boat that took him to Kinsale. From there he was escorted by a French fleet to France, where he remained for the rest of his life, a pensioner of Louis.

His stay in Ireland had been an unhappy experience, which left his supporters resentful and disillusioned. In Irish tradition he is James of the dung. His poor showing in comparison with his rival is illustrated by the well-known saying attributed to Sarsfield: 'change but kings with us and we will fight you over again'. Lord Clare thought that James would do better to spend the rest of his days praying in a cloister rather than think of commanding armies or governing a state.[72] James's unwillingness to meet Catholic demands and his preoccupation with English opinion were the subject of unfavourable comment. As one critic put it: 'he was infected with this rotten principle, provoke not your Protestant subjects'.[73] For his part James regarded the Irish with no less distaste. His instructions to his son, written in 1692, show a distrust of the Irish that is reminiscent of Henry VIII. The principal garrisons should never be

[69] Story, p. 88. There is no contemporary record of the well-known story that James said to Lady Tyrconnell 'Your countrymen, madam, can run well', and that she replied, 'Not quite so well as your majesty, for I see you have won the race'. It is in *Dublin Penny Journal*, i. 325 (1832-3).

[70] *Finch MSS*, ii. 344.

[71] *Ormonde MSS*, n.s., viii. 401-2. Another version says that the speech was made early on the following morning to the lord mayor and others (Story, p. 88).

[72] Clare to Louvois, 22 Aug. 1690 (Min. guerre, A1 1082, no. 86).

[73] *Jacobite narrative*, p. 63.

entrusted to Irish governors or Irish troops; the sons of old families should be given an English education so that they should 'be weaned from their natural hatred against the English'; schools should be set up in Ireland to teach English and 'by degrees wear out the Irish language, which would be for the advantage of the body of the inhabitants'; the Os and Macs should be firmly told that estates forfeited by James I and his predecessors could not be restored; no native of Ireland should be lord lieutenant.[74]

James's conduct was scathingly satirized in Protestant propaganda. A medal was struck, portraying him as the runaway King: on the obverse was a deer with winged feet and the Latin tag *pedibus timor addidit alas*.[75] *The royal flight, a new farce* gave dramatic form to the Boyne and its aftermath. Sarsfield is the Irish hero and James the petulant coward. His Dublin speech is reproduced, followed by his abrupt departure for the coast. James himself seems to have been conscious of the bad impression created by his flight. In his *Life* the question is discussed at length, and it is emphasized that the decision was taken on the advice of Tyrconnell and other trusted members of the Irish administration: 'that counsel was no doubt too precipitate and it is wonderful on what grounds my lord Tyrconnell thought fit to press it with so much earnestness, unless it was out of a tenderness to the queen'.[76]

In contrast, William had behaved with reckless courage, wearing his star and garter in the thick of the fight.[77] A Dutch account compared the conduct of the two kings:

the people have little tenderness for unfortunate princes or for those who show themselves more careful to preserve their persons than their dominions . . . [James is] not a man to venture himself for the recovery of [his crown], and few people are willing to assist those who are wanting to themselves . . . King William's conduct has confirmed and established his dominions . . . The reputation of a sovereign contributes very much to make his subjects considerable.[78]

[74] *James II*, ii. 636–8.
[75] 'Fear added wings to his feet.' See Hawkins, *Medallic illustrations*, i. 719.
[76] *James II*, ii. 406.
[77] *Finch MSS*, ii. 330.
[78] *The present state of Europe*, August 1690, p. 39.

William's victory was particularly opportune because it helped to offset the naval engagement of June 30 at Beachy Head, when the combined Dutch and English fleets were defeated by the French. There was panic in England and fear of a French invasion. It was not till July 7 that the news of the Boyne reached London, and the interval was agonizing for Mary who had been left in charge during William's absence.[79] Both Williamites and Jacobites thought that the French missed the opportunity of entering the Irish Sea and cutting William's communications. George Clarke observed that the frigates that convoyed James to France could otherwise have entered St George's Channel.[80] On the Jacobite side it was suggested that James had been assured by Seignelay that a fleet of French frigates would burn the shipping in the Irish Sea and keep William in Ireland, but that the French admiral, Tourville, had rejected the plan as too dangerous.[81]

5. DUBLIN CHANGES HANDS

Tyrconnell and Lauzun reached Dublin on the morning of July 2 to find James already gone and the city in confusion. The garrison had disappeared and so had the governor, Simon Luttrell. Wauchope, a Scottish officer, told Tyrconnell and Lauzun that James had left word that they should make for Kinsale or Limerick as best they could. It was decided to make for Limerick, and orders to this effect were passed to the scattered and depleted units.[82] Stevens tells how some remnants of the Jacobite army reached the northern suburbs of Dublin and were ashamed to enter the city till they could collect some more men to fill out their thin ranks. Each regiment planted its colours on a piece of high ground to attract the stragglers. When Stevens's regiment was a hundred strong it crossed the river by Bloody Bridge – as far as possible from the centre of the city – and joined the hurried and disorderly retreat to Limerick, which with many alarms they reached on July 6.[83]

[79] Her letters to William are in Dalrymple, iii (ii), pp. 131–98.
[80] *Leyborne-Popham MSS*, p. 274.   [81] *James II*, ii. 409.
[82] Lauzun to Seignelay, 16/26 July 1690 (Ranke, vi. 121).
[83] Stevens, pp. 130–8. Bloody Bridge – so called because of a riot that took place when it was first built – was on the site of the modern Rory O'More Bridge.

Most of the civilian members of the Jacobite administration also left for Limerick, and there was temporary anarchy in Dublin. The guard was removed from Trinity College, and the Protestant prisoners were free. When they came out they found crowds of Protestants in the streets intent on looting the houses abandoned by Catholics. Robert Fitzgerald, a younger son of the sixteenth earl of Kildare, took the lead in forming a provisional government. He obtained the keys of the city and the castle and organized the control of the excited mob. Finding that they had broken into Sarsfield's house 'he was forced to exercise his authority with cane and sword', and all through the night he was busy dealing with attempts at looting and arson. In the early morning of July 3 he and others dispatched a letter to William saying that they had taken charge of Dublin and that the Jacobites had left. Up to that time the Dublin Protestants had had no word of the Williamite army and did not know whether the French or Irish troops would return. At midday on July 3 Fitzgerald sent an urgent message addressed to the nearest Williamite commander asking for speedy relief as the Protestant 'rabble' was getting out of hand and there were fears that some of James's troops would return and rifle the city. This message was brought, before the earlier letter, to William himself. He remarked: 'I see I have some good friends in Dublin and am much obliged to Mr Fitzgerald . . . I will take care to send some horse as soon as I can and desire he will go on taking care of the place as he has done.'[84]

When news came that William's army was on the way the Protestants were jubilant: 'there was very great joy, and sorrow and sadness was gone away, when we crept out of our houses and found ourselves as it were in a new world'.[85] On the evening of July 4 a troop of dragoons reached Dublin and next morning the duke of Ormond came in with nine troops of horse. The same day William and the main army reached Finglas, some three miles north of the city. On the following day he rode 'in great splendour' to St Patrick's cathedral where the *Te Deum* was sung and Dean King preached 'an excellent sermon'.[86]

[84] *Full and true account; Villare Hibernicum.*

[85] *Ormonde MSS*, n.s., viii. 388.

[86] *London Gazette*, 14 July 1690. For King's experience of the Jacobite régime see his 'Diary', edited by H. J. Lawlor.

The former mayor and aldermen were present and the Protestants of Dublin gave a great welcome to their deliverer: they 'ran about shouting and embracing one another and blessing God for his wonderful deliverance as if they had been alive from the dead; the streets were filled with crowds and shouting and the poor Roman Catholics now lay in the same terrors as we had done some few days before'.[87]

[87] *True and perfect journal.*

IX

WILLIAM AT LIMERICK

~~~~~~

1. JACOBITE DISSENSION

WHEN THE Jacobite leaders reached Limerick, there was much debate about future policy. Tyrconnell appears to have taken the view that the position was hopeless and that the only prudent course was to strike a bargain with William, who might be expected to offer reasonable terms for a quick Irish settlement. Evidence for this is provided not only by Charles O'Kelly, who is a hostile witness, but by the 'Light to the blind', the writer of which is a strong supporter of Tyrconnell and argues that it would have been sensible to negotiate while there was still an Irish army in being. Both sources mention Sarsfield as the leader of the die-hard party: to O'Kelly he is the 'darling of the army'; to the other he is a 'caballing gentleman'.[1]

Tyrconnell and Sarsfield were strongly contrasted figures. Tyrconnell at sixty was an experienced politician with a long record of successful negotiation; he was in bad health and, for a man unaccustomed to physical exertion, his gallant effort at the Boyne must have been a great strain. Sarsfield at forty or less was a vigorous and dare-devil cavalry commander of fine physique and attractive manner, but lacking in subtlety and, as some people thought, in brains. Berwick described him as 'a man of an amazing stature, utterly devoid of sense, very good-natured and very brave'. James told d'Avaux that Sarsfield was very

[1] O'Kelly, pp. 57–8; *Jacobite narrative*, pp. 110–11.

brave but had no head.[2] He had all the makings of a popular hero and was regarded as one, not only by most of his own side but by the enemy. He is the one Irishman spoken of with respect and admiration in Williamite writings: the Rommel of the Jacobite war. On his father's side he belonged to a well-known, but not aristocratic, 'old English' family. His great-grandfather had been mayor of Dublin and noted for hospitality. On his mother's side he was Gaelic Irish: she was the daughter of Rory O'More, one of the leaders of the rising of 1641.[3] This gave him an advantage over Tyrconnell, who had no Gaelic background and whose wife was English. O'Kelly, who is consistently hostile to Tyrconnell, says that after the Boyne he sent his wife to France to give a pessimistic picture of the Irish situation so as to discourage further French aid.[4]

Lauzun wrote to Seignelay that Limerick was indefensible and that he and Tyrconnell doubted whether they could avoid being made prisoners of war. He said that a number of Irish had asked for military commands, but that Tyrconnell rightly suspected that they did so only to put themselves into a favourable position for bargaining with the enemy.[5] According to Stevens a council of war was held in which Tyrconnell declared that all was lost and that the only course was to negotiate for the best terms available before it was too late. This met with indignant opposition. A group of intransigent officers took control, Tyrconnell was pushed into the background, and there was talk of turning the French out of Limerick.[6] Lauzun told Louvois that he was withdrawing the French to Galway. He did not want to keep them in Limerick in close quarters with the Irish 'who hate us so much that we fear they will play some dirty trick on us'. He proposed that when the French troops were withdrawn from Ireland extra ships should be sent to bring off the best of the Irish regiments: he would be 'sorry to see them go to

---

[2] Berwick, *Memoirs*, i. 173; d'Avaux, p. 519.

[3] The best life of Sarsfield is by J. H. Todhunter (1895). There are many gaps in our knowledge of Sarsfield's life. There is no evidence when he married Honora de Burgh; it may have been in the winter of 1690, when she was 15 and Sarsfield's defence of the Shannon would have brought him to the Clanricarde castle of Portumna. She later married Berwick.

[4] O'Kelly, p. 58.

[5] Lauzun to Seignelay, 16/26 July 1690 (Ranke, vi. 122-3).

[6] Stevens, p. 144.

the Prince of Orange, particularly three cavalry regiments which are excellent'.[7]

2. WILLIAM'S DILEMMA

William did not reach the neighbourhood of Limerick until more than five weeks after the Boyne; and this gave the Jacobites time to collect their scattered forces and organize the defence of the city. They were encouraged by the resistance of Athlone, which was successfully defended by Richard Grace, a veteran of the confederate war, against an attack by Lieutenant-General Douglas. When Douglas summoned him to surrender, Grace is said to have fired his pistol as a gesture of defiance and to have declared that he would hold Athlone till he had eaten his old boots. The defenders broke the bridge and retired to the Connacht side of the Shannon. Douglas had no siege guns and spent a week in fruitless operations. He then got word that Sarsfield with 15,000 men was coming to the relief of Athlone. So he marched away and rejoined the main Williamite army.[8]

Jacobite waverers were shocked by William's uncompromising attitude, expressed in a declaration made at Finglas, near Dublin, on July 7. Its terms were drawn up in consultation with the Dublin Protestants on the assumption that the Boyne had been a crushing victory and that the Jacobites were now at William's mercy. The declaration promised pardon to poor labourers, common soldiers, tradesmen and artificers who surrendered by August 1. But as for the 'desperate leaders of the rebellion', as William was now in a position to make them sensible of their errors, they were to be left to the event of war, unless by great and manifest demonstrations they convinced him that they were deserving of his mercy.[9] Southwell, who was the draftsman, explained that the scheme was 'to invite in all of the meaner sort . . . but not to be meddling with the landed men till it appears into what posture they throw themselves or into what corners they retire'. He expected that this would bring in

[7] Lauzun to Louvois, 31 July/10 Aug. 1690 (Min. guerre, A1 962, no. 155).

[8] Story, p. 102; S. Grace, *Memoirs of the family of Grace*, p. 32.

[9] Story, pp. 93–4; the policy is discussed in Simms, 'Williamite peace-tactics' in *I.H.S.* viii. 303–23.

'the bulk of the nation and that the rest will afterwards look the more abject'.[10] This attempt to drive a wedge between the common people and the landed classes was a complete failure. Douglas's army paid no attention to the declaration and freely plundered the Catholics who had put themselves under Williamite protection. Story noted that the Ulster units 'were very dexterous at that sport'. He thought that if the declaration had been honoured the Williamites would have had 20,000 fewer enemies.[11] Another Williamite account described Douglas's army as traversing the country 'like the plague of Athens, paying no regard to declaration or protection'.[12] But whether the declaration was honoured or not its terms, which gave no guarantee of property in return for surrender, had little appeal to the better-off Catholics. The Jacobite officers complained that 'this declaration was too narrow . . . and that they were obliged to stick together as being their only safety'. Story's view was that William would have preferred a more generous declaration but was obliged to consider the English interest in Ireland.[13] The Jacobite author of 'A light to the blind' came to a similar conclusion:

But the estated gentlemen the prince excluded from his mercy. This was a foolish verdict, and the first of this kind, I believe, that ever had been; for commonly a prince, entering into a country in order to conquer it, doth in the first place encourage the principal persons to submit unto him, and when these are gained the rest do follow in course. I suppose the prince of Orange was persuaded to go against reason in favour of his great officers, who would have the Irish Catholic lords of land to be rejected from all expectation of recovering their estates, because the said officers were sure in their own conceits that the Irish army would be overcome at last, and because then they might have those lands by the prince's grant.

It was reported to France that most of the Irish officers were irritated by the declaration and were resolved to die fighting rather than accept such hard terms.[14]

It is very doubtful whether William was persuaded against his better judgement to adopt this uncompromising policy. The explanation of the Finglas declaration seems to be that William's

[10] *Finch MSS*, ii. 346. [11] Story, pp. 94, 99.
[12] T.C.D., MS V. 4. 4, p. 131. [13] Story, *Continuation*, p. 27.
[14] *Jacobite narrative*, pp. 105–6; *Gazette de France*, 2 Sept. 1690.

appreciation of the situation after the Boyne was much the same as James's, that all was over for the Jacobites. As Würtemberg put it: 'the enemy are completely scattered and it appears that the war in Ireland will soon be over'.[15] William and his troops thus helped to stiffen the resistance of the Jacobite army by showing that tolerable terms were not to be obtained from an immediate surrender: further resistance might enable better terms to be secured. William was disappointed by the poor response to his declaration of July 7 and on August 1 made a further declaration in which he assured those of superior rank that their lives would be spared if they submitted, and that if they were destitute they should have subsistence on a scale appropriate to their position. But this offer also was far less than the guarantee of property and religious freedom for which the Jacobites were looking, and it had virtually no effect.[16]

William's slow progress towards Limerick gave time to the Irish army to rally. On July 8, while he was still at Finglas, he got the news that the English and Dutch fleets had been defeated by the French at Beachy Head.[17] This created a highly dangerous situation, which might make his immediate return to England a matter of urgency. England was threatened with invasion, the French navy might cut off communication across the Irish Sea. Lord Carmarthen, William's principal English adviser, warned him that the French were preparing to send 28 frigates into Irish waters: if their main fleet followed, the French would be masters of the Irish Sea, William would find it very difficult to get back, and the situation would be ripe for a Jacobite rising in England. On July 7 the cabinet decided to ask William to send back part of his army and 'so far as it could be done with good manners' urged that William should himself return.[18] William had meanwhile marched south towards Waterford; he did not get the cabinet letter till July 16, when he was at Castledermot, County Kildare. He replied that he was sending back some units of cavalry and infantry: he would have to stay with his army for six or seven days more, but then intended to return to Dublin *en route* for England.[19]

---

[15] *Danish force*, p. 43.   [16] *Ormonde MSS*, ii. 445–6.
[17] *Danish force*, p. 46.
[18] A. Browning, *Thomas Osborne*, ii. 174, 178; *Finch MSS*, ii. 347–8.
[19] Ibid., p. 364.

When William got to Carrick-on-Suir, he sent Kirk forward to summon Waterford, which surrendered after some parleying; the example was followed by Duncannon, the fort that guarded the entrance to Waterford harbour. The defenders of Waterford at first asked for a guarantee of their estates and for religious liberty; this was contemptuously refused by William, who threatened to give no quarter if the city did not at once surrender. When it did so the garrison was allowed to march away and William took personal care to see that the citizens were not molested.[20] He had lost valuable time in his slow march on Waterford, but he had gained a safe port on the south coast which was to be of much assistance in the Munster campaign. He then made his way back to Dublin, intending to return to England and leave the Dutch general Solms to finish the campaign in Ireland. But when he got to Dublin there was better news. The French had burned the small fishing-village of Teignmouth, but had then returned to their fleet in Torbay; the English navy had not suffered as heavily at Beachy Head as had been feared. William decided to stay for some time longer, and he made for Limerick.[21]

3. THE DEFENCE OF LIMERICK

Limerick was a place of considerable natural strength. The main, or English, town was on an island in the Shannon linked to the Clare side by Thomond Bridge and to the Irish town on the County Limerick side by Ballsbridge, which spanned a branch of the river.[22] Both the English and Irish towns were walled, but the fortifications were old and decayed and, by the standards of the later seventeenth century, were inadequate to withstand a regular siege. In a celebrated phrase Lauzun is said to have remarked that Limerick could be taken with roasted apples. Stevens described it as 'almost defenceless; it had no other than an old stone wall made against bows and arrows'. Williamites treated the fortifications with greater respect.[23]

[20] Story, pp. 109–11; *Danish force*, pp. 65–6.
[21] *London Gazette*, 8 July 1690; Story, pp. 111–12.
[22] For the topography see map on p. 164.
[23] MacGeoghegan, *Histoire d'Irlande*, iii. 743; Stevens, p. 193; Story, p. 117; *Danish force*, p. 54.

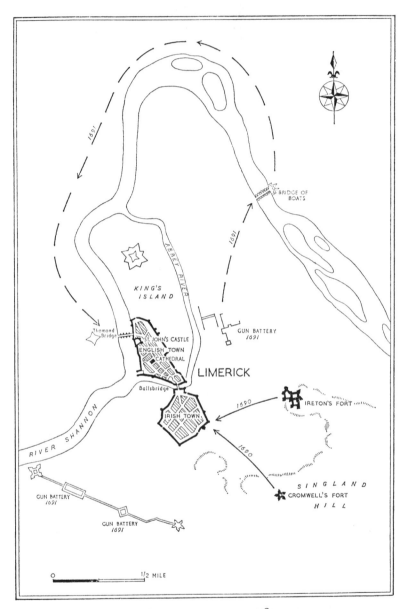

SIEGES OF LIMERICK, 1690–1

Good use was made of the interval before William's arrival to improve the defences. A ditch was dug outside the Irish town wall with a 'covered way' – a ledge cut out of the counterscarp, or outer side of the ditch, and protected by the parapet – and a palisade. Some redoubts and other outworks were made and the suburbs cleared to deny cover to the enemy.[24] Although the French troops were withdrawn, a French major-general, Boisseleau, was left as commander of the town. He was a tough and vigorous officer who had gained experience of commanding Irish troops during the previous year. His force consisted of a regiment of cavalry, a regiment of dragoons, and 28 infantry regiments. Lauzun put the strength of the infantry at 14,000, but some of them were without arms.[25] In addition, there was a cavalry force of perhaps 2,500 under Sarsfield in County Clare. Up the Shannon was a large force of Ulstermen, most of them without arms, raised by Hugh Balldearg O'Donnell, a descendant of the chiefs of Tyrconnell who had served in the Spanish army and had reached Ireland a few days after the Boyne. His arrival created much excitement, as it was prophesied that an O'Donnell with a red mark would deliver Ireland from the English.[26] One story was that Balldearg had foretold that the English would conquer till they came to the well near Singland Hill, just outside Limerick, but that after that they would be defeated and driven out of the land. His arrival thus contributed to the raising of Irish morale, though a Williamite comment was: 'it is hard to believe how this dream had obtained among the common sort'.[27]

William's strength at Limerick was less than it had been at the Boyne, as two regiments of infantry, a regiment of horse and a regiment of dragoons had been sent to England, and other detachments had been left to garrison places already occupied. His army at Limerick may be put at about 25,000. It was still very international, including the Danish force, Huguenots, Dutch and Brandenburgers. The Williamite view was that its

[24] Stevens, p. 149.   [25] Min. guerre, A1 962, nos 167, 169.

[26] He seems to have been a great-nephew of Niall Garbh O'Donnell (see J. O'Donovan, 'The O'Donnells in exile' in *Duffy's Hiberian Magazine*, 1860, pp. 50–6, 106–7). 'Balldearg' is the Irish for 'red spot'. For Balldearg O'Donnell as folklore hero see P. O Finneadh, 'Balldearg O'Donnell' in *Béaloideas*, iii. 359–62.

[27] *Finch MSS*, ii. 407.

numbers were inadequate for a complete investment of the city.[28]

On August 7 William reached Caherconlish, about eight miles south-east of Limerick. He had only field guns with him. The heavier guns required for siege operations were still on their slow journey from Dublin, a failure in logistics which Story could explain only by supposing that an immediate surrender of the town had been counted on.[29] During the following days the approaches to Limerick were reconnoitred, and there were encounters between the Williamites and the Irish who lined the thick hedges that covered the area. Williamites could hear the enemy talking 'with their damned Irish brogue on their tongues' and shouted back 'ye toads, are ye there? We'll be with you presently'.[30] The Williamite advance was towards the south-east corner of the Irish town. Their first objective was the ridge of Singland Hill, which ran in a crescent about half a mile from the wall, from which it was separated by a belt of boggy ground. On the ridge were two forts which had been built in the Cromwellian siege of 1650–1, Ireton's fort and Cromwell's fort. The Williamites succeeded in occupying both forts and the intervening ridge without resistance from the retreating Irish. William then sent a summons to the commander to surrender. According to Story a great part of the garrison was in favour of capitulating, but Boisseleau, Sarsfield and Berwick put up a strong case for resistance; they represented that the French had landed in England with 50,000 men and that William would soon have to withdraw his army from Ireland. Boisseleau sent a bold reply that he could best earn the prince of Orange's esteem by a vigorous defence of the town entrusted to him.[31]

William had thus to make a regular siege of Limerick, and waited for the arrival of the eight heavy guns that were on their way from Dublin with an accompanying procession of carts laden with ammunition and stores. On the morning of August 11 'a substantial country gentleman' named Manus O'Brien came to the Williamite camp with the news that Sarsfield had crossed the Shannon near Killaloe with the pick of the Irish

[28] Story, p. 111; *Cal. S.P. dom., 1690–1*, p. 230.
[29] Story, p. 118.
[30] Ibid., p. 114.   [31] Ibid., p. 115.

cavalry and dragoons, his objective being the siege train. It was some time before O'Brien could get a hearing. When William eventually heard his story and ordered a party to intercept Sarsfield his orders met with near-indifference – perhaps as a result of the ill-feeling between English and Dutch which paralleled the Franco-Irish dissensions on the Jacobite side. The Williamite party did not start out till 1 or 2 a.m. on the following day, and it was not long before 'they saw a great light in the air and heard a strange rumbling noise'. Sarsfield, traditionally guided by Hogan, a famous rapparee, had brought his men through the Tipperary mountains to Ballyneety, where the siege train had encamped for the night.[32] Sarsfield's ride is his most celebrated exploit. It caused an international sensation at the time and its memory is still preserved in a number of local traditions.[33] It was an enterprise of skilful timing and swift execution, which was highly damaging to the enemy. He took the convoy completely by surprise; the guns had been left out in the open, most of the horses had been turned out to grass, and very few sentries were left to guard the sleeping camp. Two of the guns were split by overcharging and it appears that Sarsfield spared the life of a Williamite gunner for his technical services in this operation. But in the process other guns were dislodged from their carriages and were left intact. Tin boats for bridging the Shannon were not completely destroyed, but holes were cut in many of them. Most of the 100 wagons of the convoy were burned and with them 12,000 pounds of powder and a great quantity of match and grenades. Carters and horses were ruthlessly cut down.[34] The carters' wives and children are said to have been among the victims, and a Williamite commentator tried to exonerate Sarsfield from personal responsibility for

[32] Ibid., pp. 119–21; Todhunter, *Life of Patrick Sarsfield*, pp. 88–94. There are two places called Ballyneety in County Limerick. This one is 14 miles south-east of Limerick.

[33] *Gazette de France*, 9 Sept. 1690, which gives a full, and somewhat inflated, account; *Coll. Hib.*, iii. 133 (reports received by the Vatican from Amsterdam and Brussels).

[34] *Finch MSS*, ii. 412; *Danish force*, pp. 55–6; R. Davies, *Journal*, p. 137; Story, p. 120. I have not discovered the origin of the story that the Williamite password for the night was 'Sarsfield', which gave him the opportunity of saying 'Sarsfield is the word and Sarsfield is the man'.

this.[35] O Bruadair praised Sarsfield's exploit with pardonable poetic licence:

> He left not a bomb or a copper pontoon
> In Baile an Fhaoitigh that he did not disperse
> Like the smoke of a candle up into the sky.[36]

The feat added greatly to Sarsfield's reputation, encouraged Irish morale, and was an invaluable support to the policy of resistance. According to O'Kelly it was less welcome to Tyrconnell, Lauzun and their partisans. It was a setback for the peace party, and the French feared that they would be kept longer in Ireland.[37] It was a severe blow to the Williamites, though in view of the shaky state of opinion in England the *London Gazette* tempered the bad news with the comforting assurance: 'this accident will only lose us three or four days, for in that time our cannon (being 24-pounders) will arrive from Waterford; in the meantime our batteries are preparing and all things are put in a posture for a vigorous attack of the town'.[38] In fact Ballyneety had badly upset the transport arrangements and the guns from Waterford did not arrive until ten days after. The delay, and even more so the loss of ammunition, were to have serious consequences for the Williamites.

Six guns salvaged from Ballyneety arrived on August 16, and during the following days the Williamites made trenches between the Singland ridge and the wall of the Irish town, and set up a battery. The Irish were pushed back from their advanced positions, though there was hard fighting before they were driven from a redoubt near the south-east corner of the wall.[39]

With the arrival of the heavy guns from Waterford the Williamites pushed their batteries nearer and nearer to the wall. This involved moving the guns across low-lying ground, which was practicable only because the season had up to then been unusually dry. Their advance was protected by woolsacks, a device introduced by Meesters, the Dutch comptroller of

[35] Parker, *Memoirs*, p. 26.
[36] O Bruadair, iii. 149.
[37] O'Kelly, p. 64.
[38] *London Gazette*, 25 Aug. 1690.
[39] *Danish force*, pp. 67–71; Story, pp. 122–4.

artillery, 'an excellent artist'.[40] August 25 brought a change in the weather. That day Sir Robert Southwell wrote: 'this morning it began to pour down at such a furious rate that some of our trenches have been two feet deep. I find by this one day's fierce rain a strange damp as to our success among many of the chief officers and that our army must draw off or be ruined if the rain should hold; nay that it would be a great task in these deep ways to get off our cannon.' He added that William himself 'in his dark and reserved way' had hinted that he was thinking of going back to England.[41] When the rain cleared the bombardment began, supplemented by carcasses (a form of incendiary bomb) and red-hot shot, which started a number of fires in the town. The defenders tried to protect the wall with woolsacks, but to no purpose; a breach was made, which according to Story was twelve yards wide. Boisseleau, the French commander, says that the breach was forty-two yards wide and that he made a retrenchment behind it, on which he mounted guns.[42]

On the afternoon of August 27 the Williamites assaulted the breach. Stevens gives a vivid account of how his regiment was led into the breach by Boisseleau himself. They could see the red-coats pouring in and at first thought that they were their own men retreating, till they noticed the green boughs that distinguished the Williamites. The Irish who had been driven from the counterscarp at first retreated hurriedly, but they were held up by dragoons and then rallied. Stevens's regiment fired effectively from the retrenchment and drove the Williamites out of the breach.[43] The French account pays tribute to this regiment and also to 'four hundred Irish of MacMahon's regiment who had no arms and threw stones, which gave considerable trouble to the enemy'.[44] Story corroborates the account and adds that the defence was assisted by 'broken bottles from the very women, who boldly stood on the breach and were nearer our men than their own'. The Danish envoy gave a similar account: 'the very women, prone as they are to violent passions,

---

[40] Southwell to Nottingham, 22 Aug. 1690 (*Finch MSS*, ii. 427). Meesters had escaped death at Ballyneety by throwing himself into a bed of nettles (ibid., p. 412).

[41] Ibid., p. 428.

[42] Story, p. 128; *Gazette de France*, quoted in *Jacobite narrative*, p. 264.

[43] Stevens, pp. 177–81.   [44] *Gazette de France*, loc. cit.

have since then become more furious; it was noted that in the attack on the counterscarp they caused as much, indeed more, damage than the garrison by throwing huge stones on the assailants, of whom a great number thus perished'.[45] After some hours' hard fighting the Williamites were driven back with heavy losses. Their casualties, killed and wounded, for the day were estimated at over 2,300.[46] On the following day, August 28, they continued to fire at the breach, but rain set in again and anxious consultations took place about a withdrawal. It was pointed out that if there was more rain the guns could not be got away and that 'the watery season would undoubtedly bring the country distemper'.[47] In any case the breach was not wide enough and, even if the Irish town were taken, the English town on its island would remain to be tackled. Würtemberg urged that the bombardment should be intensified and the breach widened. He was told that there were no more cannon-balls; with the last convoy unfilled bombs had been sent instead of balls. Ammunition that was to be shipped from London had never left, 'the French being masters of the Channel'.[48] George Clarke made a similar point: 'the ill success at Limerick is well known to be owing to the want of ammunition occasioned by Sarsfield falling upon the artillery . . . so that after a fruitless attack of a breach which we had not powder and shot to make larger the king left the army'.[49]

On August 29 it was decided to raise the siege, and next day William took the road for Waterford, a disappointed man. The withdrawal of his army was less than orderly: sick and wounded hastily evacuated, bombs and grenades abandoned with a fuse to blow them up. Stevens has a macabre account of a burning hospital full of wounded men.[50] When he reached London William wrote to the prince of Waldeck, captain-general in the Netherlands, to explain the disappointing conclusion to his Irish campaign. He had attacked Limerick rather than the easier objectives of Cork and Kinsale in the hope of completing the

[45] Story, p. 129; Fouleresse to Christian V, 29 Aug. 1690 (*N. & Q.*, 5th ser., viii. 123).

[46] *Danish force*, pp. 73–4.

[47] *Finch MSS*, ii. 435; Mullenaux, *Journal of the three months royal campaign*, p. 26.

[48] *Danish force*, p. 74; Burnet, iv. 102.

[49] *Leyland-Popham MSS*, p. 276.   [50] Story, p. 133; Stevens, p. 185.

conquest of Ireland: if Limerick with its strong garrison was taken, other places would fall of themselves. But the assault on the breach had failed; the excessive zeal of the assault troops and the strength of the enemy's retrenchment had thrown out the plan of attack. After that setback the lateness of the season and the prospect of continued rain made withdrawal inevitable; otherwise it would have been impossible to get away the heavy guns. The disappointment was the greater because, had it not been for a series of minor mishaps, the enterprise would infallibly have succeeded: but 'the good God did not will it', and William had been unable to finish the business and so was not yet in a position to give the full measure of assistance to his friends on the continent – the reason for which he had taken risks that he would not otherwise have taken.[51] Berwick later observed sarcastically that William told all Europe that continual rains had made him raise the siege: 'but I can affirm that not a single drop of rain fell for above a month before or for three weeks after'.[52]

William's conduct of the siege was subjected to some criticism: it was argued that he should have sent part of his army across the Shannon, and that he should have cut the Irish communications by breaking the Thomond Bridge on the Clare side and Ballsbridge between the English and Irish towns. On his behalf it was urged that his army was too small for such operations and that, if the Shannon rose, part of it might be cut off.[53] It was also feared that the French troops might return from Galway to reinforce the Irish.[54] Plans to bring Sir Cloudesly Shovell and a naval squadron into the Shannon were held up by postal delays and adverse winds, and Shovell did not leave the English coast till after the siege was raised and the French had left Galway.[55]

Stevens paid tribute to the bravery and resolution of the Irish, and explained why French and Irish attitudes to the defence of Limerick were so different: the French with their

[51] Ranke, vi. 278.

[52] Berwick, i. 79. His memoirs are not accurate on points of detail. Apart from Williamite references to bad weather Stevens refers to it. For a lively account of Williamite army reaction to Limerick weather see Sterne, *Tristram Shandy*, p. 295.

[53] Story, pp. 134–5.

[54] *N. & Q.*, loc. cit., p. 122.   [55] *Finch MSS*, ii. 414, 453.

experience of continental fortifications thought Limerick untenable and refused to stay in it; the Irish had never seen a well-fortified town and thought Limerick impregnable.[56] The brunt of the fighting was borne by the infantry of the garrison. Apart from the Ballyneety exploit the cavalry did little to harry the Williamites or relieve the pressure on the town. The infantry fought with spirit and tenacity and gave an account of themselves that must have astonished those who had seen them broken at the Boyne. The defence of Limerick restored their self-respect and revived a feeling of optimism, which Boisseleau is said to have tried to damp with a rather ungracious speech:

With much ado he had persuaded them to defend themselves, which with God's help they had done; but he assured them that it was not fear but prudence and policy that had made the enemy quit the siege . . . and withal he told them his opinion that the next time the enemy came they would have it.[57]

4. THE FRENCH LEAVE IRELAND

Limerick was a notable success for the Irish, won by their own courage and energy. It justified the stand taken by the resistance party and prolonged the war for over a year. Tyrconnell and the French, who had presumed that Limerick would fall, had now to modify their position. By August 24 Lauzun was contemplating the possibility that Limerick might hold out. He was still making plans to take six or seven thousand of the garrison to France. He had sounded Sarsfield and thought that he too would come if Limerick capitulated; but if it were not taken he thought that Sarsfield would keep up a guerrilla war as best he could without a regular army, which could not be formed or maintained in the prevailing conditions. The French troops were at Galway ready to sail, but he had postponed embarkation so as not to discourage the defenders of Limerick.[58]

After the siege was raised, Tyrconnell wrote to Louvois that the situation had been transformed, and that it would no longer be practicable to send an Irish force to France. He thought that resistance in Ireland could be kept up till the following spring

---

[56] Stevens, p. 194.   [57] Story, p. 133.
[58] Min. guerre, A1 962, no. 167.

and was making arrangements for the government while he himself went to France to report to James.[59] He and the French sailed about September 12, leaving the civil government in charge of twelve commissioners and the army in charge of the twenty-year-old Berwick who was to be advised by a military council, on which Sarsfield had the last place. O'Kelly suggested that Tyrconnell would have preferred to leave Sarsfield out altogether but was afraid of an army revolt.[60]

According to O'Kelly there was general surprise that Tyrconnell and Lauzun should have decided to leave Ireland when the Jacobite prospects appeared so much brighter. The reaction in Paris was much the same: 'most of the people cannot understand why, since the siege of Limerick has been raised, Tyrconnell and the French soldiers chose to leave Ireland'.[61] It is not difficult to understand Lauzun's decision. He was disgusted with Ireland: it was purgatory to be there; he had rather drive a gun-carriage in France. His orders were to withdraw his troops to France, the escorting fleet was waiting and no countermanding orders had been received.[62] Tyrconnell was no less weary of the obstruction and hostility that faced him in Ireland. His enemies intended to undermine his credit with James and he thought it prudent to get a start of them.[63]

[59] *Anal. Hib.*, xxi. 203–4.
[60] O'Kelly, p. 72.
[61] *Coll. Hib.*, iii. 136.
[62] Min. guerre, A1 962, no. 160.
[63] *James II*, ii. 420–2.

X

MARLBOROUGH AT CORK
AND KINSALE

~~~~~~~~~~~~~~~~~~~~~~~~~

I. THE MUNSTER PROJECT

ON 7 AUGUST 1690, just before the siege of Limerick began, Marlborough put before the English council a bold plan for intervention in Ireland. The proposal was that a force of about five thousand English troops under his command should sail directly to the Munster coast. The objectives were Cork and Kinsale, the ports that provided the shortest and best communication between France and Ireland. Coming after the panic of the previous month, and only three days after the French fleet had left Torbay, this proposal astonished the council and aroused strong opposition, particularly on the part of Carmarthen, its leading member. It involved stripping England of a great part of its regular troops while William was on the other side of the Irish Sea and a French attack was still imminent. However Nottingham was in favour of the plan, and so was Admiral Russell. Queen Mary referred it to William, to whom Marlborough wrote at the same time. William had hitherto not shown much liking for Marlborough; and the proposal came at an unhappy time, two days after the Ballyneety affair had damaged William's prospects of taking Limerick. But his response was surprisingly favourable. He lost no time in approving the plan: Marlborough would have to bring his own guns and ammunition, as none could be spared from Limerick, but William could send him cavalry support.[1]

William's decision left Carmarthen unconvinced: if the fleet and five thousand men set off for Ireland, England would be at the mercy of a French invasion. Nottingham was a strong supporter of the plan and had no doubt that Marlborough would soon be master of Cork and Kinsale. The escort was to be the main fleet: 42 capital ships and 10 fire-ships, together with 17 Dutch ships.[2] Marlborough and his men were on board at Portsmouth by August 30, but adverse winds held them up for over a fortnight. By that time William was already back in England, which made Marlborough's expedition less of a hazard than it had originally appeared to its critics. Marlborough finally sailed on September 17, was off Crosshaven on September 21, and two days later disembarked at Passage West, on the western shore of Cork harbour.[3]

2. THE SITUATION IN IRELAND

After William had left Ireland his army came under the command of the Dutch General Solms. The three battalions of Dutch guards were sent back to England and the rest of the army prepared to go into winter quarters. The line was withdrawn a considerable distance from the Shannon; to begin with, Tipperary town was the headquarters. Story thought it unwise to have fallen back so far, leaving to the Jacobites control of all the Shannon crossings.[4] Solms soon got permission to leave for England; his fellow-countryman Ginkel, as the senior lieutenant-general, succeeded to the command and remained in charge for the rest of the war.[5] Ginkel belonged to a prominent Dutch family, van Reede of Amerongen near Utrecht. His father had long taken an active part in the affairs of the republic, and had on a number of occasions been in opposition to William. In the post-1688 period he had been so hostile to William's supporters

[1] William to Marlborough, 14 Aug. 1690, quoted in W. S. Churchill, *Marlborough*, i. 326–7.

[2] Mary to William, 22 Aug. 1690 (Dalrymple, iii (2). 194); *Finch MSS*, ii. 431.

[3] Story, pp. 140–1; *Villare Hibernicum*, p. 26.

[4] Story, *Continuation*, p. 46.   [5] *Danish force*, p. 79.

in the Netherlands that he had been sent into 'gilded exile' as ambassador to Copenhagen.[6] The son, after a distinguished career in the Dutch army, accompanied William to England, where he gained credit for suppressing a mutinous Scottish regiment; he had then come to Ireland and had taken an active part at the Boyne and at the siege of Limerick. The instructions that William had left for Ginkel's predecessor emphasized the importance of co-operating with Marlborough and of keeping the Jacobite army away from Cork and Kinsale. Should the enemy approach they were to be attacked 'if the ground will in any way allow of it'.[7]

On the Jacobite side dissensions continued, and Berwick's position as commander was not very happy. He was only twenty and his experience of warfare outside Ireland was limited to two years fighting against the Turks in Hungary in 1686–7. He had distinguished himself there and during the Irish campaign had shown energy and initiative. In later life he was to prove an outstanding commander and to become a marshal of France. But now he was overshadowed by Sarsfield, who was at the height of his reputation and was supported by a discontented and insubordinate group of officers. Berwick's later references to Sarsfield strike a bitter note: Ballyneety had 'puffed him up so that he thought himself the greatest general in the world; Henry Luttrell turned his head and cried him up everywhere, not because he really esteemed him but to make him popular and so able to serve his own purposes'.[8]

The Jacobites took advantage of the Williamite withdrawal to cross the Shannon at Banagher and attack Birr castle, which was held by a small Williamite garrison. Berwick refers to himself as leader of the expedition and makes no mention of Sarsfield. The latter was the commander according to the Williamite accounts. The expedition was a failure, and the Jacobites withdrew before the advance of a Williamite relief force. Berwick blamed 'the unskilfulness of my gunners who never could bring their guns to bear on the castle'. The arrival of the Williamite force was a misfortune for the Birr countryside; they robbed and stripped most of the Irish, 'which made it natural for them after this to turn rapparees and do us all the mischief they could'.[9] In view

[6] S. B. Baxter, *William III*, p. 260.   [7] *Cal. S.P. dom., 1690–1*, p. 111.
[8] Berwick, *Memoirs*, i. 72–3, 96.   [9] Ibid., p. 77; Story, pp. 137–8.

of the importance of Cork and Kinsale it might have been wiser for the Jacobites to have secured the line of communication between these towns and Limerick. A half-hearted attempt was made to occupy Kilmallock, a walled town twenty-one miles south of Limerick. But the force sent was very weak, 100 foot and 100 dragoons under a French lieutenant-colonel. A major-general of the Danish force was sent with a strong detachment (400 cavalry, 200 dragoons, 500 foot and four guns), which intimidated the defenders into immediate surrender; they were allowed to get away to Limerick, without their arms and with 'their hands in their pockets'. Stevens was very contemptuous of the defenders' conduct and called it 'shameful surrender'.[10] The failure of the Jacobites to hold positions between Limerick and the south coast left the Williamite force free to invest Cork and Kinsale with little interference.

Contemporary accounts suggest that there was much dissension in the Jacobite army and that discipline and supply arrangements were very unsatisfactory. Intercepted letters from the marquis d'Albeville to James and Tyrconnell complained of insubordination on the part of officers and looting on the part of the men.[11] A deserter told the Williamites that provisions were very scarce and dear: sugar 30s. a pound; Irish soap 16s. a pound; men's shoes 30s. a pair. There was no ale or brandy; officers drank Madeira and water, soldiers drank water and occasionally milk and water.[12]

3. THE SIEGE OF CORK

Cork was the second city in Ireland, the largest and most important place left to the Jacobites. It was a walled town on a marshy island in the Lee, a little above the point where the river widens into the intricate channels of Cork harbour. Its military weakness was that it was commanded by high ground on both sides of the river. Thomas Phillips, who had made a

[10] George Clarke to Nottingham, 10 Sept. 1690 (*Finch MSS*, ii. 451); Stevens, pp. 184–5; *Danish force*, pp. 76–7. Clarke and Stevens give the number of the defenders as 200; Würtemberg put it at 400.

[11] *Finch MSS*, ii. 472–3. D'Albeville was Ignatius White, a Limerick man who had been James's ambassador at the Hague.

[12] Sidney and Coningsby to Nottingham, 5 Oct. 1690 (*Cal. S.P. dom., 1695: addenda*, p. 157).

military survey of Ireland in 1685, said that the hills dominated it 'to that degree that no person can move in the streets'. On the high ground to the north of the city was Shandon, an old castle of the Barrys. The Jacobites had lately constructed two new forts near it to guard against an approach from the north. To the south of the city was Elizabeth fort, a sixteenth-century construction. To the south of this fort was a hill called 'the Cat', where Phillips had advised the construction of an armoury. Shortly before Marlborough's arrival the Jacobites had begun to build an outpost at this point, which is referred to as 'the Cat fort'.[13]

The commander of the garrison was Colonel Roger Mac-Elligott, whom we last heard of when he escaped from the Isle of Wight after the revolution. He was an experienced soldier with a good reputation. D'Avaux thought well of him, and Stevens found his regiment to be more orderly than most in the retreat from the Boyne.[14] He commanded a garrison of about 4,500 men. Berwick is said to have taken the view that Cork was untenable and to have ordered MacElligott to burn the town and retire to Kerry.[15] An attempt by Sarsfield to move into County Cork was frustrated by the Dutch Major-General Scravenmore, who claimed to have inflicted heavy losses on the Irish near Mallow. Williamite publicity made the most of the affair and boasted that Sarsfield's exploit at Ballyneety had been avenged: 'we have given him a Roland for his Oliver'.[16]

Marlborough had sent advance information of his movements and had asked that Kirk and Lanier, the English major-generals, should be sent to support him. Ginkel, however, dispatched Scravenmore with a force of Danish and Dutch cavalry and dragoons, followed by Danish and Huguenot infantry under Würtemberg. This led to a dispute about the command, as Würtemberg claimed that he was senior to Marlborough. It is usually said that this claim was based on right of birth, but he had in fact been a lieutenant-general for several years longer than Marlborough. A compromise was

[13] N.L.I., MS 2557; B.M., Add. MS 29,878 (Cramond's diary). See map on p. 179.
[14] D'Avaux, p. 134; Stevens, p. 111. See p. 155, above.
[15] *James II*, ii. 419.
[16] R. Davies, *Journal*, p. 148; *A true and faithful account*.

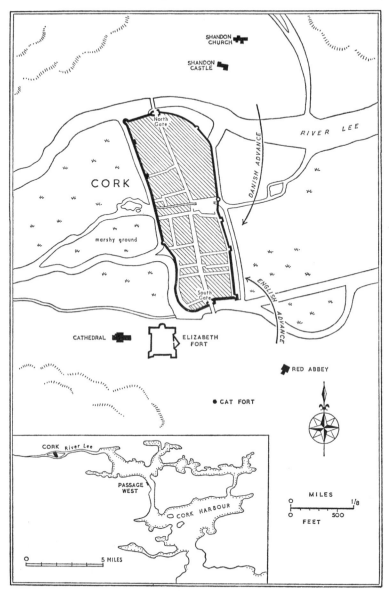

SIEGE OF CORK, 1690

reached that they should command on alternate days; Marlborough eased the situation by his tactful choice of 'Würtemberg' as his first day's password.[17] Even so there were to be
tensions and disagreements between the two commanders, and
signs of jealousy between English and continental troops.

The attack on Cork was made from both sides of the river
simultaneously. On the north side the vanguard of Scravenmore's force set up a battery on the high ground near Shandon
and prepared to attack the new forts; but the Irish immediately
abandoned them and set fire to the northern suburbs. This gave
the Williamites command of the whole area down to the north
bank of the river. Scravenmore summoned the garrison to surrender, but the commander 'sent back a very impertinent
answer'; he assured Scravenmore that he was not frightened of
his cavalry or of Marlborough's infantry and was ready to
receive them as soon as they pleased.[18]

Marlborough's first move was against the Cat fort on the
high ground south of the city. Colonel Hales with the vanguard
reached it on September 24 and exchanged some firing with the
Irish garrison. That night the Irish abandoned the Cat, which
was occupied next day by English troops.[19] Cork could thus be
bombarded from batteries set up on the high ground on both
sides of the river. A large battery at the Red Abbey south-east of
the city did damage to the eastern wall. Musketeers in the
steeple of the cathedral fired into the Elizabeth fort and 'did
good service in galling the Irish'.[20] On September 27 Mac-
Elligott let the Protestant Bishop Wetenhall out of the city with
1,300 of his co-religionists. He also wrote again to Scravenmore
proposing that envoys should be exchanged to discuss terms of
surrender. He was told that he must address himself to the
commanders Marlborough and Würtemberg.[21] When he did so
Marlborough replied that the garrison would be made prisoners
of war; Würtemberg was more lenient and replied that if the
garrison laid down their arms they would be allowed to march

---

[17] Harris, *William III*, p. 292; Würtemberg became a lieutenant-
general in 1682 at the age of twenty-three (*Danish force*, p. 142).

[18] *Danish Force*, p. 151; MacElligott to [Scravenmore], 23 Sept. 1690
(R.I.A., MS 12. I. 12, p. 46).

[19] B.M., Add. MS 29,878.   [20] Story, p. 141.

[21] R.I.A., MS 12. I. 12, p. 24; *Danish force*, p. 152.

away. Fortunately for the relations between Marlborough and Würtemberg, MacElligott kept the Williamite envoys waiting till the tide turned, and then replied that he could not accept either set of terms.[22] He hoped to be allowed to withdraw with the full honours of war.

Next day the Williamites continued their bombardment and made a considerable breach in the wall. In the early afternoon a double assault was made from both sides of the river over waterways and marshy ground, the men wading up to their armpits. The attack was supported by ships which had come up the channel on the morning tide and now fired at the breach and bombarded the city. Two hours after the attack began Mac-Elligott again asked for terms and was told that the garrison would have to be treated as prisoners of war. He was reluctant to accept the condition, and the attack continued for a short time. He then changed his mind and sent out emissaries to arrange for the surrender. The garrison were to be prisoners of war: 'no prejudice was to be done' to the officers, soldiers or inhabitants, and Marlborough would do his best to obtain clemency for them. The Elizabeth fort was to be handed over within an hour and the gates of the city next morning.[23]

This was a resounding success for the Williamites: it was the first time during this war that a large garrison had been forced to surrender as prisoners; Cork was a valuable prize for its own sake, and was an important harbour gained for William and denied to James and the French; one of the prisoners, the earl of Clancarty, was the owner of a vast estate, which was to be the largest item in the Williamite land-confiscation.[24] The treatment of the inhabitants gave grounds for complaint; 'many seamen and other loose persons' entered through the breach and plundered the city before Marlborough and Scravenmore could restore order. Charles Leslie alleged that MacElligott narrowly escaped being murdered and that the garrison were kept under guard on marshy ground, obliged to eat dead horses and afterwards confined under crowded and insanitary conditions in houses, gaols and churches.[25]

[22] Scravenmore to Clarke, 29 Sept. 1690 (Clarke corr. ii, no. 203).
[23] Story, pp. 142–3; Davies, p. 156; *Villare Hibernicum*, p. 27; *Danish force*, p. 152.
[24] Simms, *Williamite confiscation*, p. 87.   [25] Davies, p. 156; Leslie, p. 162.

D'Albeville attributed the loss of Cork to want of ammunition. He was most critical of MacElligott's handling of the situation: the governor should have taken Clancarty's advice that the garrison should burn the town and fight their way out where the enemy's strength was weakest; alternatively, he should have accepted the terms first offered; it was folly to have let the bishop and other Protestants out, as they told the English that the garrison had no more powder left.[26]

4. THE SIEGE OF KINSALE

The Williamite army lost no time in moving on Kinsale. It was again arranged that Marlborough and Würtemberg should command on alternate days.[27] Kinsale was not a walled town, but the harbour was protected by two forts, one on each side. The commander was Sir Edward Scott, a veteran of seventy who had seen service in France in Charles II's reign. He had weakened his force by sending two regiments to Cork, and not more than two thousand were left to defend Kinsale.[28] When the Williamite advance party under two brigadiers, one English and one Danish, reached Kinsale on September 29 they sent a peremptory demand for surrender: the garrison would be made prisoners of war if they capitulated at once; otherwise the commander would be hanged for resisting a victorious army. Scott gave a haughty refusal and threatened to hang the Williamite trumpeter. He ordered the town to be burned with faggots that he had already collected. But the order was not carried out in time, and the Williamites managed to save the houses, which provided their men with useful shelter from the stormy autumn weather.

The garrison and townsfolk escaped to the two forts: the old, or James's, fort on a peninsula jutting out from the west shore; and the new, or Charles's, fort on the eastern shore. Both forts were summoned, but ran up the blood-red flag of resistance.[29] The main Williamite body arrived on October 2 and drew up near Charles's fort. That fort could not be tackled till the guns came up, but Marlborough and Würtemberg agreed that an

---

[26] D'Albeville to James, 27 Oct./6 Nov. 1690 (*Finch MSS*, ii. 471).
[27] *Danish force*, p. 86.   [28] Ibid., p. 89; *Villare Hibernicum*, p. 27.
[29] Story, p. 143; *Villare Hibernicum*, p. 27; *Danish force*, p. 86.

immediate attempt should be made on the old fort on the other side of the harbour; it was a much weaker place and, according to deserters, was held by only a small force. The Danish major-general, Tettau, set out that night with a mixed force of English and continental troops. Early next morning they crossed the Bandon River in boats (a considerable feat of organization) and made a surprise attack on the old fort. The Irish garrison resisted fiercely and made good use of the fort's 46 guns; but they were overwhelmed, their commander and nearly half the garrison killed, and the survivors taken prisoner. Tettau had done well, but was not mentioned in Marlborough's somewhat ungracious report to Ginkel: 'you will excuse me that I only tell you that I took the old fort yesterday'.[30]

Charles's fort on the eastern shore of the harbour was a much larger and more formidable obstacle, built in Charles II's reign as a major contribution to the defence of Ireland. To Marlborough's summons to surrender Scott answered that it would be time enough to think of that a month later. The weather had broken and adverse winds prevented Marlborough's cannon coming by sea from Cork. They had to be dragged overland by improvised teams; the Danish cavalry had to bring cannon-balls. It was not till October 12 that the first battery was ready, and the full strength of the artillery was not in position till October 14. Heavy bombardment breached the walls in the Danish sector, and next day Scott asked for terms. Würtemberg proposed that they should be as for Cork and the garrison made prisoners; but Marlborough wanted to wind up his expedition and offered to let the garrison march off with their arms to Limerick. Lady Scott, who was a MacCarthy, was in the fort and drove out through the breach in her coach.[31]

Charles's fort had been weak in men (only 1,200), but was surprisingly well provided with foodstuffs, enough according to Story to have supported a thousand men for a year: wheat, beef, claret 'and a great quantity of sack, brandy and strong beer'.[32] According to O'Kelly, Scott had expected Berwick to relieve the pressure on Kinsale, but the latter remained inert throughout

[30] *Danish force*, pp. 86–7; *Villare Hibernicum*, p. 27; **Marlborough to Ginkel**, 4 Oct. 1690 (Amerongen Huisarchief, 336).

[31] Story, p. 145; *Danish force*, pp. 87–9; O'Kelly, p. 83.

[32] Story, p. 145.

the siege. Berwick himself wrote that he had advanced with seven or eight thousand men in the direction of Kilmallock in an attempt to relieve Kinsale but, faced with a superior enemy force, went back to his quarters.[33] Marlborough was expecting an attack and had received reports that the Jacobite cavalry were at Macroom, twenty-five miles away, waiting for Sarsfield and the infantry: 'if they come we shall be ready to receive them', he wrote to Nottingham. He was not so confident in writing to Ginkel: 'if the enemy should advance as we have intelligence they do, it will be very difficult for the few troops we have here to continue this siege unless you can make some diversion'.[34] Würtemberg informed Ginkel that Balldearg O'Donnell and his rapparees had joined Berwick and Sarsfield and that they were on their way towards Kinsale: as most of the Williamite cavalry at Kinsale were helping to bring up artillery and ammunition from Cork it would be very awkward to meet an enemy attack from the north.[35] It appears that the Jacobites mismanaged things in weakening the Kinsale garrison to reinforce their much less defensible position in Cork, and in failing to harry the besieging army even with the irregular forces of rapparees.

Marlborough immediately returned to England and was received by William with apparent warmth, though there was an edge to his compliments: 'no officer living who has seen so little service as my Lord Marlborough is so fit for great commands'.[36] To Würtemberg William wrote to express his gratitude and esteem: in a postscript he assured him that he would be in no way prejudiced by his dealings with Marlborough.[37] Although there was some friction the commanders had between them achieved a notable success in spite of bad weather and the lateness of the season. Kinsale was a good harbour and was to be much used in the following year as a port of call for English merchant fleets. Charles's fort was a strong defensive position, the most modern fort in Ireland. The Williamites thought that

[33] O'Kelly, p. 82; Berwick, *Memoirs*, i. 78.
[34] Marlborough to Nottingham, 8 Oct. 1690 (*Cal. S.P. dom., 1695: addenda*, p. 159; same to Ginkel, 10 Oct. 1690 (Amerongen Huisarchief, 336).
[35] Würtemberg to Ginkel, 9 Oct. 1690 (ibid., 338).
[36] Churchill, 1. 344. [37] *Danish force*, p. 92.

the French had made a bad mistake in not deciding to hold Kinsale in strength, 'one of the best and securest harbours in the world and by keeping of which they might have ruined our western trade'.[38]

With the departure of Marlborough Williamite activity died down, and the Irish army had the opportunity to prepare for the next campaigning season. Its efforts to do so were handicapped by internal dissent: 'when the enemy gave them some respite their whole attention was to make war upon one another'.[39] Army opinion was violently hostile to Tyrconnell and critical of Berwick, who was regarded as too young for supreme command and too much of a puppet of Tyrconnell. The legality of Tyrconnell's arrangements was challenged. It was demanded that a deputation should be allowed to go to France with the object of getting James to remove Tyrconnell from the vice-royalty and entrust authority to those in whom the army had confidence. Sarsfield appears to have been designated as the leader most acceptable to the army and to have taken an active part in putting pressure on Berwick. The deputation consisted of Henry Luttrell and his brother Simon, Nicholas Purcell, and the Catholic bishop of Cork, Peter Creagh. To counteract their influence the Scottish major-general, Thomas Maxwell, was sent in advance with a request to James not to allow Purcell and Henry Luttrell back to Ireland. Both Maxwell and the deputation were held up by adverse winds, and by the time they reached France Tyrconnell had re-established his position, obtained promise of French help, and was at Brest on his way back to Ireland.

When he heard of the arrival of the deputation, he wrote asking James to keep the delegates in France and assured him that in their absence he could control the situation in Ireland: 'for though Sarsfield's head, now that it was turned to popularity, was quite out of its usual situation, yet he hoped when he came back to set it right again, if his counsellors Henry Luttrell and Colonel Purcell were kept from him'. Tyrconnell told Louvois that he had warned James about Luttrell and Purcell, referring to them as 'mutineers' – a term he also applied to Sarsfield. According to O'Kelly, when the delegates arrived at

[38] Story, *Continuation*, p. 45.
[39] *James II*, ii. 421.

St Germain, they got a cold reception from James, who threatened to imprison them. On further consideration he decided that this would be regarded as a public affront by the Irish army and might lead it to take William's side. So he agreed to see the delegates and even took them to interview Louis, though he made every effort to prevent them from denouncing Tyrconnell. Mary of Modena supported him by saying that if she and James were satisfied with Tyrconnell there was no reason why the Irish should not be so too. The delegates argued that Tyrconnell was not fit for the responsibility of defending Ireland:

that his age and infirmity made him require more sleep than was consistent with so much business, that his want of experience in military affairs rendered him exceedingly slow in his resolves and uncapable of laying great projects . . . they insinuated also that money and employments had been given with greater regard to private ends than the King's service.

They asked for a French general, who should be given an independent command. James hesitated which side to take, and characteristically wavered between them: it was too late to recall Tyrconnell; it was too drastic to prevent the delegates from returning to Ireland. He hoped to smooth them into willingness to co-operate with Tyrconnell, but he accepted their proposal that a French general should be sent to Ireland. His efforts were 'lost labour in the end'.[40]

[40] *James II*, ii. 422–5; *Anal. Hib.*, xxi. 205; O'Kelly, pp. 83–95.

XI

WINTER 1690–1

~~~~~~

I. DISPOSITION OF FORCES

AFTER THE taking of Kinsale the two sides withdrew behind frontier lines separated by a belt of no man's land. The Jacobite frontier in the main was the line of the Shannon. This gave them Connacht and Clare as their principal base, but they also held Kerry and most of County Limerick, which were a valuable reservoir for cattle and other supplies.[1] Limerick, Athlone and Sligo were key points for the defence of the line. The Williamite frontier was well back from the Shannon, running from the Cork coast up the middle of Ireland through Cashel, Birr, Mullingar, Longford and Cavan to Enniskillen, from which it turned west along the Erne to Ballyshannon.[2] This gave them Ulster and the greater part of Leinster and Munster. Ginkel's headquarters were at Kilkenny. Douglas had the Ulster command and was stationed at Legacurry between Omagh and Dungannon, County Tyrone. Würtemberg's headquarters was Waterford, and the Danish force was scattered over south-east Ireland from Clonmel to Wexford.[3]

No man's land was raided by both sides and suffered heavily. Bands of rapparees did much damage to Williamite areas, burning and stealing with almost uninterrupted success. Both armies were badly paid and indifferently disciplined, and caused considerable hardship to the neighbourhoods in which they were

[1] Stevens, p. 191; *Danish force*, p. 90.
[2] Story, *Continuation*, pp. 46–7.   [3] *Danish force*, pp. 80–2.

quartered. O'Kelly complained of the disorders committed by the Irish army who 'lived at discretion without order or discipline'. He was particularly bitter about the commandeering that was continually carried on by the 'caterpillars and harpies' of the commissariat. He blamed Sarsfield for his easy-going readiness to sign any paper that was put in front of him.[4] According to Stevens, who was in Limerick, little of what was commandeered reached the troops, who patiently put up with short rations, scanty clothing and wretched quarters.[5] From the other side complaints were made to William of looting and damage committed by officers as well as men; both Protestants and law-abiding Catholics were victims of these disorders.[6] There were many complaints about the Danish force, whose pay was badly in arrears; they raided the shops in the towns where they were quartered, and there were protests that 'Tartars could hardly do worse'.[7]

Desultory fighting took place during the winter, but no serious engagement was fought and the basic position remained unchanged until the following summer. The Jacobites made some attempt to strengthen their key positions. At Limerick the breach in the wall of the Irish town was repaired and a new bastion made. In February French engineers arrived and under their directions a series of works was carried out: bastions and a covered way all round the Irish town, a fort on the island linked to the English town, and other protective works.[8] The defences of Athlone were strengthened and early in February an advance post was fortified at Ballymore on a lakeside ten miles east of Athlone.[9]

On the Williamite side an important development was the establishment of a civil administration in Dublin. The government was at first entrusted to two lords justices: Lord Sidney, who had been ambassador at the Hague and, at the time of the revolution, had signed the invitation to William; and Thomas Coningsby, paymaster-general of the army. Sir Charles Porter, who had been lord chancellor of Ireland in 1686 and was now reappointed by William, was soon added as a third lord justice.

---

[4] O'Kelly, pp. 96–7.   [5] Stevens, p. 193.
[6] *Cal. S.P. dom., 1690–1*, p. 154.
[7] *Danish force*, pp. 20–2.   [8] Stevens, pp. 195–6.
[9] O'Kelly, p. 121; *Cal. S.P. dom., 1690–1*, p. 264.

In December Sidney became secretary of state in England, and for the remainder of the war the chief responsibility for civil affairs in Ireland was borne by Coningsby and Porter. Coningsby was an extreme whig and disapproved of even by whigs. Burnet commented: 'Coningsby, the choice of whom was much censured, for he was a vicious man and his parts were very indifferent.' Porter was a tory and seems to have been appointed as a counterweight to Coningsby, in spite of the fact that he owed his original appointment to James.[10]

A full complement of judges, privy councillors and civil servants was appointed, and for the counties under Williamite control there were lords lieutenant with their deputies. The indicting of Jacobites for treason began and proceedings were remitted to the court of king's bench. The estates of Jacobites were seized and vested in commissioners, who gave them out on leases pending final disposal – the beginning of a long and tortuous series of land transactions, not finally wound up till 1703.[11]

2. PEACE NEGOTIATIONS

After their failure at Limerick there was a growing feeling on the Williamite side that more generous terms should be offered to the Irish to induce them to lay down their arms. Early in September Würtemberg told the king of Denmark that surreptitious efforts were being made to win over some of the more prominent Jacobites, and that if an indemnity were offered there were good prospects of the war in Ireland coming to an end; he added that the Irish openly declared 'we are fighting not for King James nor for the popish religion but for our estates'.[12] Ginkel and Bentinck were both in favour of putting an early end to the war in Ireland by the offer of liberal terms to Catholic landowners. William now accepted the desirability of a negotiated settlement, but was reluctant to

[10] Story, p. 138; *Cal. S.P. dom., 1690–1*, p. 132; H. Foxcroft, *Supplement to Burnet's history*, p. 352. Coningsby's mother was a member of the Loftus family, so that he already had a personal connection with Ireland.

[11] Story, p. 148. For the land transactions see Simms, *Williamite confiscation*.

[12] *Danish force*, p. 76.

make more concessions than necessary. He was anxious to arrive at a settlement that would leave enough confiscated land to satisfy his English parliament and himself. The winter session of 1690–1 was largely occupied with a dispute between William and the English commons about the right to dispose of confiscated land in Ireland. William claimed that it was within his discretion to grant land to his supporters as he thought fit; the commons claimed that the land should be sold and the proceeds devoted to reducing the burden that the war imposed on the English taxpayer.[13] Both king and commons were reluctant to contemplate a settlement that would leave Irish Catholics in possession of all or even most of their estates. The same reluctance was felt by Irish Protestants who hoped to acquire fresh property to compensate them for what they had suffered under the Jacobite régime.

The intermediary used by Ginkel was a Catholic barrister named Grady, who had been sent out of Limerick before the siege by the Irish peace party to find out what terms William was willing to give to Catholic landowners.[14] No further development took place till after the siege was over. Grady was then sent by the Williamites to Galway to talk to some of the leaders and find out if they were willing to make terms. He brought back the good news that there was a general desire to submit if definite assurances were given that Catholics could retain their estates and be treated as they had been during the reign of Charles II. Würtemberg, who looked at the Irish campaign from a European point of view, commented: 'a stroke of the pen could end the war in Ireland, and if the king wishes to help his allies he will have to give it'. Grady was sent to London, where he was interviewed by Bentinck and entertained by William.[15]

Towards the end of October Bentinck wrote to Ginkel that Grady was being sent back to Ireland and that negotiations should be pressed forward as energetically as possible. He did not reach Ireland till early in December, when he was sent to Limerick to find out how things had developed in the meantime. He was not authorized to offer a general indemnity: some estates were to be confiscated, but security of property was to be promised to particular individuals if they laid down their arms

---

[13] *Williamite confiscation*, pp. 82–3.
[14] Clarke corr., i, no. 78.　　　　[15] *Danish force*, pp. 79, 91, 93.

and submitted to the Williamite government. William appears to have realized that these terms were too limited to be readily acceptable. He wrote to Ginkel urging that military action should be taken against the Irish in Sligo and Kerry, as if they were not pressed it was very doubtful whether they would be willing to accept the conditions he was offering. Ginkel answered that the rebels would be reduced all the sooner if William was prepared to make some concessions. He evidently thought that William was still trying to drive too hard a bargain.[16] Ginkel's view had some effect, as Bentinck then wrote that more favourable and more general conditions might be offered: if the Irish were to be brought to terms it was important not to make them desperate. Bentinck was afraid that if no settlement was reached William's army would be locked up in Ireland for the next campaign, which would be disastrous considering the state of affairs in the Netherlands. Soon afterwards he wrote that William was so convinced of the need to use his army elsewhere that if an Irish settlement could be reached he would probably agree to give a general pardon with the exception of certain individuals. As Grady had brought proposals from the other side which amounted to more or less the same thing Ginkel was asked to send him back to the enemy with authority to treat on these lines.[17]

These offers led to a sharp division among the Jacobites. They had no appeal for the majority who had lost their land as a result of the Cromwellian and earlier confiscations; their attraction was for those who had recovered at least part of their ancestral property under the restoration settlement, and for the 'new interest' who had since bought land and resented the Jacobite repeal of the act of settlement. O'Kelly was highly critical of the last group:

some Catholics were only too anxious to submit. These were men of new interest, so called because they had purchased from usurpers the inheritance of their own countrymen . . . and these lands being all restored to the ancient proprietors by a late decree . . . the coveting purchasers, preferring their private gain before the general interest of religion and country, were for submitting to a government which they very well knew could never allow that decree.[18]

[16] Ibid., pp. 93–4; Japikse, iii. 188, 194.
[17] Ibid., pp. 196–9.   [18] O'Kelly, p. 71.

Sarsfield was strongly opposed to the negotiations and persuaded Berwick to take action against the leading members of the peace party. Lord Riverston, the secretary of state, and his brother-in-law Colonel MacDonnell, governor of Galway, were dismissed, and Judge Daly was put under arrest. Reports reached the Williamites that seven Jacobite colonels had been arrested.[19]

With the help of these firm measures the resistance movement proved too strong for the peace party. In January 1691 Grady told Ginkel that he could no longer go into the Irish quarters or even send letters there except at grave risk. On one occasion the rapparees caught him and he was with difficulty rescued by Williamite troops.[20] Balldearg O'Donnell appears to have thought that the old English were ready to accept William's terms, but that resistance might be carried on by the Gaelic Irish with French help. He sent a memorandum to d'Avaux, in which he said that William was offering to restore estates to all who held them at the death of Charles II with the exception of the earls of Clancarty and Antrim, two Gaelic magnates. He added that the agreement was to be guaranteed by the pope, the emperor and the king of Spain, and that it was attractive to the old English but stoutly opposed by the Gaels, who had regained little by the restoration settlement and still hoped to recover what they had had in 1641 or even earlier.[21] Tyrconnell in France also used the negotiations as an argument for substantial French help 'lest despair induced [the Irish officers] to accept the offers of the prince of Orange'.[22]

Religious toleration and employment under William were other points over which bargaining took place. Würtemberg referred to them in a letter he wrote to Colonel Thomas Butler of Kilcash, with whom he had previously struck up an acquaintance in Hungary; Butler replied that he and his fellow-officers were satisfied about William's good intentions, but were 'unable to endure the yoke of the English, who after his death will not fail to break their word, so hostile are they to this nation'.[23]

In the absence of any agreement Ginkel obtained authority

[19] O'Kelly, pp. 102–6; *Danish force*, p. 96.

[20] *H.M.C., rep. 4*, app., p. 318; Grady to Ginkel, 1 Jan. 1691 (Clarke corr., iv, no. 372).

[21] D'Avaux, pp. 738–9. [22] *Anal. Hib.*, xxi. 225. [23] *Danish force*, p. 99.

for a unilateral declaration in which he announced that William and Mary had no desire to oppress their Catholic subjects by persecuting them in their religion or ruining them in their estates and fortunes; they had therefore authorized Ginkel to grant reasonable terms to all who would submit. This declaration was intended as a preliminary feeler; it was much too indefinite to produce results, and the fact that it was issued in Ginkel's name and not by William or even the lords justices weakened its effect.[24] Coningsby said that it was not thought proper to offer a general amnesty in the name of the government until the temper of the Irish had been tried by Ginkel's declaration, which gave them 'all the hopes imaginable' and yet did not commit the king to anything. In spite of this somewhat cynical approach Coningsby evidently realized the advantages of concluding an immediate settlement on liberal terms: 'you know how little I am inclinable to show any favour to the Irish but . . . I cannot help wishing the war were over on any terms'.[25] The declaration produced no response, and it became clear that William's forces were committed to another campaigning season in Ireland.

3. MILITARY ACTIVITY

William's hopes of bringing the Irish to terms by military moves against Kerry and Sligo were to be disappointed. The Kerry attack was entrusted to Major-General Tettau of the Danish force. The Irish retreated before him, burning the countryside on their way, until they reached Killarney. They rallied in Ross Castle which was too strong for Tettau, who had no heavy guns or mortars. Ginkel and Würtemberg moved into County Limerick in support, but found the roads too bad to follow him into Kerry. Tettau took a small fort near Ross Castle and put most of the garrison to the sword, but bad weather and scarcity of supplies made him withdraw from Kerry with little to show for his expedition.[26] The plan to attack Sligo was even less effective. Douglas who was given the command was most

[24] Story, *Continuation*, p. 53.
[25] Coningsby to Nottingham, 17 Feb. 1691 (*Cal. S.P. dom., 1690–1*, p. 265).
[26] *Danish force*, p. 95; *H.M.C., rep. 4*, app., p. 319.

unwilling to undertake it, even though he was urged to do so by William himself. He wrote to Ginkel: 'the king has writ to me and is very desirous I should besiege Sligo. I am as willing as any mortal but, as I have told your excellency before, it is not possible to carry cannon or wagons any way from Ulster to Connacht in the winter'.[27] The lords justices were severely critical of Douglas and also of Lanier, the general who had failed to intercept Sarsfield at Ballyneety and now failed to keep control of an important crossing on the Shannon at Lanesborough. They added that Douglas 'with all the ill will in the world' had contented himself with approaching the Shannon at Jamestown and then withdrawing.[28]

Sarsfield showed considerable energy in countering Williamite threats to the line of Shannon. With his headquarters at Athlone he moved up and down the river looking to the strengthening of crossing-points and had the satisfaction of seeing the enemy retreat from the neighbourhood of the river. He claimed that a large area to the east of the Shannon was under Jacobite control and that the advanced post of Ballymore was a strong point capable of keeping the enemy in check and of resisting a siege. He described his activities to Mountcashel (Justin MacCarthy) in terms of great confidence with no hint of the deplorable conditions to which the Irish army was reduced.[29] The *Gazette de France* carried several reports of Sarsfield's exploits: 'news from Ireland that Major-General Sarsfield with a body of troops had advanced to within twelve miles of Dublin and that General Ginkel has had to draw what troops he can out of their quarters to meet him; the [Williamite] generals who hoped for success by crossing the Shannon have been very unlucky; they found General Sarsfield at the head of five thousand men who disputed the passage; he wore them out by continual skirmishes in which their men suffered heavily'.[30]

Tyrconnell returned to Ireland in January 1691, being escorted to the mouth of the Shannon by a French convoy which made the passage without sighting an English ship.

---

[27] Douglas to Ginkel, 16 Nov. 1690 (Amerongen Huisarchief, p. 342).

[28] *Cal. S.P. dom., 1690–1*, p. 226.

[29] Sarsfield to Mountcashel, 14/24 Feb. 1691 (Min. guerre, AI 1066, no. 187).

[30] *Gazette de France*, 30 Dec. 1690, 23 Feb. 1691.

William observed with asperity that the French ships might easily have been intercepted if his orders had been obeyed and some men of war had been sent to cruise off the Irish coast.[31] Berwick now left for France and Tyrconnell, in addition to taking over the civil government, regarded himself as commander-in-chief of the army, which created much friction. He brought with him the earldom of Lucan for Sarsfield, but the latter was not mollified and openly resented Tyrconnell's claim to exercise military authority. The French dispatches make it clear that there was serious unrest in the army and are not consistent with the Jacobite memoirs recorded at St Germain: 'for having brought a patent of an earl for Colonel Sarsfield it put him in a good temper enough and he being really zealous in the king's service engaged for the quiet comportment of the other mutineers and acted heartily in conjunction with the lord lieutenant while his former counsellors were absent'.[32]

A different impression is given by the letters of the French commissioner, Fumeron, who had been in Ireland in the previous year and had now returned with Tyrconnell. Writing to Louvois at the end of January he said that Sarsfield and others had been told to report at Limerick, but had not yet come. Sarsfield had pleaded ill-health, but it was stated that he was perfectly well. There were factions; some were for Tyrconnell, but the majority were for Sarsfield, and the army wished Sarsfield to be in command. Tyrconnell's own supporters were advising him to keep to civil affairs and not to put himself at the head of the army, which 'would be to spoil everything' Fumeron thought it essential to send a French general and some officers of reputation to prevent things getting worse. A further complication was created by Balldearg O'Donnell who had assembled seven or eight thousand peasants in the neighbourhood of Sligo: 'his followers pretend that it is he who will free Ireland from the occupation of the prince of Orange and they do not want to be commanded by any other general'.[33] In the

[31] *Finch MSS*, iii. 7. Tyrconnell landed at Limerick on Jan. 14; Story (*Cont.*, p. 51) and the *Jacobite narrative* (p. 128) mistakenly say he came to Galway. Fumeron's letter to Louvois of 18/28 Jan. 1691 (Min. guerre, A1 1066, no. 170) makes it clear that Limerick was the place of arrival.

[32] *James II*, ii. 434–5. 'Colonel' Sarsfield was already a major-general (Story, *Continuation*, p. 30).

[33] Min. guerre, A1 1066, no. 174.

middle of February Fumeron wrote again to say that Sarsfield's party was as opposed to Tyrconnell as ever. Sarsfield had not yet presented himself, in spite of several requests to do so. It was rumoured that he was waiting to hear what success Luttrell and Purcell had had in France, and that he hoped their efforts would secure a change in the government and a prominent role for himself. Tyrconnell's unpopularity had grown as a result of his devaluing the brass money, a measure which was regarded as in the interest of traders and unfair to the army. A few days after, letters were received from Luttrell and Purcell with the good news that James was sending six months' pay for the troops and far more supplies than had been sent with Tyrconnell. This pleased the army, and at the same time was turned into a reproach against Tyrconnell for his failure to do as much to meet military requirements. Fumeron was sure that if Luttrell and Purcell came back they would completely undermine Tyrconnell's authority, unless they were prevailed on to give up their agitation.[34]

At the beginning of March Fumeron reported that Sarsfield had at last presented himself at Limerick and appeared to be ready to accept Tyrconnell's authority: 'if he is sincere it will do much to make the army follow suit'. He added that Sarsfield had been given the royal letter creating him earl of Lucan and had been promoted 'maréchal de camp'. This corresponded to major-general, a rank which he already held; Story says that he was made a lieutenant-general, which would be more appropriate.[35] That there was no reconciliation appears from a letter from Sarsfield to Mountcashel, written in the middle of March. In it Sarsfield says that Tyrconnell has given him 'a thousand caresses and professions of friendship, but I know him too long not to be aware of how little faith I should place in his false words . . . he is very jealous and despairs of my standing and the influence I have over the army . . . we await with impatience our French general and hope he will be independent of Lord Tyrconnell'.[36] The French general who had been chosen was St Ruhe, or St Ruth as he is usually referred to, an experienced soldier who had distinguished himself in the Savoy campaign and had

[34] Min. guerre, A1 1083, no. 50.
[35] Ibid., A1 1066 no. 204; Story, *Continuation*, p. 55.
[36] Min. guerre, A1 1066, no. 211.

the reputation of being a relentless hunter of Huguenots. It is surprising that Sarsfield after his previous experience of French commanders in Ireland should have looked forward to St Ruth's arrival. The fact that Mountcashel and his Irish regiments had served under St Ruth in Savoy may have rendered him more acceptable than Rosen or Lauzun. St Ruth seems to have thought highly of Mountcashel's men and to have declared that they had 'done marvels'.[37] Fumeron told Louvois that Sarsfield's party were spreading the news that St Ruth was to command the army independently of Tyrconnell, 'which pleases almost everybody, even those who are for Lord Tyrconnell but know well that he does not understand war'.[38]

Jacobite dissensions were welcome news to the Williamites. It was reported to them that 'the Irish are all in debate among themselves; Tyrconnell and Sarsfield cannot agree; the people are all ready to mutiny for want'.[39] A Protestant who escaped from Limerick thought that the Irish depended wholly on Sarsfield: 'draw him away and they are gone; Tyrconnell and he are no great friends, neither can he abide the French; Tyrconnell never stirred abroad but once since he landed, and his countenance denotes something of despair'.[40] Tyrconnell had brought little in the way of money and supplies and found the Irish army desperately short of clothing and other necessaries. He assured the army that a fleet was coming from France with all that was required, and he wrote a series of imploring letters to Louvois, asking him to send help soon.[41] Louvois, 'a haughty and hardened minister', took little notice of Tyrconnell's supplications. Instead he pressed for recruits from Ireland for Mountcashel's regiments and expressed surprise that Tyrconnell was so indifferent to French request. The French demand for recruits was embarrassing to Tyrconnell and caused friction with the Irish commanders.[42]

[37] *Anal. Hib.*, xxi. 206; Dangeau, *Journal*, iii. 225.

[38] Min. guerre, A1 1066, no. 220.

[39] *Cal. S.P. dom., 1690–1*, p. 320.   [40] T.C.D., MS V. 4. 3, p. 98.

[41] *Jacobite narrative*, p. 129; *Anal. Hib.*, xxi. 206–14.

[42] Ibid., pp. 207, 209, 215; *James II*, ii. 437.

4. RAPPAREES

The Irish army had willing and skilful allies in the rapparees who were to be found in almost all parts of the Williamite area and did enormous damage to the persons and property of both soldiers and civilians. Nearly every number of the *Dublin Intelligence*, the official newspaper, carried stories of rapparee raids and atrocities and of punitive expeditions undertaken by the troops and by the newly-formed Protestant militia. The word rapparee, which replaced the 'tory' of an earlier period, is derived from the Irish word 'rapaire', a half-pike – the weapon with which many of them were armed. Story described the rapparees as 'such of the Irish as are not of the army but the country-people armed in a kind of hostile manner with half-pikes and skeins and some with scythes or muskets'. In an engagement the Williamites captured some silver-hilted swords and presumed that they had belonged to rapparee chiefs.[43] The rapparees enjoyed the great advantages of local knowledge and the co-operation of the Catholic population.

Story devoted much space to their exploits and says they did far more damage during the winter than 'anything that had the face of an army could pretend to'. He added that the rapparees were assisted by many of the Irish army who were sent out to shift for themselves, being given passes by their regiments to save them from the hanging that was the usual fate of captured rapparees.[44] The bog of Allen was an area that particularly favoured the rapparees. Story gives a good description of their methods:

When the rapparees have no mind to show themselves upon the bogs, they commonly sink down between two or three little hills, grown over with long grass, so that you may as soon find a hare as one of them: they conceal their arms thus, they take off the lock and put it in their pocket or hide it in some dry place; they stop the muzzle close with a cork and the touch-hole with a small quill, and then throw the piece itself into a running water or pond; you may see a hundred of them without arms, who look like the poorest humblest slaves in the world, and you may search till you are weary before you find one gun; but yet when they have a mind to do mischief they can all be

[43] Story, p. 16; *London Gazette*, 2 Oct. 1690.
[44] Story, *Continuation*, p. 49.

ready in an hour's warning, for every one knows where to go and fetch his own arms, though you do not.[45]

Individual rapparee leaders had a great reputation, and Story refers to several of them by name. One of the most celebrated was Galloping Hogan, who is said to have guided Sarsfield to Bally-neety. The fine large mare from which Hogan derived his nickname was captured by the Williamites in County Kilkenny, but Hogan himself remained at large till the end of the war, when he surrendered on promise of pardon. Ginkel then employed him to suppress other rapparees, and that proved fatal: 'for some of that sort of people murdered him afterwards'.[46] That he had a certain chivalry appears from his treatment of Story's brother, who was killed in a skirmish with Hogan's party near Birr: the Irish 'proffered to bury him honourably which they did, allowing his own drum to beat the dead march and themselves fired three volleys at his grave, acknowledging at his death certain former civilities from him, which is very rare with that sort of people'.[47] The Danish force was constantly harried by rapparees, who stole their horses, carried off unwary stragglers, killed the postal couriers and made off with the mail bags.[48]

In an effort to check co-operation between the rapparees and the Catholic population the lords justices issued a proclamation that any damage done by rapparees to Protestants would have to be paid for by the Catholics of the county: 'and in regard the popish priests had great influence over their votaries it was ordered that if any rapparees exceeding the number of ten were seen in a body no popish priest should have liberty to reside in such a county'.[49] Story hoped the 'Protestant rapparees from the north and other places' could be used as a counter-measure, and it appears that the irregular methods of the militia were more effective than army action.[50] Ginkel's correspondence has several references to the problem: 'rapparees are in so great number that we can neither find forage nor cover, which hinders much our march . . . we must see what we can do against the rapparees who will ravage us if they be not timely prevented . . . one must begin early and think what we are to do against the

[45] Story, p. 152.
[46] *Dublin Intelligence*, 19 May 1691; Story, *Continuation*, p. 270.
[47] Ibid., p. 84.   [48] *Danish force*, pp. 84, 96, 107, 110.
[49] Story, p. 149.   [50] Ibid., p. 161.

rapparees who will do us much damage'.[51] The problem of rapparees was the subject of correspondence between the lords justices and the English government and was evidently regarded as a major difficulty by the Williamite authorities.[52]

[51] Ginkel to Coningsby, 27 Dec. 1690, 13 and 18 Jan. 1691 (*H.M.C., rep. 4*, app., p. 318).

[52] *Cal. S.P. dom., 1690–1*, pp. 280, 333, 351.

XII

THE BRIDGE OF ATHLONE

~~~~~~

I. WILLIAMITE PREPARATIONS

THE FAILURE of the negotiations made it inevitable that William's army in Ireland would have to fight again. But it was hoped that the summer campaign of 1691 would finish the war. Ginkel had been a stop-gap commander and there were serious doubts of his fitness for supreme authority. He had not been altogether successful in controlling unco-operative British subordinates, and he was regarded as lacking in resolution.[1] In February 1691 Carmarthen was expressing anxiety to Nottingham about the state of affairs in Ireland. He saw no prospect of improvement unless William sent someone of quality who was 'big enough to expect obedience' and, to assist him, an officer of military experience. He suggested this double arrangement 'since his majesty has no Englishman who has both these qualifications'.[2] Evidently Marlborough was considered unacceptable. Nottingham proposed the younger Schomberg 'for his general experience in war and his particular experience in Ireland'. Early in March Sidney wrote a strong letter to William saying that the officers he had in Ireland could not do what was required.[3] There was talk of William himself coming back to Ireland, and repeated rumours of Count Schomberg's appointment. As late as April 23 Ginkel himself expected to hand over

[1] *Danish force*, p. 107.
[2] *Finch MSS*, iii. 10.
[3] Ibid., p. 17; *Cal. S.P. dom., 1690–1*, p. 295.

to Schomberg.[4] William at last decided that Ginkel should have the command. He urged him to take the field as soon as possible, presuming that Athlone would be his first objective, unless Ballymore had to be taken before that. He impressed on Ginkel that all the opponents of France in Europe were watching for the conquest of Ireland. In a postscript he added that Ginkel must be stricter than his natural disposition was inclined to be: 'you know what sort of people you have to deal with, such as cannot always be controlled by mildness'. Bentinck urged Ginkel to exert more authority over the British troops and said that it would be easier for him to do so as Douglas and Kirk were being transferred to Flanders; Mackay and Talmash were to take their place in Ireland.[5] Mackay had been William's commander-in-chief in Scotland; he had redeemed his failure at Killiecrankie by subsequent successes against the Jacobites in the Highlands. He was an argumentative but energetic soldier, whose memoirs are a valuable source for military affairs in Scotland and Ireland.

Great efforts were made to provide Ginkel with the men, munitions and equipment for the campaign. There were delays in the programme, but eventually the army was well supplied and promised to be a formidable force. The delays were the subject of much protest, and there were fears that too late a start was being made. In the middle of May the lords justices and Ginkel complained that

The army had long since taken the field if the arms, clothes, recruits and horses had been here: the want of them has made us so backward this campaign, and unless this wind brings them in we do not know when we shall be able to lie down before Athlone . . . above all the want of money is what presses us.[6]

Early in April the treasury had sanctioned enough money for four months' pay, but here again there was delay in dispatching the money to Ireland and at the end of May it had still not been received.[7]

The arrival of the artillery train at the end of May was

[4] *Danish force*, pp. 102, 105, 109; Japikse, iii. 232.

[5] William to Ginkel, 1/11 May 1691; Bentinck to Ginkel, 30 Apr./10 May 1691 (Japikse, iii. 234).

[6] *Cal. S.P. dom., 1690–1*, p. 378.   [7] Ibid., pp. 328, 392.

welcome news. It was of formidable dimensions: 36 heavy guns and 6 mortars. Story said that the train was 'such a one as had never before been seen in that kingdom'.[8] His record is punctuated with reports of cargoes arriving with arms, ammunition and uniforms. Williamite propaganda made the most of the supply build-up:

They who beheld the vast preparation for the campaign had a fair prospect of their majesties' extraordinary care and providence for the total recovery of Ireland . . . all the proper ports of the kingdom continually filled with ships and vessels, some transporting money, others recruits to the army . . . amazing quantities of provision, arms and ammunition, five hundred draught horses at a time for the carriages, and such other vast stores for the artillery.[9]

2. ST RUTH ARRIVES

On May 9 the French convoy reached Limerick and St Ruth landed.[10] He brought with him a considerable quantity of arms and ammunition, clothing and food, but no money or men. With him came two lieutenant-generals, d'Usson and de Tessé, who were to take a prominent part for the remainder of the war. Also Henry Luttrell and Purcell, the army delegates, now returned to Ireland. St Ruth's arrival was received with jubilation and for a time discouraged peace negotiations. Williamites sarcastically observed that this reinforcement was like pouring brandy down the throat of a dying man.[11] William had urged the admiralty to send a squadron to the Irish coast to intercept the French, but nothing had been done. Admiral Russell had no wish to weaken home defences: 'the danger

---

[8] *London Gazette*, 4 June 1691; Story, *Continuation*, p. 80.

[9] *An exact journal*, p. 14.

[10] This is the date given by St Ruth (Min. Guerre, A1 1066, No. 238) and by O'Kelly (p. 114); *James II*, ii. 451, has May 8.

[11] O'Kelly, p. 114; *An exact journal*, p. 13. D'Usson and de Tessé are referred to as lieutenant-generals by O'Kelly and in the military articles of Limerick. Their rank in the French army was maréchal-de-camp (major-general), to which rank both were gazetted on 30 Jan. 1691, but it was customary for French officers to be given a step in rank while serving in Ireland (Pinard, *Chronologie historique-militaire*, iii. 404, 406).

would be far greater to England than the hazard of not reducing Ireland this summer'.[12]

The arrival of St Ruth did not restore harmony among the Jacobites. Tyrconnell still claimed to exercise authority over the army, most of which insisted that St Ruth alone should command. Fumeron reported that there was open disobedience to Tyrconnell. The colonels of two regiments which he ordered to leave Limerick refused to go. A mutiny occurred when he ordered Colonel O'Donovan to surrender his regiment to another colonel. Tyrconnell had spent all his money, and had been reduced to borrowing 10,000 francs from Fumeron.[13] According to the latter St Ruth was doing his best to reconcile the dissentients but was very doubtful whether his efforts were having much effect.

There seems to have been some uncertainty about the relations between Tyrconnell and St Ruth. James apparently did not wish to put any formal limitation on the viceroy's authority, but issued instructions that tended 'to abridge his power in reference to military matters, the direction of which was vested in a manner wholly in St Ruth; so that my lord Tyrconnell who before could have made a lieutenant-general had not power now to make a colonel, which so lowered his credit in the army that little regard was had to his authority'. According to the account in the *Life of James*, Tyrconnell prudently submitted and left the management of the army to St Ruth, who was superficially on good terms with him but at bottom was prejudiced against him, influenced by Luttrell and Purcell.[14] Tyrconnell's version was that St Ruth had been appointed to command the army under the viceroy, but that the king had directed that St Ruth's advice should be followed in all that concerned the war.[15] In fact Tyrconnell was very persistent in trying to retain his connection with the army. He accompanied it to Athlone, but found that the troops refused to take orders from him and pressed for his withdrawal. The recommendation was accompanied by the threat that if he did not comply the

[12] *Finch MSS*, iii. 30, 55.

[13] Fumeron to Louvois, 11/21 May 1691 (Min. guerre, A1 1066, no. 240).

[14] *James II*, ii. 452.

[15] *Anal. Hib.*, xxi. 216.

cords of his tent would be cut.[16] Tyrconnell complained to Louvois that Luttrell and Purcell were collecting signatures from tent to tent for his withdrawal from the army. He had protested to St Ruth, who had disclaimed any knowledge of the matter. Worse still, Sarsfield and his friends had spread a rumour that Tyrconnell was selling for money the recruits that he was sending to France to join Mountcashel's regiments.[17] Sarsfield's relations with St Ruth seem to have been less cordial than he had expected them to be, and he is not mentioned in the French dispatches of this period. The Williamites heard that since St Ruth's arrival there were 'great divisions amongst them: for he commands here for the king of France, and Sarsfield and Clifford upon pretence of sickness, as is thought, keep at Portumna and have not yet been with the army'.[18]

St Ruth reported that the situation was very unsatisfactory. The authority of the government was weak and there was a general lack of confidence. No preparations had been made to provide transport to take munitions and supplies to Athlone. If the enemy attacked, Athlone would certainly fall. For lack of rations the work of strengthening the fortifications had made poor progress, but he was doing his best to expedite the work. St Ruth found a great shortage of food and was amazed at the patience of the people. More wheat was urgently needed, and he thought that there could be no greater charity than to send a consignment from France and 'save the lives of an infinity of Catholics who would rather die of hunger than live under the domination of the prince of Orange'.[19]

O'Kelly pays tribute to St Ruth's energy in organizing the supply and equipment of the army, and criticizes Tyrconnell's failure to provide boats for communication with Athlone. In spite of St Ruth's efforts it was after the middle of June before the Irish army was assembled. Stevens gives a detailed account of the movements of his regiment at this stage, and makes it clear that the army suffered from shortages of food and tents.

[16] Fumeron to Louvois, 28 June/8 July 1691 (Min. guerre, A1 1083, no. 89); *Jacobite narrative*, p. 132.

[17] *Anal. Hib.*, xxi. 215–16.

[18] George Clarke to Nottingham, 27 May 1691 (*Cal. S.P. dom., 1690–1*, p. 390).

[19] St Ruth to Louvois, 3/13 June 1691 (Min. guerre, A1 1080, no. 145).

A similar impression of bustle, shortage and improvisation is given in the Kilmallock papers, which describe the preparations made to equip a cavalry regiment at this time.[20]

3. THE FIGHT FOR ATHLONE

By the end of May the scattered Williamite forces were collected for the next advance. Mullingar was the chief assembly point, and Ginkel himself took up his position there with the Huguenot Ruvigny, who commanded the cavalry. Würtemberg and the Danish force met at Cashel and were to join Ginkel near the Shannon.[21] There had been some discussion whether to by-pass Athlone and try to cross the Shannon at Banagher, some fifteen miles to the south. But it was decided that this would be too dangerous: the Irish army might make a counter-move from Athlone and 'there was nothing to hinder them from marching even up to Dublin'.[22] It was therefore arranged to make Athlone the main objective, though the Irish advanced post at Ballymore would have to be taken on the way. On June 6 Ginkel set out from Mullingar and reached Ballymore the next day. The Irish had built a fort there on a neck of ground jutting into Lake Sunderlin. There was a garrison of about a thousand commanded by Ulick Bourke, who at first refused to surrender. Ginkel set up his batteries to bombard the fort on the landward side, and also attacked it from the lake side with four large boats filled with grenadiers. The fort soon became untenable, and on the evening of June 8 the commander surrendered at discretion. He and the garrison were made prisoners-of-war and sent to Dublin. As a security measure the other ranks were then sent to Lambay Island off the coast of County Dublin. The four hundred women and children who were crowded into Ballymore fort were set at liberty. Story commented that it was unaccountable to have left this isolated garrison without either relieving it or withdrawing it 'since they lost in it above a regiment of their best men'.[23]

Ginkel waited for ten days more at Ballymore, which was

[20] O'Kelly, pp. 116–17; Stevens, pp. 197–204; Simms, 'A Jacobite colonel: Lord Sarsfield of Kilmallock' in *Ir. Sword*, ii. 205–10.

[21] *Danish force*, p. 112. [22] Story, *Continuation*, p. 85.

[23] Ibid., pp. 87–91; *Exact journal*, p. 16; *Cal. S.P. dom., 1690–1*, p. 418.

almost certainly an error of judgement. If he had made straight
for Athlone he would have got there well in advance of St
Ruth's army. The reason for his delay was that he was waiting
for pontoons to come from England, thinking that they would
be needed for crossing the Shannon. The pontoons did not
reach Dublin till June 15, a week after Ballymore had fallen,
and they did not reach Athlone till June 23. When they did
come it was not found possible to use them to force the crossing.[24]
Ginkel left Ballymore on June 18 and that night joined up with
Würtemberg's force. The combined army, about 18,000 strong,
advanced on Athlone the following day.[25]

Athlone consisted of two walled towns – the English town on
the Leinster side of the river and the Irish town on the Connacht
side – connected by a stone bridge, which was about 70 yards
lower down than the modern bridge. In the previous year the
Irish had made no attempt to defend the English town, but now
they determined to do so. On June 20 Ginkel started his bombardment of the English town and soon made a breach in its
walls. The defenders quickly abandoned their position and
crossed the bridge over to the Irish town. There was a drawbridge at the western end of the bridge and an arch was also
broken. It has been suggested that this arch was merely a
wooden replacement for the arch broken in the previous year
and that it was therefore a relatively simple feat to demolish it.[26]
The efforts of the Williamites to close the gap and the success of
the Jacobites in keeping the gap open made the bridge the
centre of fierce and prolonged fighting, in which the Jacobites
showed great skill and determination.

The following day (June 21) St Ruth came up with the main
army and camped on a ridge a little more than two miles to the
west of Athlone. His force numbered 16,000 foot, 3,000 horse and
2,000 dragoons, and was thus somewhat larger than Ginkel's.[27]
He put Lieutenant-General d'Usson in charge of the town
and arranged for relays of regiments to relieve one another

[24] *Cal. S.P. dom., 1690–1*, p. 412; *H.M.C., rep. 4*, app., p. 320; Story,
Continuation, p. 99.

[25] Ibid., p. 94.

[26] D. Murtagh, 'The siege of Athlone' in *R.S.A.I. Jn.*, lxxxiii. 58–81
(1953).

[27] De Tessé to Louvois, 8/18 July 1691 (Min. guerre, A1 1080, no.
163).

in its defence. D'Usson wanted a regular garrison, but St Ruth wished to get as many of his men as possible accustomed to active service. His decision to keep changing the troops proved disastrous.[28] Ginkel made full use of his artillery to pound the walls of the Irish town and of 'King John's castle', which faced the river just above the bridge. The bombardment started on the night of June 21 and went on almost incessantly for ten days in what has been called the heaviest bombardment in Irish history. Story estimated that 12,000 cannon-balls were fired, besides 600 bombs and tons of stones from the mortars.[29]

By June 23 most of the castle was battered down and a large breach made in the wall.[30] The bombardment continued on the following days and reduced most of the Irish town to rubble. But there was still the problem of crossing the river, which appeared almost insoluble. Mackay in his memoirs discussed the difficulties. Crossing the broken bridge and fording the river in the face of enemy fire both presented formidable problems. It was found impossible to assemble the pontoon bridge under enemy fire. Mackay's own view was that the Shannon should be crossed either downstream at Banagher or Meelick or upstream at Lanesborough by a picked force which he was prepared to lead himself. He proposed that it should consist of Enniskillen and Derry troops because of their speed of movement. His plan was overruled, and he was critical of Ginkel's timidity and propensity for collecting conflicting opinions. The result of these deliberations was a series of attempts to cross both by the bridge and by fords above and below it.[31]

On June 24 a party was sent upstream to reconnoitre a ford of which news had been received. The party had been ordered to return as soon as they had tested the ford, but the lieutenant in charge yielded to the temptation of cattle-rustling on the Connacht side. His presence was thus made known to the Jacobites who threw up strong works at the Connacht end of the ford and frustrated the plan.[32]

A struggle for the bridge now developed. On June 26 the Williamites advanced along the bridge under cover of heavy fire and against strong resistance: in Story's words 'we labour

[28] *James II*, ii. p. 455.   [29] Story, *Continuation*, p. 115.   [30] Ibid., p. 99.
[31] Mackay, *Memoirs of the war*, pp. 145–50.
[32] Story, *Continuation*, pp. 100–1.

hard to gain the bridge, but what we got there was inch by inch as it were, the enemy sticking very close to it, though great numbers of them were slain by our guns'. The Williamites succeeded in repairing the penultimate arch, but the gap at the Connacht end still remained open. The Jacobites fired energetically from behind a breast-work on the bank, which they kept repairing with great persistence as often as it was destroyed by bombardment and burning grenades. On the night of June 27 the Williamites made strenuous efforts to close the remaining gap, and by the next morning they had spanned it with beams, partly planked over. The Jacobites countered by sending a sergeant and ten men of a Scottish regiment to throw down the beams. A French engineer says that they were grenadiers who volunteered to carry lighted faggots and burn the Williamite breast-work – made out of fascines (bundles of faggots) and woolsacks – and that they did this successfully and also threw down the three beams which had been laid across the open arch.[33] The sergeant's name is given as Custume, and he is commemorated in the present-day barracks at Athlone.[34] In the account of a Williamite engineer the sergeant and his ten men were immediately killed, but they were followed by a lieutenant and twenty men 'who all but two were killed, who threw our planks and some of our beams into the river and escaped among the fire and smoke'. Stevens was on the bank just above the bridge and said that it was the 'hottest place' he ever saw during his military service – a 'mere hell upon earth'.[35]

The last hope for the Williamites was the ford below the bridge. Deserters had informed them of it and it had been used by some of the retreating Irish when the English town was taken. On June 27 three Danes under sentence of death had been sent to try the ford. Under cover of continuous firing overhead they had made the double trip and reported that the river was fordable for sixteen men marching abreast.[36] At a council of war held on June 30 grave doubts were expressed about the possibility of continuing the Athlone operation. But Würtemberg

[33] Ibid., pp. 102–3; Noblesse to Louvois, 13/23 July 1691 (Min. guerre, A1 1080, no. 165).

[34] *James II*, ii. 459.

[35] *A diary of the siege of Athlone*; Stevens, pp. 208–9.

[36] Mackay, p. 142; *Danish force*, pp. 16–17, 117; Parker, *Memoirs*, p. 30.

and Mackay urged that the risk should be taken of fording the river at Athlone. The inevitable deserters gave valuable information. Two officers swam over and told Ginkel that the Jacobites were over-confident after their success at the bridge and that the town was guarded only by three indifferent regiments.[37]

On the evening of June 30 the assault began; the church bell was rung to give the signal for the grenadiers to enter the water, which came up to their breasts. Each man had been given a guinea to whet his courage. Under cover of a heavy cannonade they made for the breach just below the castle. Here the river bank was of soft black earth and the assailants had a slippery climb to make, which put them at a disadvantage.[38] But they met no resistance. That day the position was held by O'Gara's regiment, composed of raw recruits who broke and ran for it. D'Usson then came forward towards the breach with Mac-Mahon's regiment, which also consisted of inexperienced troops. The flight of O'Gara's men proved infectious and both regiments stampeded. Tyrconnell declared that they were the two worst regiments in the army. D'Usson himself was knocked down and trampled under foot and had to be carried unconscious to the camp.[39] In less than half an hour the Williamites were masters of the Irish town. The ramparts on the western side, over which many of the fugitives clambered, made an effective barrier which prevented St Ruth from reinforcing the town with his main army. St Ruth had proposed to demolish the western ramparts to allow of the rapid entry of relief forces, but the suggestion was opposed by the French engineer. The latter said it would be wrong to demolish fortifications that would be needed if the enemy should cross the river above the town; that Athlone had been so battered and cut up that rapid relief would be impossible; and that what was needed was a good regiment to man the breach. According to O'Kelly St Ruth gave a belated order to demolish the ramparts but d'Usson neglected

[37] Mackay, pp. 143–4; Story, *Continuation*, pp. 145–6.

[38] *London Gazette*, 6 July 1691; *Diary of the siege of Athlone*; Mackay, p. 154.

[39] D'Usson to Louvois, 5/15 July 1691 (Min. guerre, A1 1080, no. 152); Noblesse to Louvois, 13/23 July 1691 (ibid., no. 165); *Anal. Hib.*, xxi. 217; *Jacobite narrative*, pp. 134–5.

to carry it out.[40] The Williamites thought that if the ramparts had been broken St Ruth would have had no difficulty in throwing back the comparatively small Williamite force – no more than 2,000 – who had by then crossed the river.[41]

O'Kelly put the chief blame on the Scottish Major-General Maxwell, who was a supporter of Tyrconnell and had gone to France in the winter of 1690 to counter the mission of Luttrell and Purcell. According to O'Kelly's account Sarsfield had recently denounced Maxwell for his anti-Irish attitude in France: after this affront it was dangerous to have entrusted the defence of a critical point to Maxwell, but St Ruth had yielded to Tyrconnell's pressure. O'Kelly accused Maxwell of treachery on several grounds: an officer of his regiment had swum across to assure Ginkel that the garrison was off its guard; a request for ammunition was contemptuously turned down by Maxwell – 'would they shoot birds'; he assured the men that there would be no action till nightfall and told them to rest. Corroboration of the second charge comes from an Irish officer who quoted Maxwell as asking whether they would 'kill lavracks'.[42] Maxwell was taken prisoner at the breach, and Ginkel found him quick to complain about St Ruth's failure to be at the scene of action.[43]

The Williamite losses in the action were very light; the estimate was 13 killed and 35 wounded. 500 Jacobites were estimated to have been killed that day and 1,200 during the whole siege. Many were butchered during mopping-up operations: 'the Danes found many of them under tubs and in dark corners, most of which they put to the sword'. An eye-witness gave a gruesome description of the scenes: 'one could not set down his foot at the end of the bridge, or castle, but on dead bodies; many lay half buried under the rubbish, and more under faggots, and many not to be seen under the ruins, whereby the stink is insufferable'.[44]

The fall of Athlone produced a dramatic change in the

[40] Min. guerre, A1 1080, no. 165; O'Kelly, p. 122.

[41] Mackay, p. 156.

[42] O'Kelly, pp. 122–3; Felix O'Neill to countess of Antrim, 10 July 1691 (*Rawdon papers*, p. 346).

[43] Mackay, p. 154; Ginkel to William, 11 July 1691 (*Cal. S.P. dom., 1690–1*, pp. 441–2).

[44] *Dublin Intelligence*, 7 July 1691; *Diary of the siege of Athlone.*

situation. Control of the Shannon crossing was a valuable gain to the Williamites and threatened the whole Jacobite position. After their courageous and successful defence of the bridge the ignominious loss of the town created consternation in the Irish army, and there were bitter complaints over the failure to defend the breach: 'never was a town which was so well defended before so basely lost'.[45] Up to the final day the Irish had fought with a spirit that impressed both the Williamites and the French officers. Treachery seems to have played a part in the concluding stages. But it was also a mistake to have put an inexperienced regiment in the breach and to have made no adequate arrangement for a second line of defence. The Irish town of Athlone should have been harder to assault than the Irish town of Limerick had been in the previous year.

4. PEACE TERMS PROCLAIMED

In spite of the poor response to Ginkel's peace overtures the Williamites did not give up hope that a favourable offer might induce the Irish to come to terms. In May 1691 Bentinck wrote to Ginkel that if the Irish thought of surrendering, as there was some ground for hoping, he should not hesitate to give them quite generous terms, as nothing could be more helpful than to see the end of the war in Ireland.[46] Ginkel accordingly went up to Dublin and discussed the matter with the lords justices, Porter and Coningsby. He convinced them that the issue of a proclamation offering generous terms held out the best hope of bringing the war in Ireland to an early end. At the same time the lords justices were acutely aware of the opposition shown by influential Protestants in Ireland to the grant of concessions to Catholics. They drafted a proclamation (which, as William was in Holland, they wished to be issued in the queen's name) offering pardon and restoration of estates to all those in arms who surrendered, and promising Catholics such freedom to practise their religion as they had enjoyed in the reign of Charles II. The draft proposed to specify a particular year of Charles's reign for determining the privileges of Catholics. When it was

[45] Mort O'Brien to Sir Donough O'Brien, 6 July 1691 (*Inchiquin MSS* (I.M.C.), p. 30).
[46] Bentinck to Ginkel, 11/21 May 1691 (Japikse, iii. 236).

sent over to England Porter observed: 'it will be absolutely necessary upon any terms to end the war in Ireland this summer, and the most probable means will be by giving the large terms mentioned in the proclamation. The English here will be offended that the Irish are not quite beggared, and what the house of commons will say when they see those lands gone which they designed for the payment of the army you can better judge than I.' In their official letter transmitting the draft the two lords justices expressed the conviction that all the forfeited estates in Ireland were not worth one-tenth the hazard and expense of another summer's war, and that as there was a party among the Irish which was opposed to any negotiation it was necessary that the proclamation should leave no room for suspicion; terms less generous than those proposed would be useless. They proposed that the proclamation should be published 'when it shall please God to give us the first considerable advantage over the enemy, which we hope we may expect in a short time, either by beating the army if they dispute the passage of the Shannon, which they seem to intend, or otherwise by the taking of Athlone'. The precise moment for publication would be left to Ginkel.[47] The question of estates had gained importance with the treason proceedings that had occupied the Williamite courts in Ireland for several months and resulted in the outlawry of over two thousand Jacobites, many (though by no means all) of whom were owners or lessees of land.[48]

Queen Mary replied to the lords justices that the proclamation should be issued in their name as they could best judge the circumstances. It should be as general as they thought proper and should contain a time-limit – three weeks was suggested. They could also issue another proclamation promising a reward as well as pardon to anyone who surrendered a fort or came over with a number of men.[49] These orders placed a heavy responsibility on the lords justices; Ginkel was pressing for a general pardon, while Protestant opinion in Dublin was for restricting the terms within the narrowest possible limits.

After a good deal of discussion a modified version of the proclamation was given to Ginkel to publish at a favourable

[47] *Cal. S.P. dom., 1690–1*, pp. 393–6.
[48] Simms, *Williamite confiscation*, pp. 30–7.
[49] Queen to lords justices, 6 June 1691 (*Finch MSS*, iii. 102).

moment. The capture of Athlone and the evident consternation that it produced among the Irish officers gave Ginkel his opportunity. He issued the proclamation on July 9, perhaps a few days late for maximum effect. It differed considerably from the original draft. Officers to qualify for pardon were not only to surrender themselves within three weeks but to deliver up any towns, forts or garrisons in their charge, or to bring over their regiments or troops or a considerable portion of them. The terms of the proclamation were, however, extended to cover the civilian inhabitants of Limerick and Galway who should be instrumental in procuring the surrender of those towns.

As published by Ginkel, the proclamation seems to have made no reference to religion. Such a reference was, however, added by the lords justices to an amended version of the proclamation dated July 7.[50] The clause was much weaker than it had been in the original draft sent over to England in May. No assurance was given that Catholics should have the freedom to practise religion that they had enjoyed in Charles II's reign. It was merely stated that as soon as possible William and Mary would summon a parliament in Ireland and endeavour to procure for Catholics such further security as might preserve them from any disturbance on account of their religion. Ginkel was dissatisfied with the new clause. He observed that it promised Catholics nothing, and he was afraid it would do more harm than good: 'since the promise is so sparing . . . it would better be passed over in silence'.[51] The lords justices replied that they had made more specific provision for religious toleration in the draft originally sent to England. That, however, had not been approved and they had been directed to publish 'only such proclamation as we should think necessary, which has put a great difficulty upon us'. They could only suggest that the question might be made the subject of a supplementary proclamation to be published later.[52]

The immediate effect of the proclamation on Irish Catholics was inconsiderable; that on Protestants was much more pronounced. It was alleged that the draft proclamation had been

[50] Story, *Continuation*, pp. 117–20, gives the text of this version.
[51] Ginkel to lords justices, 8 and 11 July 1691; same to Coningsby, 10 July 1691 (*H.M.C., rep. 4*, app., pp. 321–2).
[52] Lords justices to Ginkel, 13 July 1691 (Clarke corr., ix, no. 735).

unanimously rejected by the Irish privy council, in spite of which the lords justices and the general had persisted in issuing it; that its terms had been studiously concealed from the Protestants of Ireland; and that 'the lords justices and their secretaries will not confess anything relating to it or so much as speak of it to a Protestant'.[53] The reaction in England also seems to have been unfavourable. Blathwayt, the secretary-at-war, wrote to George Clarke, secretary-at-war for Ireland: 'the lords justices' proclamation gives occasion of great talk here and of some dissatisfaction; as you know it is impossible to please all at once'.[54] Ginkel himself thought the terms inadequate and raised with the lords justices the desirability of offering a general pardon. The lords justices thought that they had already gone as far as they were authorized to do and saw no advantage in extending the terms: 'should we publish a general pardon we give away the estates of all those persons who have submitted already upon easier terms, others who are in France and of divers others in no condition to serve or dis-serve their majesties' interest'.[55]

Though the proclamation found little favour with either Catholics or Protestants it led to a series of negotiations; and eventually it provided a basis for the discussions that ended in the treaty of Limerick.

[53] Comments on back of a copy of the proclamation in T.C.D., MS V. 4. 10, pp. 149–51; *Finch MSS*, iii. 232.

[54] Blathwayt to Clarke, 30 July 1691 (Clarke corr., ix, no. 798).

[55] Lords justices to Ginkel, 9 July 1691 (ibid., no. 717).

XIII

AUGHRIM

~~~~~~~~~~~~~~~~~~~~~~~~~~~~~~~~~~~~~

1. ST RUTH'S DECISION TO GIVE BATTLE

THE MAIN Irish army had played no part in the last day's fighting at Athlone. But the fate of the regiments in the town and the dramatic collapse of the resistance had created something like panic. John Stevens describes the confusion in which the Jacobites withdrew next day: 'such a panic fear has seized our men that the very noise of ten horsemen would have dispersed as many of our battalions, above half the soldiers scattering by the way without any other thing but their own apprehensions to fright them'.[1] Deserters told the Williamites that the Irish were 'now in as great a consternation as they were after the breach of the Boyne'.[2] But it was not long before the situation improved; stragglers drifted back to the ranks, and the Jacobite army was again to show its remarkable power of rapid recovery. St Ruth fell back on Ballinasloe without interference from the Williamite army. He took effective measures to stop desertion and to reassure the troops, with whom he seems to have made himself personally popular. Story says that he set out to be 'very kind to and familiar with the Irish officers, whom formerly he had treated with disrespect and contempt; and to caress the soldiers, though a little before he would hang a dozen of them in a morning'.[3]

[1] Stevens, p. 211.
[2] *Dublin Intelligence*, 15 July 1691.
[3] Fumeron to Louvois, 9/19 July 1691 (Min. guerre, A1 1080, no. 164); Story, *Continuation*, p. 114.

According to O'Kelly a council of war was held, which showed a division of opinion. Some were for defending the crossing of the Suck at Ballinasloe; they were supported by St Ruth, who was anxious to redeem his reputation by winning a battle. Sarsfield and others were opposed to this on the ground that the Williamite army was stronger and better disciplined than the ill-equipped, unpaid and discouraged Irish army. Sarsfield's plan was to hold Limerick and Galway in strength, to leave the rest of Connacht open to the Williamite forces and to cross the Shannon and devastate Leinster and Munster in Ginkel's rear; there was even talk of sacking Dublin. St Ruth was under strong pressure to accept this plan, but made his own decision to give battle on the high ground near Aughrim, about five miles south-west of Ballinasloe.[4] O'Kelly's account is corroborated by the French Lieutenant-General d'Usson, who reported that St Ruth had it in mind to give battle. D'Usson himself was in favour of a defensive strategy, holding walled towns with the best troops, disbanding the rest of the infantry and using the cavalry and dragoons to harass the enemy's convoys. He said that there was widespread panic among the officers, which extended up to the generals, and that the morale of the infantry was so low that St Ruth himself agreed that it could not be relied on: the 32 battalions that had filed over Ballinasloe bridge had not totalled more than 7,000.[5] D'Usson, who had been in disagreement with St Ruth at Athlone, was sent to defend Galway; de Tessé was retained as second-in-command for the coming battle at Aughrim.

The site selected by St Ruth was on the eastern slopes of Kilcommodon Hill, a good position protected by a belt of bog along the whole front except for two narrow passes to the north and south of the bog. St Ruth seems to have taken up his position on July 8, which, as things turned out, meant that he had four days in which to prepare his dispositions.[6] His line stretched from beyond Kilcommodon Church on his right to Aughrim Castle which commanded the pass on his left, a distance of nearly two miles. Hedges and ditches covered the

[4] O'Kelly, pp. 129–31.
[5] D'Usson to Louvois, 8/18 July 1691 (Min. guerre, A1 1080, no. 163 *bis*).
[6] Stevens, p. 213. See the map on p. 218.

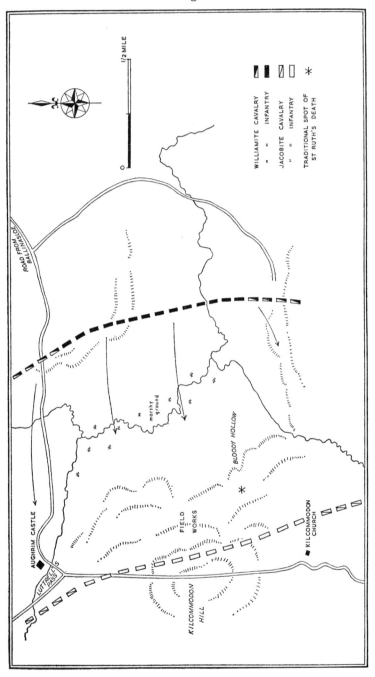

BATTLE OF AUGHRIM, 1691

lower slopes of the hill; some of these were adapted to serve as field-works, others were levelled to give the Jacobite army a clear approach to the passes that led across the bog.[7]

The Jacobite army had had time to reform and recover its numbers and its spirits. There are varying estimates of its strength. O'Kelly put it as low as 10,000 foot and 4,000 cavalry and dragoons. The large number of casualties suggests that this figure is much too low. Story's estimate is 'nigh 20,000 foot and 5,000 horse and dragoons'. Würtemberg put it at 19,000 foot and 8,000 cavalry and dragoons, which seems to be an over-estimate.[8] A prisoner gave the Williamites a list of 37 regiments of infantry, 11 of cavalry and 8 of dragoons. They were certainly not at full strength, and the total may be put at about 20,000, about the same as that of the Williamite army.[9]

On the day of the battle the Jacobites were drawn up in two lines, with cavalry on either wing. There are discrepancies in the accounts of the order of battle, and in particular the role of Sarsfield is obscure. O'Kelly says that de Tessé was on the right wing and Sarsfield on the left; the 'Light to the blind' that de Tessé and Sarsfield were both on the right. De Tessé says that he himself was posted on the left of the front line; he does not mention Sarsfield. According to a Williamite officer Sarsfield was in the rear behind the centre with positive directions not to stir till he received orders.[10]

St Ruth seems to have paid special attention to morale and to have relied on the clergy to instil a crusading fervour in the army. As the battle was fought on Sunday it was natural that the day should begin with mass. But Story adds that the priests assured the men of a glorious victory and told them to give no quarter. He quotes, with some reserve, the speech that St Ruth is said to have delivered on the previous day – allegedly taken from the copy found afterwards on the body of his secretary. The speech referred to St Ruth's own services in suppressing

[7] *Rawdon papers*, p. 353.

[8] O'Kelly, p. 131; Story, *Continuation*, p. 141; *Danish force*, p. 122.

[9] *Rawdon papers*, pp. 359–60. The lists of cavalry and dragoon regiments are followed by a note that 8 regiments were not at Aughrim, but at Galway and Limerick. This is probably a reference to infantry regiments, of which 45 in all are listed.

[10] O'Kelly, p. 132; *Jacobite narrative*, p. 138; Min. guerre, A1 1080, no. 171; Parker, *Memoirs*, p. 35.

heresy and to his mission to preserve the church in Ireland. It called on the soldiers to fight for their families, their liberties and their property, but above all for the propagation of the holy faith and the suppression of heresy: 'you may be assured that King James will love and reward you; Louis the great will protect you; all good Catholics will applaud you; I myself will command you; the church will pray for you; your posterity will bless you; God will make you all saints and his Holy Mother will lay you in her bosom'.[11] We may suspect the authenticity of this address, but there is other evidence that St Ruth made some kind of speech to his men, and there is no doubt that the clergy were present in force. The Catholic bishop of Cork wrote that 80 priests were killed at Aughrim, crucifix in hand, while urging on the troops to fight for their faith. Among them was the learned Dr Alexius Stafford, chaplain of the royal regiment of foot guards and dean of Christ Church.[12] The crusading spirit must have made its contribution to the courage and resolution with which the Irish fought at Aughrim.

2. GINKEL'S ADVANCE

The prolonged bombardment of Athlone had exhausted Ginkel's stock of ammunition, and it was over a week before sufficient supplies arrived. The interval was occupied in clearing some of the ruins of Athlone, strengthening the defences, and patching up houses to serve as magazines. Ginkel was very uncertain about St Ruth's intentions. Deserters brought reports of an impending battle, but Ginkel's chief preoccupation was guarding against cavalry raids in the area to his rear. The Irish cavalry were successful in preventing Ginkel's scouts from finding out the dispositions of the enemy forces. A Williamite party that set out on July 4 under the guidance of an ex-priest fell into an ambush and suffered heavy losses.[13] As late as July 10 Ginkel's information was that the enemy had retired to Galway, from which he concluded that they declined to give battle; there were reports that many of their infantry were deserting.

---

[11] Story, *Continuation*, pp. 123–5.

[12] *Jacobite narrative*, pp. 138, 279; Bellesheim, *Geschichte der Katholischen Kirche in Irland*, iii. 1.

[13] Story, *Continuation*, p. 116.

Ginkel himself marched that day with an advance party towards Ballinasloe, even though the expected convoy of ammunition had not yet arrived from Dublin. He had evidently no suspicion that the main Jacobite army was so near, as he announced his intention of moving down from Ballinasloe to Portumna to get command of the Shannon crossing. On July 11 he wrote to the lords justices that the enemy planned to divide their infantry into three sections and to hold Limerick, Galway and Sligo, while their cavalry and dragoons threatened the Williamite rear. Four Williamite regiments were kept at Kilkenny to guard the approach to Dublin, and plans were made to occupy the Shannon crossings that were still open to the Jacobites.[14]

The ammunition convoy, escorted by Lord Portland's regiment of horse, seems to have reached Athlone on July 11, and the main army advanced that day to Ballinasloe. Reconnaissance then showed the Jacobite army drawn up on the side of Kilcommodon hill, though a dip behind the first brow prevented a complete view. Story describes the impression that the scene made on the Williamites:

The enemy's camp lay along the ridge of a hill . . . from thence to the bog below was nigh half a mile, and this cut into a great many small enclosures which the enemy had ordered so as to make a communication from one of them to another, and had lined all these very thick with small shot; this showed a great deal of dexterity in M. St Ruth in making choice of such a piece of ground as nature itself could not furnish him with a better, considering all circumstances; for he knew that the Irish naturally loved a breastwork between them and bullets, and here they were fitted to the purpose with hedges and ditches to the very edge of the bog.

Ginkel was taken aback by the strength of the enemy's position: he found it no easy matter to attack them.[15] He was greatly helped by members of the Huguenot family of Trench, who were owners of Garbally, between Ballinasloe and Aughrim. They acted as guides to the Williamite army, and it was presumably from them that Ginkel got the map of the ground with which he was provided.[16]

[14] *H.M.C.*, *rep. 4*, app., p. 322.   [15] Story, *Continuation*, p. 122.
[16] Story, *Continuation*, p. 122; Clancarty, *Memoir of the le Poer Trench family*, pp. 4–5.

In spite of the strength of the Jacobite position Ginkel decided to advance without further delay. Early on the morning of Sunday, July 12, his army crossed the Suck at Ballinasloe, leaving their tents and baggage behind them. The infantry marched over the bridge; the horse and dragoons crossed by fords, English and Huguenot above the bridge, Dutch and Danish below it. Fog slowed up the Williamite advance. When it cleared there was skirmishing with the enemy's cavalry. The action began on a small scale, but more troops on both sides were soon engaged and fighting continued for about an hour before the Jacobites withdrew beyond the bog. A Williamite account suggests that there might have been no engagement that day had it not been for some over-enthusiastic dragoons who disobeyed orders and engaged a party of the enemy.[17]

By 3 p.m. the Williamite army had taken up its position facing its opponents. Story gives the line of battle: 28 battalions of infantry and 47 squadrons of horse in two lines, with infantry in the centre, English horse on the right, Danish, Dutch and most of the Huguenot horse on the left. To these the three squadrons of Lord Portland's horse were subsequently added. Another account says that the wings were a mixture of horse and foot.[18] According to Story the total strength of the Williamite army was not above 17,000. Würtemberg, writing a few days after the battle, gives the same figure, saying that it was no higher 'because of the many parties detached on convoy duty' and because of the need to garrison Athlone. Burnet says that the army was not more than 20,000.[19] Modern commentators, faced with varying estimates for both armies, have concluded that their strength was approximately equal.[20]

[17] Story, *Continuation*, p. 127; *Rawdon papers*, p. 353. The dragoons were Conyngham's Donegal men (*Danish force*, p. 121).

[18] Story, *Continuation*, facing p. 124; *Rawdon papers*, pp. 356–8.

[19] Story, *Continuation*, p. 141; *Danish Force*, p. 122; Burnet, iv. 136.

[20] See the accounts by G. A. Hayes-McCoy in *Galway Arch. Soc. Jn.*, xx. 1–30 (1942) and Diarmuid Murtagh in *The Irish at war*, ed. Hayes-McCoy (1964). Murtagh's estimate is 20,000. Ginkel's battalions were much below full strength (806 privates). D'Usson, who saw the Williamite army at Galway, said the battalions had only 450 privates and the squadrons 100 troopers (Min. guerre, A1 1080, no. 183). Allowing for officers and the Aughrim casualties, this would give a figure of not much less than 20,000.

3. THE BATTLE

Ginkel was in some doubt whether to launch his main attack that day. A council of war was held, in which some opinions were in favour of putting off the attack till next day. Against this view it was argued that the preliminary fighting had thrown the Irish army into some disorder and that St Ruth might withdraw during the night. It was therefore decided to attack, adopting a plan advocated by the Scottish Major-General Mackay. This was to begin pressure on the Williamite left, in the hope of drawing some of the enemy strength away from Aughrim Castle on the other flank. The Williamite right would then try to force the northern pass towards the castle.[21]

The course of the fighting was confused and it is not easy to reconcile the conflicting accounts. On the Jacobite side the most detailed descriptions are de Tessé's dispatch, the 'Light to the blind' and a contemporary Latin poem.[22] On the Williamite side there are the official version published in Dublin, Würtemberg's report, and the accounts of Story, Mackay, Major Tempest and Captain Parker.[23]

The advance on the Williamite left began about 5 p.m. and met determined resistance: 'the Irish behaved themselves like men of another nation, defending their ditches stoutly: for they would maintain one side till our men put their pieces over at the other and then, having lines of communication from one ditch to another, they would presently post themselves again and flank us'. The Huguenot and Danish troops bore the brunt of the fighting on this wing, and found it very hard going over the bog with sun and wind in their faces. Fighting continued on the Williamite left flank for about an hour and a half, during which their centre and right wing were not engaged except for artillery fire. The Williamites brought into action eighteen cannon, to which St Ruth's nine guns replied effectively.[24]

[21] Story, *Continuation*, p. 128.
[22] *Jacobite narrative*, pp. 139–48; Poema de Hibernia (extract about Aughrim in *Jacobite narrative*, pp. 275–826); Min. guerre, A1 1080, no. 171.
[23] *A particular and full account of the routing the whole Irish army at Aghrim*; *Danish Force*, pp. 120–3; Story, *Continuation*, pp. 121–47; Mackay, *Memoirs*, pp. 160–6; *Rawdon papers*, pp. 352–60; Parker, *Memoirs*, pp. 34–6.
[24] Story, *Continuation*, p. 129; *Danish force*, pp. 121–2. The tradition of this fighting is preserved in the name 'Bloody Hollow'.

To meet the pressure on his right St Ruth switched units of both cavalry and infantry from the direction of Aughrim Castle on his left wing. The Williamites could see this manœuvre, and took advantage of it to launch an infantry attack with English troops across the northern sector of the bog. Four regiments struggled through the swamp and a stream that ran through it, 'most of them up to their middles in mud and water'. They established a footing on the lowest slope of the hill, but were then overwhelmed by Irish cavalry and infantry which drove them back across the bog with heavy losses; two of the English colonels were captured.[25] The Irish pursued their enemies as far as the Williamite guns beyond the bog. One Jacobite account claims that Colonel Gordon O'Neill captured some of the guns, but he does not seem to have succeeded in carrying any of them away.[26] St Ruth, delighted at the repulse of the English is said to have called out 'le jour est à nous, mes enfants', and to have boasted that he would drive the enemy to the gates of Dublin.[27] The Williamites had been roughly handled, but they were able to check the Irish advance with 'turnpikes' (chevaux de frise).[28] Ginkel was able to bring up sufficient reinforcements to support the hard-pressed English regiments. His next move was to send a cavalry force to probe the northern pass towards Aughrim Castle – a move which was countered by St Ruth ordering the left wing of his cavalry to hold the pass. St Ruth himself moved over to his left to superintend the operation. As he did so, a cannon shot from a Williamite battery hit him and carried off his head.[29] A cloak was thrown over him and his body carried over the brow of the hill. His final resting-place is unknown. One account says he was buried in Loughrea, twelve miles to the south-west. Another tradition is that he was buried in the graveyard of Kilcommodon Church, but that the body was later removed.[30]

[25] Story, *Continuation*, pp. 129–30. The confusion is illustrated by the fact that one of the colonels escaped, was retaken and again escaped.

[26] *Jacobite narrative*, p. 141; another version says O'Neill left his scar on the guns (ibid., p. 277); de Tessé says the enemy were pushed back 'very near their cannon' (Min. guerre, A1 1080, no. 171).

[27] *Jacobite narrative*, p. 141.   [28] *Rawdon papers*, p. 354.

[29] *Jacobite narrative*, pp. 142–3; Story, *Continuation*, p. 133.

[30] *Jacobite narrative*, p. 143; J. O'Donovan, Ordnance Survey letters for County Galway, i. 566.

The news of St Ruth's death quickly reached the cavalry and created consternation; the infantry remained for some time in ignorance of what had happened. The Jacobite accounts suggest that Ginkel either guessed or was informed that St Ruth had been killed and therefore ordered an attack. In fact, he seems not to have known about it, and even on the next day had no definite information.[31] Soon after St Ruth had been killed the Jacobite cavalry rode away from the northern pass. The 'Light to the blind' puts the blame on Henry Luttrell, who was detailed to hold a causeway near Aughrim Castle, and on Sheldon who commanded the left wing of the Jacobite cavalry. The writer describes the place as 'an old broken causeway only large enough for two horses to pass it at a time, and sixty yards long'. He says that Luttrell withdrew after 'a small resistance', and that Sheldon followed him off the field. This account argues that St Ruth had given specific orders to hold the causeway, that the orders did not lapse with St Ruth's death, and that by abandoning their position the commanders concerned were either traitors or cowards: 'and so let them keep their priding cavalry to stop bottles with'.[32] The author of the Latin poem had no doubt that there was treachery: 'trickery and grave treachery were shown by the officer who stood at your walls, fatal Aughrim, in a narrow passage, stationed as an insuperable obstacle to the enemy, had not the guard been removed'. The poet goes on to accuse this officer of being 'bought with filthy lucre (if the story is true)'.[33] The way past Aughrim Castle is locally known as Luttrell's Pass, and there is a tradition that Luttrell's action was dictated by treachery. Although he had been a leading figure in the anti-Tyrconnell resistance movement of 1690 he seems to have come to the view that further fighting was useless. Not long afterwards he was discovered to be in correspondence with Ginkel, and subsequently he received a Williamite pension. It is, of course, possible that it was these later developments that gave rise to the story of treachery; but there seems no doubt that negligible resistance was offered at the causeway and that this was fatal for the whole Jacobite army. The crossing of the causeway was followed by the taking

[31] *Jacobite narrative*, p. 143; O'Kelly, p. 133; Ginkel to William, 13 July 1691 (*Cal. S.P. dom., 1690–1*, p. 444).
[32] *Jacobite narrative*, pp. 138, 143–6.   [33] Ibid., pp. 280–1.

of Aughrim Castle: many of the garrison were put to death; Walter Burke, the commander, and other officers were taken prisoner. Meanwhile the Williamite cavalry had been able to ride along the contour of Kilcommodon Hill and take the Jacobite infantry in the rear. The retreat, which began on the Jacobite left, soon spread all along the line. The arrival of English ball which would not fit French-calibre muskets added to the confusion.[34]

De Tessé, to whom the command passed after St Ruth's death, described the chaos that set in. The infantry in the Jacobite centre began to break, and all efforts to rally them failed. De Tessé then saw the enemy squadrons who had 'already passed by the centre of our line'; these were presumably the Williamite cavalry who had come over the causeway near Aughrim Castle. De Tessé himself headed a force of cavalry to charge them; but his men, seeing that flight was general, followed suit. He was wounded in three places with pistol shots. The wounds were not serious and he was able to get away; but he seems not to have remained in command or to have made provision for a successor.[35] There is evidence from both Jacobite and Williamite sources that Sarsfield was not given authority to take charge. He and Lord Galmoy are said to have covered the retreat as well as could have been expected.[36]

But that is not saying very much. The last stages of the battle were marked by something like a massacre, from which the remnants of the Irish army were saved by nightfall. As they ran they threw their muskets away. According to Story, Ginkel began by offering sixpence apiece for them, but so many came in that he reduced the price to twopence.[37] Würtemberg wrote that the Williamite cavalry cut down the flying foot-soldiers and would have destroyed them all if there had been two hours more of daylight left. Story corroborates him: 'the night, and also the bog, saved the lives of many thousands of their foot, for

[34] *Jacobite narrative*, p. 147.

[35] Min. guerre, A1 1080, no. 171.

[36] 'When the commander was killed the password and order of battle had been committed to none of the leaders, not to Lucan himself' (poem quoted in *Jacobite narrative*, p. 280); 'Sarsfield would not stir from his post, still expecting his general's orders' (Parker, p. 36); *Jacobite narrative*, p. 147.

[37] Story, *Continuation*, p. 148.

our foreigners, and especially the Danish horse, are excellent pursuers'.[38] When the Irish prisoners were ordered to bury their dead comrades, it was recorded that over 7,000 had been killed. It was the most disastrous battle in Irish history.[39] Story described the gruesome scene: corpses scattered for almost four miles round; ditches full of bodies, lying where they had been shot. 400 officers were killed, of whom Lord Galway (a son of the seventh earl of Clanricarde) was the most notable. The 450 prisoners included many of the Jacobite aristocracy; among them were Lord Bophin (Lord Galway's brother), Lord Bellew of Duleek (who died of wounds), Lords Slane and Kenmare, Colonels Gordon O'Neill and Butler of Kilcash. All the guns and baggage were captured, together with 11 horse standards and 32 regimental colours. Ginkel's triumph was complete.[40]

The Williamites paid tribute to the resolution shown by their opponents in the earlier stages of the battle. Würtemberg wrote that they had resisted much more vigorously than had been expected and that the issue was in doubt for two hours; he made special reference to the bravery of King James's regiment of guards, and to Irish officers 'who were so full of valour that they leaped over our chevaux-de-frise'. Story's verdict was that 'the Irish, before they began to shrink, had behaved themselves beyond all expectation and had fought longer than ordinary'. In the generous words of another Williamite writer: 'it was the last effort, *pro aris et focis*, in which the gasping honour of all the Catholic nobility and gentry of the kingdom struggled to do its utmost.'[41]

[38] *Danish force*, p. 123.

[39] *Dublin Intelligence*, 22 July 1691; Würtemberg within a few days of the battle gave the same figure. The *Jacobite narrative*, pp. 147-8, estimates 2,000 killed and 600 wounded on the Irish side and above 5,000 Williamites killed. *James II*, ii. 458, puts the Irish deaths at 'nigh 4,000, nor was that of the English much inferior'. The Williamites, who supervised the burials, were in a better position to know the figures. Story, who gives a detailed breakdown, puts Williamite losses at 673 killed and 1,071 wounded (*Continuation*, p. 138).

[40] Story, *Continuation*, pp. 136-7; *Danish force*, p. 123; Lord Galway's head and those 'of other great men' killed at Aughrim were kept at Kilconnell Abbey and shown to Molyneux in 1709. There is a tradition that St Ruth was buried there, but Molyneux does not mention him ('A journey into Connacht in 1709' in *Ir. Arch. Misc.*, i. 161-78).

[41] *Danish force*, pp. 122-3; Story, *Continuation*, p. 134; *Exact journal*, p, 21.

Outside Ireland the battle was regarded as less sensational than the Boyne. Numbers on each side were fewer, the kings had departed, and there was a sense that the main issue had already been settled. It has been claimed that this was not so; that 'much had been lost, but all might yet be regained'; that the course of Irish, and even European, history might have been changed by an Irish victory.[42] The death of St Ruth undoubtedly altered the immediate situation, but the relative resources of the two sides were such that the Jacobites, if victorious, could hardly have regained control of what they had lost since the war began. The Williamites had great advantages in experienced and disciplined troops, and a well-organized system of supplies. They were backed by the resources of England, to which Ireland was of much greater importance than it was to France. Louvois was no friend to the Irish alliance, but he was a great administrator, and his death, a few days before Aughrim, left a vacuum in the organization of the French military effort. The Irish were handicapped by lack of money, supplies and equipment, and by their own internal disagreements. These handicaps were neutralized at Aughrim by the strength of their position and by the desperate resolution with which they seized what might be their last opportunity. But it seems unlikely that they could have mustered the means for a large-scale offensive operation. The initial phase of the battle resulted in the Williamite attack being repulsed with considerable loss. But the prospect at that stage was not that Ginkel would be routed, but that he would fail to dislodge St Ruth's army from its strong position. This might well have led to a prolonging of the war into the following year, or to the granting of more favourable peace terms.

For the Irish Aughrim was a shattering blow. O'Kelly describes the grief and despair created by this disaster, in which the Irish lost 'the flower of their army and nation'. He makes an unexpectedly fervent eulogy of St Ruth: 'never was general better beloved by any army, and no captain was ever more fond of his soldiers than he'.[43] Tyrconnell was less enthusiastic: St Ruth 'was of a temperament ill suited to the Irish situation'; if

[42] Murtagh, 'The battle of Aughrim' in *The Irish at war*, p. 59; Hayes-McCoy, p. 1.
[43] O'Kelly, pp. 134-5.

he had consulted Tyrconnell there would not have been a battle, and neither St Ruth nor his army would have perished.[44] The disaster was long remembered in Irish poetry and tradition. To quote from a contemporary poet:

> In Aughrim of the slaughter they rest;
> Their skeletons lying there, uncoffined,
> Have caused the women of Ireland to beat their hands,
> The children to be neglected, and the fugitives to wail.[45]

'It isn't the loss of Aughrim' became a proverb for bearable misfortunes.

[44] *Anal. Hib.*, xxi. 219.
[45] Séamas Dall MacCuart (1647–1732), 'Elegy for Sorley MacDonnell'. in S. Laoide, ed., *Duanaire na Midhe*, p. 88. For Aughrim traditions see P. Egan, *The parish of Ballinasloe*, pp. 105–8.

XIV

THE SURRENDER OF GALWAY

~~~~~~~~~~~~~~~~~~~~~~~~~~~~~~~~~~~~~~~

1. 'THE NEW INTEREST'

GALWAY HAD long been regarded as the weak spot in the Jacobite resistance. Its citizens had fared surprisingly well in the great land-changes of the seventeenth century. They had acquired large estates throughout Connacht by lending money on mortgage to an older stratum of impoverished owners. During the commonwealth régime they had succeeded in retaining much of this land and had added to it by buying up lands assigned to transplanters from other provinces. Their titles were confirmed by the restoration acts of settlement, and during Charles II's reign they acquired more land by purchase. They had thus a strong interest in the maintenance of the settlement, and they had formed an active pressure-group to oppose its repeal by the Jacobite parliament of 1689. In the autumn of that year d'Avaux had reported to Louis that he was worried about the Galway situation as there were many Catholic malcontents in the town whose property had been adversely affected by the repeal of the settlement.[1] Galway landowners played a prominent part in the response to Ginkel's peace-feelers during the winter of 1690–1. They represented the 'new interest' which O'Kelly condemned for preferring private gain to the general interest of religion and country.[2]

In the interval between the fall of Athlone and the battle of Aughrim Ginkel had hopes that Galway would surrender on

[1] D'Avaux, p. 533. [2] O'Kelly, p. 71.

terms. He thought that the townsmen would be encouraged to do so if a Williamite fleet appeared in Galway Bay. The lords justices agreed and instructed Captain Matthew Aylmer, who commanded a squadron at Kinsale, to sail for Galway with power to bargain with the governor or garrison on 'such advantageous terms as, if they have any inclination to save their lives and estates, will invite them to submit'. Aylmer replied that he had no provisions for a voyage to Galway: the navy commissioners had not sent the promised supply. The lords justices then applied to Admiral Russell, suggesting that he might himself sail to Galway and offer similar terms: 'the citizens of Gallaway are said to be much inclined to submit, and nothing will more contribute to it than the appearance of a considerable fleet'.[3] A Dublin official was very hopeful 'that the town of Galway would give up upon promise of half that six and fifty thousand pounds a year which is the value of their property in land'.[4] Nottingham supported the lords justices, though he nervously disclaimed any intention of giving positive orders to Admiral Russell, who clearly disliked the idea. He left matters to Russell's discretion with the remark: 'in short, the speedy taking of Galway is of vast importance to their majesties' service and therefore must be promoted by all means that will consist with the safety of the fleet'. In the event the fleet did not appear before Galway till after it had surrendered.[5]

A few days after the battle Ginkel moved his camp to Athenry, half-way between Aughrim and Galway. Several of the towns-men came out to his camp and gave him an account of the situation: d'Usson was the chief military commander; the governor of the town was Lord Dillon; the garrison consisted of seven regiments, below strength and poorly equipped; opinion was divided on whether to surrender or resist, and much depended on whether Balldearg O'Donnell and his Ulstermen would come to the relief of the town.[6] A message was sent by Sir John Kirwan, a leading citizen and former mayor, that

---

[3] Lords justices to Ginkel, 6 July 1691 (Clarke corr., viii, no. 698); same to Russell, 8 July 1691 (*Finch MSS*, iii. 148).

[4] Israel Fielding to Ginkel, 5 July 1691 (Clarke corr., viii, no. 689).

[5] Nottingham to Russell, 10 July 1691 (*Finch MSS*, iii. 150); Story, *Continuation*, p. 174.

[6] Ibid., p. 151.

Ginkel need not bring up his artillery, as the town would capitulate at the first sight of his army. The current mayor, Arthur French, was also in favour of negotiation, sent the town clerk to Ginkel, and was himself put under arrest by d'Usson's orders.[7] One of those who joined Ginkel at Athenry was Judge Daly, who had taken a leading part in opposing the repeal of the settlement and in the peace negotiations of the previous winter. Ginkel paid tribute to Daly's share in getting Galway to surrender: 'he has told all the Irish intrigues there'. Another negotiator was Richard Martin, who seems to have played an active part in advising Ginkel on how to bring about the surrender.[8]

2. CAPITULATION

Ginkel's Protestant advisers professed to distrust the bona fides of the Galway negotiators, and Ginkel was in considerable doubt whether to wait for his heavy artillery to come up from Athlone or to advance on Galway without it. He decided on the latter course, and on July 19 marched the greater part of his army on Galway; the Irish offered no opposition, but retired to the town after burning the suburbs. Ginkel then sent a trumpet offering the terms of the July proclamation if the town would surrender immediately. Dillon, the governor, replied on behalf of himself, d'Usson and the other officers that they were resolved to defend Galway to the last.[9] D'Usson claimed for himself the credit of persuading a council of war to adopt this bold decision: he thought that Ginkel's troops had marched to within musket shot of the walls with an air of great confidence, as if the gates were to be opened to them. Another French observer remarked that Ginkel's army approached Galway 'in battle order within musket range with such recklessness that they seem quite sure of the state of mind of the troops and of the population'.[10]

The walled town of Galway lay to the east of the Corrib river, where it flows out into the bay. It was surrounded by

[7] B.M., Add. MS 38, 153, f. 19; O'Kelly, pp. 135–6; *Danish force*, p. 125.
[8] *H.M.C. rep. 4*, app., p. 322; *Cal. S.P. dom., 1694–5*, pp. 506–7.
[9] Story, *Continuation*, pp. 159–62.
[10] D'Usson to Louvois, 23 July/2 Aug. 1691 (Min. guerre, A1 1080, no. 183); *Danish force*, p. 124.

water on three sides, but to the east it was commanded by a ridge of high ground. Some outworks had been made on this ridge, but they were on too small a scale to protect the town adequately on that side. The chief strength of the fortifications was the citadel, which stood within the walled town towards the eastern section and was armed with eight guns. On the night of July 19/20 Ginkel sent a party in tin boats across the Corrib above Galway, and thus effectively barred the way for Balldearg O'Donnell, who retired into Mayo. Early on the morning of July 20 the outworks on the ridge were attacked and the defenders, after making very little resistance, were driven back into the town. This was followed by a message from the governor proposing that negotiations for surrender should be started.[11]

D'Usson's report to France drew a picture of general defeatism against which he had found it impossible to prevail. He had asked Tyrconnell and Sarsfield for 1,500 men, which were refused on the ground that none could be spared. Clanricarde had withdrawn a detachment of his men from the threatened outwork on the ridge in spite of d'Usson's written order 'in English'. As soon as the outworks had been abandoned Dillon had called a second council of war, this time without d'Usson. This decided that resistance was hopeless, and sent d'Usson the reasons: the walls were weak and could be breached within 24 hours; the troops had no spirit; there was a shortage of gunners and hardly any ammunition; there was obvious defeatism among the townsmen, many of whom had gone over to the enemy. D'Usson added that the principal clergy were in favour of surrender. He referred in particular to the archbishop of Tuam, the bishop of Elphin and 'the dean, who has great influence in the town'; he may have been the warden of the collegiate church.[12]

There was hard bargaining over the terms to be offered to Galway. Ginkel was pressed to agree to the inclusion of some individuals who were not in the town at the time, including Lord Bophin, Clanricarde's brother, who had been taken prisoner at Aughrim. There were several prominent landowners of the county who were not in Galway town but were engaged in negotiating with Ginkel; they also demanded to be included.[13]

[11] Story, *Continuation*, pp. 162–4.   [12] Min. guerre, A1 1080, no. 183.
[13] Annesley MSS, xx. 1–10; xxvii. 153.

The articles of the capitulation as finally agreed upon allowed the garrison to choose whether to stay in Galway or go to their homes or else to march to Limerick with full honours of war. The eighth article promised pardon to the city officials, freemen and inhabitants. The ninth guaranteed their property to the garrison as well as to the officials, freemen and inhabitants. The wording of the ninth article made no distinction between those of the garrison who went to Limerick and those who stayed behind. Gentlemen of the town and garrison were to be allowed to keep a gun for self-defence and to carry a sword and a case of pistols. Catholic lawyers were to be allowed freedom to practise as in Charles II's time. These two clauses were an advance on the July proclamation and were to be repeated in the articles of Limerick. The names of priests were to be given to Ginkel, and they and the laity of Galway were to have freedom for the private practice of their religion 'without being prosecuted on any penal laws for the same'; the clergy were to have protection for themselves and their property.[14]

These terms went a good deal beyond the July proclamation, and Ginkel had some hesitation in agreeing to them. He wrote twice to William to express the hope that in the special circumstances his action would be approved.[15] Some years later he recalled that the drafting of the eighth and ninth articles (which offered pardon and security of property) had given him particular trouble, and that it was a long time before he could bring himself to agree to them. He was induced to do so by the consideration that prolonging the siege would have put him in a difficult position, and that it would have taken eight or ten days to bring up his heavy guns from Athlone to make a breach in the walls. He had therefore agreed to a liberal form of words and had given special assurances to four or five of the citizens who were not then in the town of Galway.[16]

English reaction to the Galway articles was critical. Bentinck wrote to Ginkel that the English thought he had given Galway

[14] Story, *Continuation*, pp. 166–9.

[15] Ginkel to William, 22 July, 8 Aug. 1691 (*Cal. S.P. dom., 1690–1*, pp. 455, 475).

[16] Ginkel to Blathwayt, 6/16 Aug. 1697 (Annesley MSS, xxvii. 153). For a later controversy about the Galway articles see Simms, *Williamite confiscation*, pp. 67–72.

unnecessarily favourable terms.[17] Nottingham sent a copy of the articles to Sidney, who was with William in Holland, with a somewhat apologetic explanation: 'perhaps your lordship will think they are very large concessions, and they are censured here as such, especially by the gentlemen of Ireland'. He gave Ginkel's reasons, which were that the navy had not convoyed provision ships to Galway, that the heavy guns were at Athlone, and that it was important to gain as much time as possible to deal with Limerick.[18] Queen Mary approved Ginkel's proceedings and hoped that they would lead to the surrender of Limerick.[19]

The French officers professed themselves disgusted by the failure of Galway to hold out. D'Usson declared that the Irish would have contributed more than the enemy to the ruin of the country. He said that the army was very unreliable: 'he who today is ready to die rather than submit to the prince of Orange will tomorrow talk loudly about the need for a settlement'.[20] Fumeron, the French commissary, attributed the rapid surrender of Galway to the demoralization that had set in after Aughrim.[21] Before the Galway articles were signed on 21 July 1691 a copy had been sent to Tyrconnell with two Irish officers, who on their return are said to have had a private conference with Ginkel.[22] The latter was apparently sounding them on Tyrconnell's attitude to the negotiations. He sent a communication to Tyrconnell, but got no reply. Ginkel seems to have thought Tyrconnell more likely to compromise than Sarsfield 'who with Luttrell and Purcell are the drivers and certainly have pensions from France'.[23] O'Kelly suggests that the Galway peace-party were encouraged by the knowledge that Tyrconnell would support them and that perhaps James himself would not be ill pleased.[24] The author of the 'Light to the blind' took the opposite view: according to him Tyrconnell had counted on

[17] Japikse, iii. 249.

[18] Nottingham to Sidney, 28 July 1691 (*Finch MSS*, iii. 180–1).

[19] Nottingham to Ginkel, 28 July 1691 (ibid., p. 182).

[20] Min. guerre, A1 1080, no. 185.   [21] Ibid., A1 1080, no. 175.

[22] *Dublin Intelligence*, 29 July 1691.

[23] Ginkel to lords justices, 28 July 1691 (P.R.O.N.I., de Ros MSS, 12/99). Ginkel's view was a misapprehension based on 1690 attitudes, which had been reversed (cf. pp. 241–2 below).

[24] O'Kelly, p. 138.

Galway holding out for a long time, which would have made it too late in the year for the siege of Limerick to be undertaken.[25] Tyrconnell himself wrote to Louis blaming the surrender on St Ruth's neglect to provide supplies for Galway and on the inadequate condition of the defences.[26]

The surrender of Galway was a notable gain for the Williamites. It divided the Irish-held area beyond the Shannon, and limited the main resistance to Limerick and County Clare. Story observed that, with a good garrison, Galway 'might have given us more trouble and so have postponed the siege of Limerick'. He says there was a good store of ammunition left in the town, 'besides 800 hogsheads of meal and other things of value'.[27] The failure to provide protective works on the east ridge contributed to the surrender, but the decisive factor was morale. The leading townsmen were unwilling to stand a siege, which was unlikely to be successful, would destroy their town, and would hazard their extensive investment in landed estates. The Williamites found the merchants and townsmen of Galway 'well pleased that the English government is again restored among them'. Most of the townsmen remained in Galway and Ginkel received a civic welcome.[28]

3. O'DONNELL CHANGES SIDES

Balldearg O'Donnell had become very disillusioned about his reception in Ireland and attributed most of his troubles to the hostility of Tyrconnell. He felt that he was not given the status to which he was entitled by his military experience and the number of Ulstermen he had raised. Instead of a major-general's commission he was given that of brigadier when Tyrconnell returned to Ireland in January 1691. Arms and clothing were refused to his men until the arrival of St Ruth, who 'of his own authority . . . gave him 500 coats, 50 muskets and 400 swords'.[29] This would not go very far: a French document dated 10 June 1691 details the units of O'Donnell's brigade, 'which are not

---

[25] *Jacobite narrative*, p. 152.   [26] *Anal. Hib.*, xxi. 220–1.

[27] Story, *Continuation*, pp. 172–3.

[28] *Dublin Intelligence*, 11 Aug. 1691; Story, *Continuation*, p. 173.

[29] 'Account of Balldearg O'Donnell's conduct' in J. O'Donovan, 'The O'Donnells in exile' (*Duffy's Hibernian Magazine*, i. 50–6).

being supplied with arms or clothing'. The list contains thirteen battalions of infantry and three squadrons of cavalry, a total of 9,100.[30]

O'Donnell took no part at Aughrim. Story commented that 'the heat of expectation from this Irish deliverer was now pretty well cooled'.[31] His horde of Ulstermen with their accompanying wives, children and cattle must have been a heavy burden on the over-taxed resources of Connacht. The *Life of James* refers to them as 'a rabble that destroyed the country, ruined the inhabitants and prevented the regular forces from drawing that subsistence that they might otherwise have had from the people'. O'Donnell was suspected of plotting to restore an independent Gaelic Ireland.[32] At the time of Aughrim he claimed to have orders from St Ruth to burn or garrison all the strong houses or castles he should think fit, and to retire farther into the country. Soon after the battle he burned Tuam, apparently on the ground that it was preparing to receive the Williamite army.[33] His earlier offer to reinforce Galway had been rejected, but on a request from d'Usson he made a belated approach from the north, only to find himself barred by part of Ginkel's army. Story thought that O'Donnell had made no serious effort to relieve Galway and 'that his design was to keep among the mountains till he could make terms for himself, upon which account he writ to the general before our army removed from Galway'.[34] According to O'Kelly, O'Donnell heard that he was being blamed for failing to come in time to the aid of Galway, and this, together with his acute shortage of supplies, induced him to bargain with Ginkel.[35] O'Donnell's demands were that his Ulstermen should be employed in William's forces in Flanders, and that he himself should be given the rank of brigadier, receive a sum of money to satisfy his creditors, and be recommended by Ginkel for the grant of the estate and title formerly enjoyed by his ancestors.[36] Ginkel wrote to William to ask for orders and said that in the meantime he had arranged a truce with O'Donnell and had asked him to keep in the neighbourhood of Sligo. He added that O'Donnell's

[30] Min. guerre, A1 1083, no. 75.
[31] Story, *Continuation*, p. 151.
[32] *James II*, ii. pp. 434, 461.
[33] Story, *Continuation*, p. 152.
[34] Ibid.
[35] O'Kelly, p. 141.
[36] Amerongen Huisarchief, 342.

submission would be an important gain and 'that the people of Ulster have great confidence in him'.[37]

Ginkel's negotiations with O'Donnell had some effect on the situation in Sligo, which was still held by Sir Teague O'Regan and secured the Jacobite position in north Connacht.[38] Sligo was under strong pressure from a Williamite force advancing from Donegal under the command of Colonel John Mitchelburne, who had taken a leading part in the siege of Derry. Mitchelburne sent O'Regan a copy of the July proclamation (accompanied by a bottle of usquebaugh and a packet of snuff) and suggested that he should take advantage of the terms by surrendering Sligo. O'Regan agreed to surrender if he were not relieved within ten days, and he obtained Sarsfield's approval to his action. At the same time he wrote to O'Donnell, who had no objection to showing the Williamites that he and his Ulstermen were a force to be reckoned with. O'Donnell moved his men to the neighbourhood of Sligo, Mitchelburne retired, and O'Regan regarded himself as freed from the undertaking to surrender. William was informed that 'the foolishness of Colonel Mitchelburne before Sligo had encouraged that place to defend itself and O'Donnell to play one of his Irish tricks instead of submitting as he intended'.[39]

O'Donnell had made his point and soon afterwards came to an agreement with Ginkel on terms satisfactory to himself, though his abandonment of the Jacobite cause was not to the liking of many of his followers. O'Kelly tried to dissuade him, but without success: 'revolting from his natural prince, he unhappily joined with the sworn enemies of his country'.[40] O'Donnell now agreed to take part in the Williamite attack on Sligo, collaborating in an advance from the south with Sir Albert Conyngham: an unusual partnership of Donegal Gael and Donegal planter. The correspondence of the Williamite officers shows that O'Donnell's men mutinied and demanded to be allowed to join Sarsfield. The distribution of guineas and threats of seizing mutineers' cattle enabled O'Donnell to rally

[37] *Cal. S.P. dom., 1690–1*, pp. 475–6.

[38] See Simms, 'Sligo in the Jacobite war' in *Ir. Sword*, vii. 132–5.

[39] Carmarthen to William, 28 Aug. 1691 (*Cal. S.P. dom., 1690–1*, p. 501).

[40] O'Kelly, p. 143.

part of his force, but it is clear that his Ulstermen put little value on the peace terms offered by the Williamites. O'Regan's men made a successful sally from Sligo on a foggy September morning and took Conyngham and O'Donnell by surprise. Conyngham was killed; O'Donnell 'escaped the nearest ever man did and if they had got him he had been presently hanged'.[41]

Sligo was now heavily invested from all sides. Mitchelburne succeeded in entering the town, and the resistance was confined to the 'green fort on the hill'. This was threatened by fresh forces advancing from the south under Lord Granard, who had transferred his allegiance to William. O'Regan finally decided to surrender and the articles were signed on September 14.[42] The garrison was allowed to march out with full honours of war and made its way to Limerick, the only place of consequence still left to the Jacobites. Those of the inhabitants who wished to stay behind were to have protection for their persons and property; protection was also extended to the clergy of the district.

[41] Clarke corr., xi, nos 1065, 1069, 1089, 1097, 1105, 1111.
[42] A copy of the agreement is in Amerongen Huisarchief, 356.

XV

THE TREATY OF LIMERICK

~~~~~~

1. TYRCONNELL'S LAST DAYS

IMMEDIATELY AFTER Aughrim Tyrconnell had written to
James that help from France must be sent at once, or else the
Irish must be allowed to make terms. The French decided to
send help.[1] They hoped to keep the war in Ireland going, so as
to lock up a Williamite army over the winter of 1691–2.

The main Irish army was now concentrated in the neighbourhood of Limerick, the only place of consequence left to it after
the surrender of Galway. Garrisons were put into Clare Castle
and Ross Castle with the object of keeping the counties of Clare
and Kerry under Jacobite control.[2] When part of the Galway
garrison had joined it the manpower of the army was considerable, but only half the number had arms. At a review held
at the beginning of August there were found to be 18,000
infantry, 3,000 cavalry and 2,500 dragoons. But morale was
low. The French commissary, Fumeron, reported that there
was general consternation and that both troops and civilians
thought the war as good as lost, now that Limerick was the
only place left to them: 'if they hold out till October, as we are
urging them to do so as to gain the winter, it is only in the hope
that some have of getting help from France to enable them to
drive out the enemy, and that others have that the king will

---

[1] *James II*, ii. 459.
[2] Min. guerre, A1 1080, no. 178.

send enough ships to bring them to France'.[3] The French generals, d'Usson and de Tessé, were equally pessimistic. They told Louvois's son and successor that the position was unbelievably ramshackle (*délabré*), and that they were dealing with people who changed their minds from one day to the next.[4] They told Louis that the cavalry were alarmed at the shortage of forage, and that the infantry were no less alarmed by their officers' talk of capitulation as the sole alternative to prolonged misery. They thought the only solution was to send a French army and take Irish troops to France in exchange. Tyrconnell wrote to Louis that the whole army was tired of serving without pay. He was afraid that a number of individuals might try to settle their own terms with the enemy, and so he was making all the officers and men, beginning with himself, take an oath of fidelity. They were to swear not to make individual bargains and not to capitulate without James's permission. The French generals thought this step would do more harm than good: it would frighten the troops and shake their confidence.[5] Fumeron was also doubtful of its effectiveness. Henry Luttrell and Purcell were among those who were persuading others not to take the oath.[6]

Next came the sensational news that Luttrell had been arrested on a charge of corresponding with the enemy. The French generals would have hanged him on the spot; they sympathized with the position of Tyrconnell, who was doing his best and unable to trust any of the army. They thought it fortunate that Sarsfield was on the spot: Luttrell was his friend, but like a good soldier Sarsfield had obeyed the order to put him under arrest.[7] When Luttrell was court-martialled the majority of the court held that he did not deserve the death penalty, but Tyrconnell who presided kept him under arrest in the castle, where he remained till Limerick surrendered.[8]

[3] Fumeron to Barbesieux, 7/17 Aug. 1691 (ibid. no. 192).

[4] D'Usson and de Tessé to Barbesieux, 7/17 Aug. 1691 (ibid., no. 198).

[5] Same to Louis, 7/17 Aug. 1691 (ibid., no. 199); Tyrconnell to Louis, 5/15 Aug. 1691 (*Anal.Hib.*, xxi. 220).

[6] Min. guerre, A1 1080, no. 192.

[7] D'Usson and de Tessé to Louis, 7/17 Aug. 1691 (ibid., no. 202); same to Barbesieux, 7/17 Aug. 1691 (ibid., 1083, no. 96).

[8] *Jacobite narrative*, p. 149.

Ginkel threatened reprisals against his Irish prisoners if Luttrell or anyone else who proposed to make terms were shot.[9]

A few days after Luttrell's arrest Tyrconnell was taken ill after dining with d'Usson – apparently the result of drinking ratafia (crushed apricot stones in brandy). The stroke proved fatal; he died on August 14, and it was rumoured that he had been poisoned.[10] Porter, one of the Williamite lords justices, thought that Tyrconnell's death would bring the war to an early end: 'it is his authority and countenance that attached the Irish to the French interest'.[11] The writer of the 'Light to the blind' also thought that the loss of Tyrconnell was a fatal blow to the Jacobite cause. O'Kelly, who made no reference to Luttrell's arrest, took the view that Tyrconnell and his supporters were all along anxious to settle with William: 'his death was much lamented by his friends, and not less by the English who cried him up for an honest man and a lover of peace; they gave out that he was poisoned by Sarsfield and the French commanders'.[12]

James had issued a sealed commission appointing Tyrconnell's successors. The civil government was entrusted to three lords justices – the lord chancellor (Alexander Fitton, Lord Gawsworth), Francis Plowden (one of the revenue commissioners), and Sir Richard Nagle. It was remarked that the first two were Englishmen and therefore unpopular. The army was put under the control of d'Usson, the senior French general.[13] There was no place for Sarsfield in these arrangements The new administration had no more success in resolving the differences of opinion on the Jacobite side. Tyrconnell's opponents continued to agitate against French policy. As part of their campaign they distributed copies of Tyrconnell's 'will', a strongly-worded piece of anti-French propaganda, which began:

My dear fellow-countrymen, if ever you are capable of thought it is now more needed than ever, as you are on the verge of ruin; to wait for help from France is a mere chimera. . . . I do not doubt that some

[9] *Finch MSS*, iii. 212.

[10] Story, *Continuation*, p. 187.

[11] Porter to Clarke, 19 Aug. 1691 (Clarke corr., x, no. 875).

[12] *Jacobite narrative*, p. 155; O'Kelly, p. 144.

[13] *Jacobite narrative*, p. 282; d'Usson and de Tessé to Barbesieux, 15/25 Aug. 1691 (Min. guerre, A1 1083, no. 97).

who have more loyalty than sense say 'let us wait for the king's consent'. I have myself made the same proposal in public, not that I thought it reasonable, but because I knew that Lord Lucan and Luttrell were looking for an opportunity to ruin my reputation with the deluded masses.[14]

This propaganda was so bad for morale that the Jacobite lords justices asked the French for money to distribute to the troops in order to convince them that the French really meant to help them. The cavalry and dragoons were beginning to desert, and the army was a whole was very short of supplies. To meet the critical situation the French reluctantly parted with 50,000 livres (*c.* £4000).[15]

2. LIMERICK INVESTED

Ginkel showed his usual caution, and did not establish his position before the walls of Limerick till over a month after the surrender of Galway. He was very reluctant to undertake active siege operations. William's failure of the previous year and the difficulty of transporting the artillery from Athlone weighed heavily with him, and he hoped that the Irish might be induced to surrender without further fighting. At the most he favoured a blockade, rather than formal siege operations. He told the Dublin lords justices that he was in favour of granting really generous terms: 'my opinion was always to finish the war by giving the Irish a free pardon, if it could be done soonest that way; for one summer's war costs the king more than all the forfeitures will amount to'.[16] The lords justices were well aware that Protestants in Ireland had no liking for generosity to Catholics and hoped that the war would be ended by force of arms, supported by the minimum of concessions. They put considerable pressure on Ginkel to begin operations against Limerick; they favoured a formal siege rather than a blockade, which would be a sign of weakness and 'induce the factious to hold out, reconcile their animosities and expect help from France; and before they can be starved out the year will be so

[14] *Anal. Hib.*, xxi. 226–7.

[15] Fumeron to Barbesieux, 8/18 Sept. 1691 (Min. guerre, A1 1081, no. 155).

[16] Ginkel to lords justices, 24 July 1691 (*H.M.C.*, *rep. 4*, app., p. 322).

far gone that it will be too late to send any of the forces hence to any part of the world'.[17]

Ginkel's cautious advance took him back across the Shannon by Banagher Bridge and on through Birr and Nenagh towards Limerick. At Nenagh he was joined by Coningsby, who was anxious to keep a watch on Ginkel's progress: he was afraid that the weather would break and that the war would be still unfinished at the end of the campaigning season.[18] News came in that the Irish were inclined to accept the terms of the July proclamation, but had 'surmises of the parliament not making it good'.[19] To encourage the peace party Ginkel issued a further declaration at Nenagh on August 11, extending his previous offer by another ten days and promising to those who brought in troops or surrendered a town or castle 'the same or a better post or employment in the army than they left and a reward suitable to the merit of the service'. Copies of the declaration were distributed by Williamite spies to the Irish army.[20] A trickle of deserters came over, but there was no general response to the offer.

Bad weather and the slow movement of the guns delayed the approach to Limerick. As usual Ginkel hesitated. He called a council of war to advise him whether to make a regular siege or to content himself with a blockade. The Danish commander was strongly in favour of active operations and though it would have a bad effect, on both military and political grounds, to do nothing more than blockade Limerick.[21] The majority of the generals voted against a regular siege, and Ginkel himself was anxious to avoid it; he thought that the position of the defence at Limerick was very strong and that the Williamite army might suffer heavily. His reluctance to attack was critically received by William, and he was urged to take more vigorous measures.[22]

[17] Lords justices to Ginkel, 27 July 1691 (*H.M.C, rep. 4,* app. p. 323).

[18] Story, *Continuation,* pp. 181–2; Clarke to Ginkel, 1 Aug. 1691 (Clarke corr., x, no. 804.)

[19] Capt Peter Poore to Major Malcolm Hamilton, 8 Aug. 1691 (ibid., no. 875).

[20] Story, *Continuation,* pp. 184–5, 190.

[21] *Danish force,* pp. 127–8.

[22] Ginkel to Coningsby, 29 Aug. 1691 (de Ros MSS 12/106); same to lords justices, 7 Sept. 1691 (ibid., 12/109); Bentinck to Ginkel, 17/27 Aug., 8/18 Sept. 1691 (Japikse, iii. 251–2).

It was not till August 25 that Ginkel made his approach to Limerick in force. The Irish made little effort to hold positions outside the walls, and Ginkel had no difficulty in occupying the two forts – Ireton's and Cromwell's – to the south-east and south of the Irish town. Lines were drawn round the Irish town and batteries set up. The wet weather had made the ground swampy and Ginkel could not move his guns close to the walls as William had done in 1690. His first line of attack was from the south-west, which had the advantage of contact with a Williamite fleet that had come into the Shannon. The ships brought stores and also some heavy guns and mortars which added to Ginkel's firepower. A bombardment began, which damaged houses and started fires, but had little effect on the walls. It was therefore decided to try a new approach from the east, setting up a battery to fire at the English town across the Abbey river (the branch of the Shannon which enclosed the King's Island). This was ready on September 8. There were twenty-five heavy guns (24- and 18-pounders) to batter the walls, field-pieces to fire red-hot shot, and mortars to lob in bombs.[23] Story described the cannonade: 'it put the Irish in such a fright that a great many of them wished themselves in another place, never having heard such a noise before'.[24] A sizeable breach was made in the English-town wall and much damage was done to houses. Fires were started, one of which set a store ablaze in which there were eighty-four barrels of brandy.[25]

The Irish reacted strongly to Ginkel's attack. They had a battery of eight guns on the island, which fired briskly at the Williamites. An Irish party crossed the Abbey river in boats and burned the woolsacks that the Williamites had planned to use for the crossing. To replace the woolsacks floats were made out of empty barrels, but Ginkel decided not to use them: he was put off by reports of a well-palisaded ditch outside the English-town wall and by the general strength of the King's Island position.[26]

[23] Story, *Continuation*, pp. 188–210. See map on p. 164.

[24] Story, *Continuation*, p. 210.

[25] De Tessé to Barbesieux, 16/26 Sept. 1691 (Min. guerre, A1 1081, no. 166).

[26] Story, *Continuation*, pp. 209–13.

The French commissary was encouraged by the slowness of Ginkel's progress: 'as they have already been fifteen days before the town without having come nearer than they were the first day I do not think they have resolved to take it by force, but that they count on their intelligence or that they will content themselves with bombarding us'.[27] He emphasized that it was very important that the French fleet should be sent soon, as otherwise the Irish would capitulate and it would be very difficult to get any of them to come to France: they were afraid that they would lose their property and that their families in Ireland would be badly treated.[28]

On the night of September 15/16 the Williamites crossed the main stream of the Shannon above Limerick. The tin boats that Ginkel had brought from Athlone were laid across to an island from which the water could be forded to the Clare side. In the morning the Williamites reached the farther bank, meeting only token resistance from Brigadier Clifford's dragoons, whose commander was more than suspected of treachery. O'Kelly claimed that he had warned Sarsfield that Clifford was unreliable, and had urged him to take command himself or to send a trustworthy officer to guard the crossing. Fumeron said there was every reason to suspect Clifford who, without firing a shot or warning other units, had let the enemy cross the river. Clifford was put under arrest and his failure to stop the crossing was one of the major arguments for the subsequent capitulation. The Irish dragoons and a weak infantry force which was also in the area fled before the Williamite advance, some making for the Thomond bridge which joined the English town to the Clare side, and others scattering into the countryside. The Irish cavalry, which was not far off, retreated hastily in the direction of Ennis. At the time the Williamites did not try to exploit their success, otherwise than to post a battalion at the Clare end of the bridge of boats. The rest of the force crossed back to the Limerick side of the river.[29]

---

[27] Fumeron to Barbesieux, 8/18 Sept. 1691 (Min. guerre, A1 1081, no. 155).

[28] Fumeron to Barbesieux, 16/26 Sept. 1691 (ibid., no. 164).

[29] Ibid.; O'Kelly, pp. 151–3; Story, *Continuation*, pp. 216–18; *Jacobite narrative*, pp. 161–2.

The same day – September 16 – Ginkel published another declaration, giving a final eight days' extension to the offer of July. He assured the Irish that parliament had done nothing to invalidate the offer, 'as they are falsely made to believe by some persons who live by sacrificing their country to the tyranny and ambition of France'. He ended with a solemn warning: 'if they should still continue obstinate and neglect to lay hold on this favour, which is the last that will be offered them, they must be answerable for the blood and destruction they draw upon themselves; for I hereby acquit myself before God and the world and wash my hands of it'.[30]

The declaration had an immediate effect on Irish opinion. Next day the French generals told Louis that everyone was thinking of capitulation, and that Sarsfield told them they had waited too long. The generals did their best to reassure the infantry in Limerick and went round the posts promising further distributions of pay. They thought the morale of the infantry was holding, but were less confident of the cavalry and dragoons who were in County Clare away from French influence.[31]

Everything now turned on whether relief from France would arrive in time. Ginkel wrote to the lords justices in Dublin that the reduction of Ireland entirely depended on intercepting the French relief force. He would do what he could to put pressure on the Irish, but if the French were not stopped at sea he took no responsibility for the consequences.[32] It was fortunate for the Williamites that the dispatch of the French convoy was so badly delayed. A series of letters from the port official at Brest to the minister of war in Paris tells a story of administrative confusion and procrastination. On August 24/September 3 it was reported that the convoy could not sail till September 2/12 or 5/15. On September 1/11 it was still hoped that it would sail that week. But on September 28/October 8 it had not yet left Brest; arms were still being loaded, though Admiral Chateaurenault had received orders to sail at once. On October 2/12 provisions were still awaited, and it was feared that the convoy would not be able to sail till the end of the month. In fact it left Camaret Bay

[30] Story, *Continuation*, pp. 219–30.

[31] D'Usson and de Tessé to Louis, 17/27 Sept. 1691 (Min. guerre, A1 1081, no. 168).

[32] Ginkel to lords justices, 18 Sept. 1691 (*H.M.C., rep. 4*, app., p. 323).

247

on October 13/23, ten days after the treaty of Limerick had been signed. The ships did not come into the Shannon till October 20/30.[33] The great delay in the dispatch of the convoy effectively stultified French policy and was a major factor in bringing about the surrender of Limerick. The Williamites had little hope of being able to intercept the French ships and their naval officers were reluctant to patrol the stormy Irish coast.[34]

Ginkel's position was not easy. It was already much later in the season than when the previous year's siege of Limerick was raised. He was running short of cannon balls and began to put his heavy guns on the ships – an indication of impending withdrawal. He decided that his best plan was to exploit the crossing of the Shannon, which was still covered by the Williamite battalion without challenge from the Irish army. Deserters told him that he could not hope to take Limerick unless he cut its communications with County Clare.[35] On September 22 he himself crossed the bridge of boats with a considerable force and pushed forward along the Clare bank of the river to the Irish works at the approaches to Thomond bridge. There was a sharp fight, and the Irish were supported by fire from King John's castle and the walls. But the Williamite grenadiers showed great spirit and pushed the Irish back to the bridge. A French major pulled up the drawbridge and left the retreating Irish cut off. They suffered heavy casualties: 'before the killing was over they were laid in heaps upon the bridge higher than the ledges of it'. A number were pushed into the gap left by raising the drawbridge and were drowned.[36] This success still left Ginkel with the river between him and the English town, but he had now cut the garrison off from the cavalry and the Clare countryside. The disaster at the bridge had a great effect

[33] Min. guerre, AI 1081, nos 1, 14, 36, 45, 61; Fumeron to Barbesieux, 6/16 Nov. 1691 (ibid., no. 200). The French evidence contradicts a report that 33 French ships put into Dingle Bay about Oct. 7 (*Dublin Intelligence*, 20 Oct. 1691; Story, *Continuation*, p. 273).

[34] Nottingham to lords justices, 28 Aug. 1691 (*Finch MSS*, iii. 237).

[35] Ginkel to lords justices, 18 Sept. 1691 (*H.M.C., rep. 4*, app., p. 323); Story, *Continuation*, p. 224.

[36] Ibid., pp. 224–5; *Jacobite narrative*, pp. 166, 295–6. There is a good contemporary picture of the bridge and walls, made by Thomas Phillips in 1685 (N.L.I., MS 3037).

on Irish morale and increased ill feeling between the Irish and the French.

3. NEGOTIATIONS BEGIN

On the next day – September 23 – the Jacobites held a council of war at which all the generals, French and Irish, were present. There are two versions of the proceedings, in English and in French. They are identical except for the titles. The English version is headed: 'the reasons the French generals gave Major-General Wauchope and Lord Lucan for the capitulation'. The French version is headed: 'motives that led the Irish to capitulate, the general officers being assembled in council of war'.[37] The Irish blamed the French and the French blamed the Irish. Great stress was laid on Clifford having allowed the Williamites to bridge the Shannon and cross to the Clare side. It was also stated that provisions were running short, that there was no news of the convoy leaving Brest, and that it was not certain that the convoy would be able to get past the English ships in the Shannon and their batteries on the shore.

All these reasons maturely examined made us desire General Ginkel to let us retire into France with such of the troops as had a mind to go... having no hopes to establish the king but by going into France there to make the war, being not able to make it here. And if we had stayed to the last day of our food we could not obtain any capitulation and the enemy might therefore have our troops: whereas now by passing them into France we may be in a condition not only to oppose the common enemy but also to make a descent into England or Scotland, if it pleased God to give the French fleet such a victory over the enemies' fleet as it had last season.

That day (September 23) Ginkel had written to the lords justices that he still hoped to take Limerick provided help did not come from France, but that it was impossible for him to take the town by assault. He had seen how vigorously the Irish had defended themselves the previous day: 'they do not fear fire and were very steady in the charge'. That evening he sent a second letter to report a dramatic change in the situation. Sarsfield and Wauchope had just asked for a capitulation and a cease-fire.

[37] B.M., Eg. MS 2618, f. 171; Min. guerre, A1 1081, no. 178. Wauchope was a Scottish Jacobite.

Ginkel now hoped for a rapid and satisfactory end to the war; he asked the lords justices to come to Kilkenny, where they could see the proposed terms, and then to come on to Limerick to conclude them.[38]

The leading part in the negotiations was taken by Sarsfield (Lord Lucan), who had been the centre of resistance in the previous year. His chief interest seems to have been in getting permission for the Irish army to go to France. According to George Clarke, the Williamite secretary-at-war, the first question put by the Irish was whether they might 'go and serve where they would'. Ginkel at once agreed and the truce was begun on that understanding.[39] Letting the Irish go to France was not an aspect that had so far been considered by the Williamites. Their peace terms had been confined to toleration and restoration of land, coupled with an offer of serving on William's side. To allow the Irish army to continue the war in France might have seemed an unacceptable demand. But Ginkel made no difficulty about granting it and agreeing to provide the transport. He seems to have regarded this part of the negotiations (the military articles) as entirely within his own province, for which he neither sought nor obtained the concurrence of the lords justices. It was over the treatment of those who were to stay in Ireland (the civil articles) that the hard bargaining took place. Any extension of the terms offered in the July proclamation would have to be within the limits set by government policy. Queen Mary had authorized the lords justices to use their discretion in the grant of terms if Ginkel was unable to take Limerick before winter set in. She approved of them going to Limerick to negotiate, provided that the terms to be granted were consistent with the laws of Ireland as they were in Charles II's reign.[40]

Preliminary discussions took place on the following days between Ginkel and the Irish leaders. The latter, besides Sarsfield, included the Catholic archbishops of Armagh and Cashel and Sir Toby Butler, the solicitor-general.[41] The dis-

---

[38] Ginkel to lords justices, 23 Sept. 1691 – two letters (*H.M.C., rep. 4,* app., p. 323).

[39] *Leyborne-Popham MSS*, p. 281.

[40] Queen to lords justices, 28 Aug. 1691 (*Finch MSS*, iii. 237).

[41] Story, *Continuation*, pp. 228–32.

cussions were conducted with great courtesy. Ginkel recognized Sarsfield's Jacobite title; Sarsfield brought a boatload of claret for the Williamite officers.[42] The archbishops as well as the laity dined with Ginkel. On September 26 it was agreed that there should be regular negotiations, and hostages were exchanged. Four senior Williamite officers were sent into Limerick, and four of the Irish nobility were sent out to the Williamite camp.[43] On September 27 the Irish sent out their proposals for a settlement. They were as follows:

1. a complete indemnity;

2. restoration of all Irish Catholics to the estates they held before the revolution;

3. free liberty of worship and a priest for each parish;

4. the right of Irish Catholics to follow all professions and hold military and civil offices;

5. the maintenance of the Irish army in William's service, in case they were willing to fight against France or any other enemy;

6. the right of Irish Catholics to be members of corporations and to enjoy trading rights in towns and cities;

7. ratification of the above terms by act of parliament.

According to Story these proposals were pressed with particular vigour by Dominick Maguire, the archbishop of Armagh. He appears to have returned from a recent mission to France, during which he had discussed the Irish situation with James and had received assurances that help would be forthcoming. This may have encouraged him to hold out for much more favourable terms than had previously been offered.[44]

The Irish demands would have given Catholics much better treatment than they had had in Charles II's reign, and they were rejected out of hand. Ginkel answered that 'though he was in a manner a stranger to the laws of England, yet he understood that those things they insisted on were so far contradictory to them and dishonourable to himself that he could not grant any such terms'.[45] The Irish asked him what he would agree to,

[42] *Rawdon papers*, pp. 361–2.

[43] Story, *Continuation*, p. 230. The Irish hostages were Lords Westmeath, Iveagh, Trimleston and Louth.

[44] Story, *Continuation*, pp. 230–1; *Coll. Hib.*, iv. 15–16.

[45] Story, *Continuation*, p. 231.

and he sent them twelve propositions, which formed the basis of the civil articles. A full conference was held next day at Ginkel's headquarters, attended by Sarsfield, Wauchope, Purcell, the archbishops of Armagh and Cashel, and by three lawyers, Garrett Dillon, Sir Toby Butler and Colonel John Browne of Westport; all the Williamite general officers were also present. It is to be noted that the Jacobite lords justices took no part in the negotiations. A long debate took place on Ginkel's proposals. Sir Toby Butler asked what was meant by the title: 'articles granted by Lieutenant-General Ginkel to all persons now in the city of Limerick and in the Irish army, that is in the counties of Clare, Kerry, Cork and Mayo and other garrisons that are in their possession'. George Clarke answered that the terms were being offered to those who were still in a condition to offer opposition, a definition that would exclude the civilian population in the Irish-held countryside. Sarsfield objected to this and said he 'would lay his bones in these old walls rather than not take care of those who stuck by them all along'. The terms were therefore extended to include all those under the protection of the Irish army in the counties named. This extension, which was found to be omitted from the final copy, was the celebrated 'missing clause', over which there was to be much argument.[46]

This point decided, the discussions were on matters of detail and were settled without much difficulty. The first article laid down the standard of religious toleration to be extended to Catholics in Ireland as a whole. They were to have the same privileges in the practice of their religion as they had enjoyed in Charles II's reign or as were consistent with the laws of Ireland. As soon as possible an Irish parliament would be held, in which William and Mary would endeavour to procure such further security for Catholics 'in that particular as may preserve them from any disturbance upon the account of their said religion'. The second and fifth articles laid down conditions for the inhabitants of Limerick or any other garrison still held by the Irish army; for those under the protection of the Irish army in the four counties named, to which County Limerick was now added; and for all officers and soldiers still in arms. If they were

[46] *Leyborne-Popham MSS*, p. 280; Simms, 'The original draft of the civil articles of Limerick' in *I.H.S..*, viii. 37–44.

prepared to submit to William and Mary and take a simple oath of allegiance, they would be pardoned, and be allowed to keep their property and carry on their professions as freely as they had done in Charles II's reign. If they were gentlemen, they could ride with a sword and a case of pistols and keep a gun in their houses. The terms were not extended to those who had been killed or captured or had already surrendered unconditionally. The requirement of submission and an oath of allegiance meant that those who chose to go to France were excluded from the benefit of the terms, and would be liable to lose their property. The third and fourth articles dealt with particular cases of persons who were out of Ireland at the time. The sixth article prescribed that, in the interests of peace, no law-suits should lie for acts committed by either side during the war. In the course of the negotiations the form of the articles was changed. What had been a unilateral grant of terms by Ginkel was altered to an agreement between the lords justices and Ginkel on the one side and 'the right honourable Patrick Earl of Lucan, Piercy Viscount Galmoy, Colonel Nicholas Purcell, Colonel Nicholas Cusack, Sir Toby Butler, Colonel Garrett Dillon and Colonel John Browne on the other'. The Williamite signatories undertook that William and Mary would ratify the articles within eight months and 'use their utmost endeavours that the same shall be ratified and confirmed in parliament'.

These changes were made to meet Irish suspicions that terms granted by Ginkel might be repudiated by the civil authority. The lords justices reached the camp on the evening of October 1. On the next day all the points of drafting were settled and orders given to prepare the final copy, which was signed on October 3.[47] A belated addition was made for the benefit of John Browne (one of the signatories) who in addition to being a colonel and a lawyer was the owner of iron-works in County Mayo. Sarsfield and Tyrconnell had commandeered Browne's products, which he claimed had been pledged as security for loans he had taken from Protestants. He therefore got a clause inserted in the articles levying a charge on every estate restored to a Catholic under the treaty. This clause had a long subsequent history,

[47] *The diary of the siege and surrender of Limerick*, p. 17.

involving complicated accounts and several acts of Parliament.[48]

Ginkel found Sarsfield a surprisingly reasonable negotiator. From their experience of the previous year the Williamites had expected that he would be the most intransigent of the Irish leaders and that even if Limerick surrendered they might be faced with a long guerrilla war against forces led by Sarsfield. It was debated whether in these circumstances the war should be regarded as still in progress or whether Sarsfield and his followers should be treated as mere rebels and if captured denied the status of prisoners of war.[49] It was therefore a great relief to Ginkel to find that Sarsfield had initiated the peace-talks. He had been authorized by William to promise Sarsfield an estate if satisfactory terms were concluded. Sarsfield, however, was bent on making a career for himself in France, so that the grant of a Irish estate would not suit him. But he was not averse from gaining some financial advantage and he asked that he might be allowed to send back wine and other French goods on the ships that were returning after taking the Irish troops to France. Ginkel undertook to recommend the request and a quota of three hundred tons was fixed. The agreement was honoured, and several of Sarsfield's cargoes which were seized as enemy property by the customs officers were released on William's orders.[50] We need not suppose that this privilege affected Sarsfield's attitude to the negotiations. The primary considerations for a soldier must have been the fact that an Irish army could be kept in being and continue the fight in France.

According to O'Kelly there was general astonishment at the 'sudden, unexpected, prodigious change'. Sarsfield, 'who (as they all believed) would be the last man to hearken to a treaty, was now the most earnest to press it on: a mystery which requires some further time to unravel'.[51] George Clarke thought that Sarsfield was moved by personal ambition: 'he reckoned on

[48] The texts of the military and civil articles are given in Story, *Continuation*, pp. 239–56. A recent version of both articles is in *English historical documents*, viii. 765–70.

[49] Nottingham to Sidney, 28 July 1691 (*Finch MSS*, iii. 181).

[50] Ginkel to lords justices, 28 Sept. 1691 (B.M., Harl. MS 7524, f. 99); *Cal. treas. papers, 1697–1702*, p. 114; *Cal. S.P. dom., 1693*, p. 5.

[51] O'Kelly, pp. 154–5.

making himself considerable in France by bringing over such a body of troops'.[52]

4. REASONS FOR THE SURRENDER

The motives for the surrender were the subject of much speculation on the part of both Jacobites and Williamites. The views expressed on both sides point to the conclusion that psychological rather than military reasons were responsible for the capitulation. When fighting ceased, Ginkel was as far from being able to take Limerick by assault as he was at the beginning of the siege. The only breach was in the wall of the English town on King's Island, and the garrison continued to conduct a vigorous defence up to the time of the cease-fire. The season was getting late and Ginkel would soon have had to withdraw. Though there are references to an impending shortage of supplies, both Jacobite and Williamite writers agree that food would have lasted for a considerable time longer. Limerick was never reduced to the plight of Derry. A major cause was army discontent, particularly among the cavalry officers in County Clare, hemmed in and short of forage. Many of them had estates which might be saved by bargaining before it was too late. The disaster at Aughrim, the example of Galway, and the reflection that Limerick was the only place of consequence left had a depressing effect on Irish morale generally. The failure of the promised help to arrive from France was an important contributory cause. It is evident that there was no love lost between the allies, and that the idea of prolonging resistance into the winter simply to suit French long-term strategy had little appeal for the Irish. Paradoxically the French, who had so often complained of Irish characteristics, were eager to bring as many Irish as possible to France, and a great many of the Irish were ready to accept the offer.

One of the few subjects on which O'Kelly and the writer of the 'Light to the blind' agree is that the decision to accept Ginkel's terms was disastrous and unnecessary. O'Kelly says that he himself was deliberately excluded from the negotiations as it was known that he would oppose them.[53] The writer of the

[52] *Leyborne-Popham MSS*, p. 281.
[53] O'Kelly, pp. 154–6.

'Light to the blind' in a long and interesting analysis discusses the pros and cons of the surrender and concludes that it would not have taken place if Tyrconnell had lived. He makes no mention at all of Sarsfield's part in the negotiations. He argues that the defences of Limerick were stronger in 1691 than they had been at the time of William's siege in the previous year; that Ginkel gained no advantage by crossing to the Clare side of the Shannon, a move that over-extended his resources; and that separation from the cavalry did not affect the garrison of a walled town. There were plenty of provisions and ammunition, and a fleet from France was daily expected. The writer called it a 'mock siege' and attributed the capitulation to the lack of a leader: 'there wanted a *pater patriae*, a father of the country, that is a man all on fire with zeal to preserve his country, his religion, his liberty and his king's prerogative, and at the same time a man commissioned with the highest power. . . . If the duke of Tyrconnell were then alive . . . he would not hearken to any offer of a surrender, because he expected to retrieve the country by spinning out the war.' The Jacobite lords justices had 'loyalty enough and zeal for the welfare of the Catholic people; but whether they had skill enough to over-rule the remonstrances for a surrender which the great officers of the army made is the question'.[54]

On the Williamite side George Clarke commented: 'it may appear very strange that a numerous garrison, not oppressed by any want, should give up a town which nobody was in a condition to take from them, at a time when those who lay before it had actually drawn off their guns and were preparing to march away, and when that garrison did daily expect a squadron of ships to come to their relief, if they had needed any'. He thought that the prospect of a military career in France was the deciding factor. Other causes were the cutting of communications between the cavalry and the town, and disappointment with French help; also the French officers were tired of Ireland and glad of an excuse to get away.[55]

Story thought the Irish could well have held Limerick. They had as many infantry in it as were in the besieging army: 'and notwithstanding all the stories told us by deserters about the

[54] *Jacobite narrative*, pp. 158, 175-6.
[55] *Leyborne-Popham MSS*, pp. 279-81.

scarcity of provisions they had a quantity of the finest French biscuit I ever tasted, sufficient for the whole garrison for two months'. He also refers to a church heaped full of oats. His conclusion was that the Irish were either weary of war or jealous of one another, or both.[56]

Should the Irish have stood out for better terms? The writer of the 'Light to the blind' thought that the negotiators agreed too easily with Ginkel and that they should have insisted on the free exercise of their religion and the restoration to Catholics of all the estates and rights they enjoyed in the reign of Charles II.[57] The first article gave the impression that there would be no less, and possibly more, religious toleration than in Charles II's reign. But in fact the laws of Ireland guaranteed no religious privileges to Catholics. The act of uniformity required all to conform to the established church, and such tolerance as was granted was by connivance and not by right. O'Kelly had ground for saying that 'the articles were not so warily drawn but room was left for captious exceptions; neither was any article made for assuring the true worship'.[58] The first article held out hopes that the laws would be amended in favour of Catholics, but they can hardly have felt much confidence that these hopes would be fulfilled.

Ginkel could not agree to terms inconsistent with the law. But he might have been pressed harder on the question of estates. The restoration of all lands held by Catholics at the end of Charles II's reign would have been a reasonable price to pay for the winding up of an exhausting and expensive campaign. The restriction of the benefit of the second article to those who were holding out at the end was in some ways anomalous. Premature submission was penalized, obstinate resistance was rewarded. But Ginkel was well aware of the importance attached to the forfeiture of lands, and it would have been hard to get him to go beyond the terms of the second article. As it was, the reaction of Protestants in Ireland was generally unfavourable. The terms were regarded as needlessly generous, and it was argued that the opportunity should have been taken to assure the permanent security of the English interest by the complete suppression of the Irish.[59] Archbishop Narcissus

[56] Story, *Continuation*, pp. 256, 279.   [57] *Jacobite narrative*, pp. 176–7.
[58] O'Kelly, p. 156.   [59] Story, *Continuation*, pp. 273–4.

Marsh was shocked by the unhappy conditions that (he knew not how or why) had been granted to a rebellious people that were not able to defend themselves. Bishop Dopping preached a sermon in which he urged his hearers not to rely on the treacherous promises or submissions of the Irish.[60]

In fact the settlement was greatly to William's advantage. It enabled him to wind up the Irish campaign (which had proved very expensive in money and resources), and to transfer his army to the continent where it was badly needed for next season's fighting.

5. THE FATE OF THE TREATY

The first part of the treaty to be implemented was the military articles. The first of these allowed all who wished, without exception, to leave Ireland for any destination outside Britain with their families and household goods. Under other articles the officers and men of the Irish army (including 'those called rapparees or volunteers') who wished to go to France were allowed to do so and were promised free transport. Ginkel undertook to supply up to seventy ships for the purpose. Till transport was available the Irish army was to remain in control of the English town of Limerick. It was an astonishing arrangement. An army in being, with its own commanders, arms, ammunition and even horses, was to be transported at William's expense to a hostile country where they were to be used in an attempt to restore William's rival to the throne.

Ginkel was criticized for having entered into such an undertaking. Bentinck wrote to him: 'what is difficult in the capitulation is to send as it were an army to the king of France, and to be obliged to transport it'. He suggested that William's own troops should first be shipped to the continent, and that the consequent delay might make the Irish army think better of going to France 'to be butchered for bread and a sou a day'.[61]

---

[60] Marsh's diary in *Ir. Ecc. Jn.*, v. 148; T.C.D., MS Q.3.7, p. 108. The lords justices denounced Dopping's sermon as 'bitter invective', and asked for some mark of William's disapproval; Dopping was temporarily removed from the privy council (*Finch MSS*, iii. 304; *Cal. S.P. dom., 1691-2*, pp. 28, 430).

[61] Bentinck to Ginkel, 22 Oct./1 Nov. 1691 (Japikse, iii. 264).

Orders had already been given to Ginkel to hold up the shipping but they did not reach him till the Irish had already embarked. He rejoined that he could not understand why the Irish should be stopped from sailing, and he pointed out that William's troops could not be withdrawn while the Irish army remained in Limerick.[62] For the internal security of Williamite Ireland there were advantages in getting rid of numbers of the Irish army.

Individual soldiers were to elect whether to go to France or not, and great efforts were made on both sides to influence them. Sarsfield urged them to come with him and guaranteed that next year they would be back in England or Ireland with a powerful army; sermons and brandy reinforced his arguments. Ginkel countered with offers of employment in William's service.[63] It was a hard decision: exile, or the bleak prospect of life in a Williamite Ireland. There was much hesitation; reports that the first arrivals in France had been badly treated caused some last-minute changes of mind.[64] But the majority opted for France. Ginkel honoured the commitment to transport them, though there were arguments about his obligation to provide shipping for women and children. Sarsfield wrote him a sharp letter to say that difficulties were being made on this point. The letter seems to have been effective, as women and children are particularly mentioned as accompanying Sarsfield from Cork.[65] A fortnight before he left he released Ginkel from any obligation to provide further shipping. Harrowing scenes, when some women were prevented from boarding, seem to have been the result of a last-minute rush for the boats.[66] Chateaurenault's fleet came into the Shannon on October 20 and anchored off Scattery Island near the mouth of the estuary. It provided a valuable supplement to Ginkel's ships and is said to have brought off 10,000 Irish, including 4,000 women, children and old men. The Jacobite lords justices also travelled with the

[62] Nottingham to lords justices and Ginkel, 13 Oct. 1691 (*Finch MSS*, iii. 287); Ginkel to Coningsby, 23 Oct. 1691 (de Ros MSS, 12/113).

[63] Story, *Continuation*, pp. 259–61.

[64] *Dublin Intelligence*, 22 Dec. 1691.

[65] Sarsfield to Ginkel, 17 Oct. 1691 (Clarke corr., xiii, no. 1270); *Coll. Hib.*, iv. 31.

[66] Story, *Continuation*, pp. 292–3; O'Kelly, p. 157–8.

French fleet.[67] The English town of Limerick was handed over to Ginkel on November 1, but it was not till December 22 that the final contingent sailed from Cork with Sarsfield.

It was estimated that 12,000 soldiers went to France.[68] They provided James with an army of his own, paid for by Louis, until the treaty of Ryswick in 1697; after that they were absorbed into the French army. In the spring of 1692 they were posted at Boulogne, ready for the invasion of Britain. The defeat of the French fleet at La Hogue destroyed James's hopes of returning to England, but the Irish army distinguished itself that summer at Steenkirk. Sarsfield was mentioned in dispatches as having shown 'the valour of which he gave such proofs in Ireland'.[69] In the following year (1693) he was mortally wounded at Landen. He had his critics, even among his admirers. But he was the nearest approach to a hero that the war in Ireland produced on the Jacobite side; and the publicity that his opponents gave to him is the best evidence of their respect.

William did not long retain those Irish who had opted to enter his service. Early in 1692 eighteen regiments of them were disbanded, 1,400 of the likeliest men were kept and sent to William's ally, the emperor, under the command of Lord Iveagh. Balldearg O'Donnell tried to get the command for himself, but without success. He was given a pension of £500 a year and returned to the service of Spain.[70]

Irish regiments formed part of the French army up to the revolution, and numerous Irishmen gained distinction in it. They included many who were brought up in Ireland after the treaty of Limerick and left to seek their fortunes abroad.[71] The 'wild geese' kept alive in Ireland the idea of a Stuart restoration and the Jacobite cause was romanticized by poets whose theme

[67] *Coll. Hib.*, iv. 26; *London Gazette*, 4 Jan. 1692; Fumeron to Barbesieux, 6/16 Nov. 1691 (Min. guerre, A1 1081, no. 200).

[68] Story, *Continuation*, p. 292; *Coll. Hib.*, iv. 30–1.

[69] Todhunter, *Life of Patrick Sarsfield*, p. 199.

[70] *Dublin Intelligence*, 16 Feb. 1692; the number sent to the emperor was later increased to 2,000 (*Finch MSS*, iv. 246); ibid., iv. 486.

[71] The standard account is J. C. O'Callaghan, *History of the Irish brigades in the service of France* (1870). A convenient book of reference is R. Hayes, *Biographical dictionary of Irishmen in France* (1949). With the outbreak of the war of the Spanish succession Irish regiments were formed to fight in Spain for the French claimant and continued as part of the Spanish army.

was the vision (aisling) of Ireland as a damsel in distress, waiting for a restored Stuart to rescue her.

The Catholic church helped to inspire similar sentiments. Both James II and his son kept close contact with the Irish bishops and the latter did their best to rally support for the Jacobite movement. The archbishops of Armagh and Tuam and four diocesan bishops were at St Germain in the beginning of 1692 and appealed to the pope to take up James's cause. James II nominated a number of Irish bishops in the post-war period, and after his death his son as James III continued the practice. The Vatican recognized both in turn up to 1760 in the briefs of appointment of Irish bishops.[72] Many Irish clerics got their education in France, and the links between Ireland and Catholic Europe generally remained strong throughout the eighteenth century.

The activities of Irish soldiers and priests in Europe, and the evident sympathy shown by their kinsmen at home, confirmed the suspicions of Protestants. They were convinced that those Catholics who had remained in Ireland were not genuinely reconciled to the Protestant régime and were waiting for a favourable opportunity to overthrow it. Apprehension, as well as vindictiveness, was responsible for the demand for penal laws. The Limerick settlement appeared to leave Catholics in a dangerously strong position, and there was much opposition to the parliamentary ratification of the civil articles.

William and his government made efforts to implement the treaty, and it was given some consideration in the penal legislation that was imposed in instalments during the remainder of his reign. For a time at any rate, William preserved an uneasy balance in the attention he paid to the reproaches of his Catholic allies and to the intolerant demands of Protestant politicians. With the conclusion of the war in Europe in 1697, the influence of the allies waned and Protestant pressure prevailed.

Controversy over the treaty began almost immediately. No sooner had Ginkel's son left for England with the signed copy of

---

[72] Moran, *Spicil. Ossor.*, ii. 304; C. Giblin, 'The *processus datariae* and the appointment of Irish bishops in the seventeenth century' in Franciscan Fathers, ed. *Luke Wadding*, pp. 508–616; M. Wall, *The penal laws, 1691–1760*, p. 65.

the articles than it was noticed that the words 'and all those under their protection in the said counties' had been left out. When Ginkel reached England he explained that the omission was an accident, but a majority of the privy council was opposed to restoring the missing clause. William, however, took Ginkel's advice and incorporated the words in his ratification of the articles. But this did not end the argument, and the Irish parliament never accepted the clause.[73]

The hearing of claims under the second article began in the spring of 1692 and almost all the applications were granted. Successful claimants whose estates had been seized got them back in consequence. But the parliament (which was of course an all-Protestant body) that met in the autumn of that year was bitterly opposed to the ratification of the articles and showed such hostility to the government that it was dissolved in less than a month. It was not till 1697 that William's government felt itself in a position to put the confirmation of the civil articles before the Irish parliament; and the form in which the bill was drafted bore very little resemblance to the original articles. There was no reference at all to the first article, by which Catholics in general were to have the privileges in the practice of their religion that they had had in Charles II's reign. The second article, in favour of the Irish army and the inhabitants of Limerick, was set out without the missing clause. Even so, this was the most effective of the articles. It regained or preserved property rights for several hundred of the Catholic gentry and substantially limited the area confiscated from James's supporters. By the beginning of Anne's reign the Catholic share of the land, which had been 22 per cent in 1688 was still 14 per cent. The failure to ratify the 'missing clause' had less effect in practice than Catholics had feared.[74]

But those who kept their property by this means were before long subjected to the penal restrictions of Anne's reign. The 'popery act' of 1704 severely curtailed rights and interests that had been lawfully enjoyed in the time of Charles II. A Catholic could not leave his estate to his eldest son, unless the latter turned Protestant; if the son had already done so, his father was

[73] For a discussion of this question see Simms, *Williamite confiscation*, pp. 55–65.

[74] Ibid., pp. 63–5, 195.

reduced to the status of a tenant-for-life, with no power to dispose of the property. Catholics could not buy land or take leases of more than thirty-one years. Sir Toby Butler argued in vain at the bar of the house of commons that these provisions would make for 'the destroying of the said articles granted upon the most valuable consideration of surrendering the said garrisons at a time when they had the sword in their hand and for anything that appeared to the contrary might have been in a condition to hold out much longer'. In the debate that followed several members of the commons admitted that the articles of Limerick had been granted on the public faith and that if the bill contravened them it ought to be rejected. They argued, however, that there was no contravention: there were no laws in Charles II's reign that restricted the passing of future legislation. This argument overlooked the fact that the second article specifically preserved the rights that Catholics were entitled to under the laws that were in force in Charles II's reign. It was also urged that the disloyalty of Catholics made the bill necessary for the quiet, security and well-being of the public, and that these objects were 'consonant to all laws heretofore made or that were in force either in the reign of King Charles or at any time since'.[75] Protestants were able to salve their consciences in this way. They were determined to pass the bill, which they regarded as essential for the protection of the Protestant régime during a war with France in which the sympathy of the Catholic population was strongly suspected of being with the enemy. As a result of the penal laws against property most of the Catholic land-holding families became Protestant in the course of the eighteenth century. In 1776 Arthur Young estimated that no more than 5 per cent of the land was owned by Catholics.

Although the first article, with its offer of religious toleration, was ignored in the act for the confirmation of the articles, it had been accepted by William. It was therefore a shock to Catholics that in 1697 William and his council should have approved of a bill to banish bishops and regular clergy. The emperor instructed his ambassador to remonstrate with William and urged that the bill was a violation of the treaty of Limerick. The imperial envoy pointed out that if there were no bishops there

[75] *An impartial relation of the several arguments of Sir Stephen Rice, Sir Theobald Butler and Counsellor Malone,* 1704.

could be no replenishment of the clergy, and that as they died off the Catholic church in Ireland would come to an end.[76]

The emperor's intervention was unsuccessful, perhaps because it coincided with the Ryswick negotiations and the end of the war. Several bishops were expelled; others lived a precarious life, depending on the shelter provided by courageous members of their flock. Archbishop Comerford of Cashel wrote to the pope in 1698: 'several of our brethren have stayed, hiding in cisterns, in mountains, caves and holes. I am sustained by the bread of tribulation and the water of scarcity, but I have not given up my office and will not do so'.[77] He remained in his diocese till his death in 1710. The Catholic church did not die away as the emperor had feared and as some Protestants had hoped.[78] New bishops were appointed and came to Ireland, sometimes going under false names to elude the authorities.

An act of 1704 provided for the registration of parish priests, and in this way gave a certain recognition to the Catholic church. Over a thousand priests were registered under this act, but very few were prepared to comply with a subsequent act of 1709, which required them to take the oath of abjuration. This oath denied the claim of the pretender and asserted that Anne was lawful and rightful queen. The requirement was a breach of the ninth article of Limerick, which prescribed that Catholics should not be made to take an oath other than that of allegiance. Protestants argued that those who gave sincere allegiance to Anne could have no objection to abjuring her rival. Catholics drew a distinction between allegiance *de jure* and allegiance *de facto*.[79]

The civil articles were a very defective instrument, hastily and imprecisely drafted. They did little but preserve from confiscation the estates of a number of individuals. They did not give Catholics religious toleration or safeguard them from the political and economic consequences of the penal laws. Catholics resented their treatment as a gross breach of faith. Protestants contended that allegiance to William and his successors was an

---

[76] O. Klopp, *Der Fall des Hauses Stuart*, vii. 474.

[77] Moran, *Spicil Ossor.*, ii. 345.

[78] J. Dunton, *Conversation in Ireland*, pp. 556-7.

[79] For the penal laws as they affected the Catholic Church at this time see Wall, *Penal laws*, pp. 13-24.

integral part of the bargain, and that Catholics' sympathy for the Stuart cause made them a security risk, from which the Protestant administration had to protect itself by all the means at its disposal. Religion and politics were inseparable, and the favourable attitude of Rome to the Jacobite cause was bound to affect the political views of Catholics and to arouse the suspicions of Protestants. From the beginning there was an absence of trust on either side. The military articles, which gave James an Irish army, were not easy to reconcile with the civil articles which offered toleration to Irish Catholics in return for allegiance to William. But the surrender of Limerick had given a real advantage to William and his allies. The treaty concessions were offered as a price worth paying for the advantage gained by ending the war before the winter of 1691. Whatever sympathies Catholics in Ireland may have felt, there was nothing in their conduct to justify the penal legislation that was so soon to follow the signing of the treaty.

XVI

EPILOGUE

IN LESS than seven years the wheel had turned full circle. The high hopes that Catholics had had at James's accession had come to nothing. Their support of the legitimate monarchy had left them worse off than they had been in 1685. All that they had gained under Tyrconnell's administration had been lost. The Protestants, whose ascendancy was now restored, were embittered by the humiliations and deprivations inflicted on them by the Jacobite government, and by the losses suffered in three years of war. They were determined that these experiences should not recur; the penal code that followed was an expression of that determination.

Priests and people had expected too much and had rejoiced too soon over the apparent success of Tyrconnell's take-over. They had not taken into account the weakness of James and the strength of English hostility to the revival of Irish Catholic power. Religion had become the principal dividing-line in Ireland. The English interest was identified with Protestantism; Catholics of whatever origin were regarded as Irish, by themselves as well as by others. The distinction between 'old English' and Gaelic Irish was still discernible, but it was rapidly disappearing. In the Irish context the religious animosities of contemporary Europe were reinforced by bitter memories of conflicts at home. If Catholics remembered Cromwell and the 'popish plot', Protestants had not forgotten 1641. Tyrconnell's drastic reversal of the Irish balance of power built up a strong reaction on the part of Protestants both in England and Ireland, and this undoubtedly contributed to the fall of James.

When James was driven from England, Irish hopes rested on France. But French help was relatively ineffective. Louis XIV had little interest in action outside continental Europe; Louvois and Seignelay were at loggerheads. The intervention of France drew Ireland within the periphery of a European war, but it brought little prospect beyond the prolonging of a frustrating struggle that damaged the country and diverted William's army from the protection of Holland. Williamites were able to accuse the Irish, not only of supporting James, but of calling to their aid the chief enemy of England.

Even if French help had been greater, it is not likely that the final result would have been very different. Lack of unity and inability to keep up a sustained resistance were serious dis-advantages on the Irish side. On occasions the Irish troops fought well, and later generations could look back with pride on the defence of Limerick and Athlone. Fortune did not favour them; the balance of advantage at Derry and Aughrim might well have tipped the other way. But William was a formidable organizer, and in the last resort England was prepared to devote more resources to the reconquest of Ireland than it was worth France's while to give to the cause of James.

The surrender of Limerick was in form a compromise; in fact it was a Williamite victory. It led to a Protestant ascendancy which paid little regard to the spirit in which Ginkel had bar-gained with Sarsfield and his fellow-negotiators. The Irish Jacobites were soon aware of the bleak prospect that lay before them. O'Kelly lamented the 'public calamity' of his country-men and could not 'pursue that remnant of a woeful history that requires ink mixed with the writer's tears'.[1] O Bruadair, who in 1687 had, too soon, celebrated the 'triumph of Tadhg', bewailed the fate of Ireland in a poem called 'the shipwreck'.[2] It was to be many years before Catholics regained the status and oppor-tunities that they had briefly enjoyed under a Jacobite adminis-tration.

[1] O'Kelly, p. 159.
[2] O Bruadair, iii. 164–79.

BIBLIOGRAPHY

~~~~~~

SYNOPSIS

A. SOURCES

I. *Manuscript material*

1. National Library of Ireland, Dublin
2. Royal Irish Academy, Dublin
3. Trinity College, Dublin
4. Corporation Library, Pearse Street, Dublin
5. Public Record Office of Northern Ireland, Belfast
6. Public Record Office, London
7. British Museum, London
8. Bodleian Library, Oxford
9. Bibliothèque Nationale, Paris
10. Amerongen Castle, Utrecht
11. Austrian National Library, Vienna
12. Rigsarkivet, Copenhagen

II. *Printed material*

1. Record publications
2. Publications of the Irish Manuscripts Commission
3. Publications of the Historical Manuscripts Commission
4. Other documentary material
5. Newspapers and periodicals
6. Pamphlets and other contemporary writings

B. LATER WORKS

269

Bibliography

INTRODUCTION

It is over fifty years since this period of Irish history was treated in detail by R. H. Murray, *Revolutionary Ireland and its settlement* (1911). The book is superficial and badly arranged, and its author is clearly Williamite in sympathy. But he made use of a wide range of sources, manuscript as well as printed, and paid particular attention to the European aspects of his subject. There is an impressive array of references, and a substantial bibliography. Murray drew largely on the contemporary and near-contemporary accounts that must form the basis for any history of Ireland during this period.

On the Jacobite side these are:

1. J. T. Gilbert, ed., *A Jacobite narrative of the war in Ireland, 1688–91*, edition of an account attributed to a member of the Plunkett family and known as the Fingall manuscript; it was written about 1711 and is strongly pro-Tyrconnell in sympathy;
2. C. O'Kelly, *Macariae excidium, or the destruction of Cyprus*, the work of a County Galway Catholic gentleman who played some part in the war and was extremely hostile to Tyrconnell; it was completed shortly after the end of the war.
3. The journal of John Stevens, an English officer in the Jacobite army; it was later edited by Murray (1912);
4. J. S. Clarke, *The life of James the second*, an edition of the biography compiled early in the eighteenth century at the court of the exiled Stuarts and incorporating some of James's memoirs (see Appendix).

On the Williamite side the most important sources of this kind are:

1. G. Story, *An impartial history of the wars of Ireland* and *A continuation of the impartial history*, written by a chaplain in the Williamite army who arrived in Ireland with Schomberg's expedition in August 1689 and with one break remained till the end of the war; it is a detailed and relatively objective account of the campaign, though the author's sympathies are undisguisedly Williamite;
2. W. King, *The state of the Protestants under the late King James's government*, by a future archbishop who was in Dublin under Jacobite rule and was violently hostile to James;
3. a reply to it by Charles Leslie, the non-juror;
4. accounts of Derry and Enniskillen by writers who were present during the fighting and were of strongly anti-Jacobite sympathies;
5. other accounts by Williamite officers who took part in the campaign in Ireland.

In addition, Murray used the published correspondence of Clarendon, viceroy in 1686, and of d'Avaux, French ambassador in Ireland in 1689–90, as well as a number of other sources, notably the *Calendars of state papers, domestic series* and the correspondence of George Clarke, Williamite secretary-at-war, which is in Trinity College, Dublin.

Much the same material was used by R. Bagwell in the third volume of *Ireland under the Stuarts* (1916), which stops in July 1690, just after the battle of the Boyne. He also is Williamite in sympathy. His writing is pedestrian, but he is more systematic than Murray, and for the period he covers his is the standard history. D. C. Boulger, *The battle of the Boyne* (1911) is wider than its title suggests; it extends from the revolution of 1688 to the treaty of Ryswick in 1697. It is largely based on the French archives, but rarely particularizes the source for its statement; it is strongly Jacobite in tone. P. W. Sergeant, *Little Jennings and fighting Dick Talbot*, 2 vols (1913), is a biography of Tyrconnell which has been described as better than its title. Most of its statements are supported by detailed evidence from sources similar to those used by Murray; Tyrconnell is very much the hero of the book.

This unusual concentration of interest has not up till now been followed by any detailed treatment of the period as a whole. In the interval a number of additional sources have been published or otherwise been made easily available. The most important are:

1. H.M.C. *Ormonde MSS*, new series, viii (1920), which has an interesting diary kept by a Protestant in Dublin during the whole of the Jacobite régime;
2. H.M.C., *Finch MSS*, ii (1922), iii (1957), which contain the correspondence of Nottingham, the Williamite secretary of state concerned with Ireland, for 1690 and 1691;
3. N. Japikse, ed., *Correspondentie van Willem III en Hans Willem Bentinck, eersten Graf van Portland*, iii (1927), which has a number of letters written by William and Bentinck on matters relating to Ireland;
4. Tyrconnell's letters, published in *Analecta Hibernica*, i (1930), iv (1934);
5. *Poems of David O Bruadair*, iii (1917), ed. J. C. MacErlean, which is valuable as an illustration of the Gaelic point of view;
6. *Analecta Hibernica*, xxi: Franco-Irish correspondence, December 1688–August 1691 (1959), which contains a large number of letters about Ireland in the French archives up to August 1689, with a few of Tyrconnell's letters for the following two years; they are taken from the archives of the French ministry of war, which are an invaluable source for the Jacobite war in Ireland and have not hitherto had adequate attention; a further instalment is to be published by the Irish Manuscripts Commission;
7. K. Danaher and J. G. Simms, ed., *The Danish force in Ireland, 1690–1* (1962), which contains the correspondence of Würtemberg and other officers of the force hired by William from the king of Denmark; the writers give much valuable information on military affairs; and their comments on the political situation have a certain detachment, appropriate to their mercenary status; the letters have been preserved in Copenhagen and have not previously been used in the writing of Irish history;

8. *Calendars of state papers, domestic series, 1685* (1960) and *1686–7* (1964) fill what had long been a gap between the published papers of Charles II's reign and that of William III.

A. SOURCES

I. MANUSCRIPT MATERIAL

1. *National Library of Ireland, Dublin*

   Correspondence of William Robinson (MS 13,654)
   Fingall MS: 'A light to the blind' (MSS 476–7)
   Survey of Ireland by Thomas Phillips, 1685 (MSS 2557, 3037)
   Tyrconnell papers (MS 37)

N.L.I. has microfilms of MSS in many countries (see R. J. Hayes, ed., *Manuscript sources . . . of Irish civilization*, xi) MSS listed in sections 9, 10, 12, are among those available on microfilm.

2. *Royal Irish Academy, Dublin*
   Documents on the reduction of Ireland, 1689–91 (MS 24. G. 1–7)
   Ordnance Survey letters of John O'Donovan (typescript)
   Southwell papers (MS 12. I. 12)

3. *Trinity College, Dublin*
   Correspondence and papers of George Clarke, secretary at war
     (MSS K. 5. 1–13)
   Letters of James II (MS E. 2. 19)
   Sermons of Bishop Dopping (MS Q. 3. 7)
   Southwell papers (MSS I. 4. 17, V. 4. 3–4)

4. *Corporation Library, Pearse Street, Dublin*
   Poema de Hibernia
     Long narrative poem, apparently by a lawyer who held office
   during the Jacobite régime (see H.M.C., *rep. 8*, app., p. 493)

5. *Public Record Office of Northern Ireland, Belfast*
   De Ros MSS (Ginkel correspondence)
   Manuscripts of the Annesley collection, formerly in Castlewellan,
     County Down

6. *Public Record Office, London*
   State papers, Ireland, Elizabeth to George III, vol. 340 (S.P. 63/340)
   Transcripts by Armand Baschet of French ambassadors' dispatches

7. *British Museum, London*
   Correspondence of John Cary (Add. MS 5540)
   Correspondence and papers of George Clarke (Eg. MS 2618)
   Diary of Ensign Cramond (Add. MS 29,878)
   Ginkel letter (Harl. MS 7524)
   Letter-book of John Wallis: deciphered letters (Add. MS 32, 499)

Bibliography

Malet papers: Tyrconnell letters (Add. MS 32,095)
Southwell papers (Add. MS 38,153, Eg. MS 917)

8. *Bodleian Library, Oxford*
Carte MSS, clxxxi

9. *Bibliothèque Nationale, Paris*
Ministère de la guerre, archives anciennes, A1, vols, 893–5, 960–3, 1066, 1080–3

10. *Amerongen Castle, Utrecht*
Huisarchief (Ginkel's correspondence)

11. *Austrian National Library, Vienna*
A collection of poems, lampoons, etc., 1670–90 (MS 14,090)

12. *Rigsarkivet, Copenhagen*
England B diplomatic reports (letter of Fouleresse to Christian V)

II. PRINTED MATERIAL

1. *Record publications*

Acts of the Irish parliament, Dublin, 1689
Official Jacobite publications
Calendar of state papers, domestic Series, 1673–95, London, 1895–1964
Calendar of treasury papers, 1697–1702, London, 1871
Cobbett's parliamentary history of England, v, London, 1809
Journals of the house of commons, x
Statutes at large passed in the parliaments held in Ireland, Dublin, 1786

2. *Publications of the Irish Manuscripts Commission*

Analecta Hibernica
    i (Report on Bodl. Rawl. MS A. 253), 1930;
    iv (Tyrconnell's letter-book), 1932;
    xxi (Franco-Irish correspondence, 1688–91), 1959
Books of survey and distribution, i. County of Roscommon, ed. R. C. Simington, 1930
The Danish force in Ireland, 1690–1, ed. K. Danaher and J. G. Simms, 1962
The Inchiquin manuscripts, ed. J. Ainsworth, 1961
Négociations de M. le comte d'Avaux en Irlande, 1689–90, ed. J. Hogan, 1934
—, supplementary volume, 1958
The Tanner letters, ed., C. MacNeill, 1943

3. *Publications of the Historical Manuscripts Commission*

Fourth report, appendix (Ginkel corr., de Ros MSS), 1874
Eighth report, appendix i, section ii (MSS of Lord Talbot de Malahide) 1881
Eleventh report, appendix v (Dartmouth MSS), 1887

Bibliography

Twelfth report, appendix (House of lords MSS, 1689–90), 1889
—, appendix vii (Le Fleming MSS), 1890
Buccleuch MSS, ii. (Shrewsbury corr.), 1903
Finch MSS, ii, iii, iv (Nottingham corr.), 1922–65.
Leyborne-Popham MSS (George Clarke's autobiography), 1899
Ormonde MSS, i, 1895; ii, 1899; new series, vi, vii, viii, 1911–20
Stuart MSS, vi, 1916

4. *Other documentary material*

Barbe, L., 'The battle of the Boyne' and 'The siege of Limerick' in
   Notes and Queries, 5th series, viii. 21–3, 121–3 (1877)
Letters of Jean Payen de la Fouleresse to Christian V of Denmark
Calendar of the ancient records of Dublin, v, ed. J. T. Gilbert, Dublin, 1895
Campana de Cavelli, Marquise de, *Les derniers Stuarts*. 2 vols, Paris,
   1871
Clarendon and Rochester correspondence, ed. S. W. Singer, 2 vols,
   London, 1828
Collectanea Hibernica, iii, iv, Dublin 1960–1
Davies, Rowland, *Journal*, ed. R. Caulfield, London, 1857
Ellis, H., *Original letters*, second series, London, 1827
English historical documents, viii (1660–1714), ed. A. Browning, Lon-
   don, 1953
Evelyn, John, *Diary*, ed. E. S. de Beer, 6 vols, Oxford, 1955
Facsimiles of the national manuscripts of Ireland, part iv (ii), ed. J. T.
   Gilbert, London, 1884
James II's charter to Dublin
Japikse, N., ed., *Correspondentie van Willem III en Hans Willem Bentinck,
   eersten Graf van Portland*, iii, Hague, 1927
Macpherson, J., *Original papers*, 2 vols, London 1775
Montgomery manuscripts, ed. G. Hill, Belfast, 1869
Moran, P. F., *Spicilegium Ossoriense*, 3 vols, Dublin, 1874–84
O Duigennain, M., 'Three seventeenth-century documents' in *Galway
   Archaeological and Historical Society Journal*, xvii. 154–61 (1936)
Petty papers, ed. Lansdowne, 2 vols., London, 1927
Petty-Southwell correspondence, ed. Lansdowne, London, 1928
Rawdon papers, ed. E. Berwick, London, 1820
Sidney, H., *Diary of the times of Charles II*, ed. R. W. Blencowe, 2
   vols., London, 1843
Simms, J. G., 'A Letter to Sarsfield', in *Irish Sword*, ii. 109 (1955)
Stevens, John, *Journal*, ed. R. H. Murray, London, 1912
Witherow, T., *Two diaries of Derry in 1689*, Londonderry, 1888

5. *Newspapers and periodicals*

Dublin Intelligence
Gazette de France
London Gazette
The Present State of Europe, or Historical and Political Mercury

6. *Pamphlets and other contemporary writings*

An account of King William's royal heading of the men of Inniskillin, London, 1690

An account of the late action . . . with a large and full account of the state of King James's affairs in Dublin, London, 1690

An account of the present miserable state of affairs in Ireland, London, 1689

An account of the present state Ireland is in under King James, London, 1660

An address given in to the late King James by the titular archbishop of Dublin, London, 1690

Ailesbury, Thomas Bruce, Earl of, *Memoirs,* London, 1890

Aphorisms relating to the kingdom of Ireland, London, 1689

An apology for the Protestants of Ireland, London, 1689

Berwick, James Fitzjames, duke of, *Memoirs,* 2 vols, London, 1779

Brune, Jean de la, *Histoire de la révolution d'Irlande arrivée sous Guillaume III,* Amsterdam, 1691

Burnet, G., *History of his own time,* 6 vols, Oxford, 1823

The Derry complaint, London, 1699

A diary of the siege of Athlone, London, 1691

A diary of the siege and surrender of Limerick, London, 1691

An exact account of the royal army under the duke of Schomberg with particulars of the defeat of the Irish army near Boyle, London, 1689

An exact journal of the victorious progress of their majesties' forces under the command of General Ginckle, this summer in Ireland, London, 1691

An exact list of the lords spiritual and temporal who sat in the pretended parliament at Dublin, London, 1689

An exact relation of the glorious victory obtained upon the French and Irish army before Londonderry, on Sunday 2 June 1689, London, 1689

An exact relation of the persecutions, robberies and losses sustained by the Protestants of Killmare in Ireland, London, 1689

A faithful history of the northern affairs of Ireland. London, 1690

[French, N.], *The narrative of the settlement and sale of Ireland,* Louvain, 1668

A full and impartial account of all the secret consults . . . of the Romish party in Ireland, London, 1689

A full and impartial relation of the brave and great actions that happened between the Inniskilling men and the French Protestants on the one hand and the Irish rebels commanded by Sarsfield on the other, London, 1689

A full and true account of the late revolution in Dublin, London, 1690

Gilbert, J. T., ed., *A Jacobite narrative of the war in Ireland, 1688–91,* Dublin, 1892

Great news from the army under the command of Duke Schomberg, London, 1689

Great news of a bloody fight in Newton in Ireland, London, 1689

Great news from Dublin, London, 1690

Great news from the duke of Schomberg's Army, London, 1689

Great news from Ireland, London, 1690

Great news from the port of Kingsale in Ireland, London, 1689

Bibliography

Hamill, W., *A view of the danger and folly of being public-spirited*, London, 1721

Hamilton, A., *A true relation of the actions of the Inniskilling men*, London, 1690

An impartial relation of the several arguments of Sir Stephen Rice, Sir Theobald Butler and Counsellor Malone, Dublin, 1704

Ireland's lamentation, London, 1689

A journal of the proceedings of the parliament in Ireland, London, 1689

A journal of the proceedings of the pretended parliament in Dublin from the 7th to the 20th of this instant May, London, 1689

[King, W.], *The state of the Protestants of Ireland under the late King James's government*, London, 1691

King, W., *Diary . . . during his imprisonment in Dublin Castle, 1689*, ed. H. J. Lawlor, Dublin, 1903 (reprinted from *R.S.A.I. Jn.*).

Lawrence, R., *The interest of Ireland in its trade and wealth stated*, Dublin, 1682

[Leslie, C.], *An answer to a book intituled The state of the Protestants in Ireland under the late King James's government*, London, 1692

A letter from Liverpool, London, 1689

McCarmick, W., *A farther impartial account of the actions of the Inniskilling Men*, London, 1691

Mackay, H., *Memoirs of the war carried on in Scotland and Ireland*, Edinburgh, 1833

Mackenzie, J., *A narrative of the siege of Londonderry*, London, 1690

McCuart. Séamas Dall, 'Elegy for Sorley MacDonnell' in S. Laoide, ed., *Duanaire na Midhe*, Dublin, 1914

Marsh, N., 'Diary', in *Irish Ecclesiastical Journal*, v (1848)

More good news from Ireland, giving a faithful account . . . of the English army there under the command of his grace Duke Schomberg, London, 1689

Mullenaux, S., *Journal of the three months' royal campaign of his majesty in Ireland*, London, 1690

Molyneux, Thomas [*recte* Samuel], 'Journey to Connaught, April 1709', ed. A. Smith, in *Irish Archaeological Miscellany* i. 161–78 (1846)

O Bruadair, D., *Poems*, ed. J. C. MacErlean, 3 vols, London, 1910–17

O'Kelly, C., *Macariae excidium, or the destruction of Cyprus*, ed. J. C. O'Callaghan, Dublin, 1850

Parker, R., *Memoirs of the military transactions . . . from 1683 to 1718*, London, 1747

Petty, W., *The political anatomy of Ireland*, London, 1691

Phillips, G., *The interest of England in the preservation of Ireland*, London, 1689

The present dangerous condition of the Protestants in Ireland, London, 1689

The present miserable condition of Ireland, London, 1689

The present state of affairs in Ireland, London, 1690

Reflections on a paper pretending to be an apology for the failure charged on Mr Walker's account of the siege of Londonderry, London, 1689

A relation of what most remarkably happened during the last campaign in Ireland, Dublin, 1689

The royal flight, a new farce, London, 1690

Seasonable advice to the electors of County Armagh, Dublin, 1753

The speech of King James II, 7 May 1689, and Irish acts, London, 1689

Story, G., *A continuation of the impartial history of the wars of Ireland*, London, 1693

[Story, G.], *A true and impartial history of the most material occurrences in the kingdom of Ireland during the last two years*, London, 1691

A true account of the whole proceedings of the parliament in Ireland, London, 1689

A true and faithful account of the present state and condition of the kingdom of Ireland, London, 1690

A true and impartial account of their majesties' army in Ireland, London, 1690

A true and impartial account of the most material passages in Ireland since December 1688, London, 1689

A true and perfect journal of the affairs in Ireland since his majesty's arrival, London, 1690

Villare Hibernicum, London, 1690

A vindication of the present government of Ireland under Richard, earl of Tyrconnell, London, 1688

Walker, G., *A true account of the siege of Londonderry*, London, 1689

Walsh, P., *The history and vindication of the loyal formulary or Irish remonstrance*, Dublin, 1679

B. LATER WORKS

Bagwell, R., *Ireland under the Stuarts*, 3 vols, London, 1910–16

Baxter, S. B., *William III*, London, 1966

Bellesheim, A., *Geschichte der Katholischen Kirche in Irland*, 3 vols, Mannheim, 1890–1

Belloc, H., *James II*, London, 1928

Boulger, D. C., *The battle of the Boyne*, London, 1911

Browning, A., *Thomas Osborne, earl of Danby*, 3 vols, London, 1944–51

Carte, T., *The life of James, first duke of Ormond*, 6 vols, Oxford, 1851

Churchill, W. S., *Marlborough, his life and times*, 4 vols, London, 1933–8

Clancarty, Richard le Poer Trench, second earl of, *Memoir of the le Poer Trench family*, Dublin, 1874

Clark, G. N., *The later Stuarts*, 2nd ed., Oxford, 1955

Clark, R., *Anthony Hamilton, his life and works*, London, 1921

Clarke, J. S., *The life of James the second*, 2 vols, London, 1816

Collectanea Hibernica, iii, iv, Dublin, 1960–1

Connell, K., *The population of Ireland, 1750–1845*, Oxford, 1950

Cullen, L. M., *Anglo-Irish trade, 1660–1800*, Manchester, 1968

—, ed., *The formation of the Irish economy*, Cork, 1969

Dalrymple, J., *Memoirs of Great Britain and Ireland*, 4th ed., 3 vols, Dublin, 1773

Dalton, C., *Irish army lists, 1661–85*, London, 1907

Davis, Thomas, *The patriot parliament of 1689*, ed. C. Gavan Duffy, London, 1893

Dunton, J., *Conversation in Ireland*, London, 1818

Egan, P., *The parish of Ballinasloe*, Dublin, 1960

Foxcroft, H. C., *Supplement to Burnet's history of his own time*, Oxford, 1902

Froude, J. A., *The English in Ireland in the eighteenth century*, 3 vols, London, 1887

Garland, J. L., 'The Regiment of MacElligott, 1688-9', in *Irish Sword*, i. 121-7 (1950-1)

Giblin, C., 'The *processus datariae* and the appointment of Irish bishops in the seventeenth century', in Franciscan Fathers, ed. *Luke Wadding*, Dublin, 1957

Gill, C., *The rise of the Irish linen industry*, Oxford, 1925

Goodbody, O. M., 'Anthony Sharp', in *Dublin Historical Record*, xiv. 12-19 (1955)

Grace, S., *Memoirs of the family of Grace*, London, 1823

Grattan, H., *The speeches of the right honourable Henry Grattan, edited by his son*, 4 vols, Dublin, 1822

Harris, W., *The history of the life and reign of William-Henry . . . king of England, Scotland, France and Ireland, etc.*, Dublin, 1749

Hawkins, E., *Medallic illustrations of the history of Great Britain and Ireland*, 2 vols, London, 1885

Hay, M. V., *Winston Churchill and James II*, London, 1934

Hayes, R., *Biographical dictionary of Irishmen in France*, Dublin, 1949

Hayes, R. J., ed., *Manuscript sources of the history of Irish civilisation*, 11 vols, Boston, 1965

Kazner, J. F. A., *Leben Friedrichs von Schomberg oder Schoenberg*, 2 vols, Mannheim, 1789

Kenyon, J. P., *Robert Spencer, earl of Sunderland, 1641-1702*, London, 1958

Kiernan, T. J., *History of the financial administration of Ireland to 1817*, London, 1930

Klopp, O., *Der Fall des Hauses Stuart*, 14 vols, Vienna, 1875-88

Lavisse, E., *Histoire de France*, viii, Paris, 1911

Martin-Leake, S., *The life of Sir John Leake*, ed. G. A. R. Callender (Navy Records Society), 2 vols, 1920

Lecky, W. E. H., *History of Ireland in the eighteenth century*, 5 vols, London 1892

Macaulay, T. B., *The history of England from the accession of James II*, 3 vols, London, 1906 (Everyman ed.)

Hayes-McCoy, G. A., 'The battle of Aughrim, 1691', in *Galway Archaeological and Historical Society Journal*, xx. 1-20 (1942)

Mason, W. M., *History . . . of the . . . cathedral church of St Patrick*, Dublin, 1820

Milligan, C. D., *The history of the siege of Londonderry*, Belfast, 1951

Moody, T. W., 'Redmond O'Hanlon', in *Proceedings of the Belfast Natural History and Philosophical Society*, 2nd series, i. 17-33 (1937)

Murphy, J. A., *Justin MacCarthy, Lord Mountcashel*, Cork, 1959

Murray, R. H., *Revolutionary Ireland and its settlement*, London, 1911

Bibliography

Murtagh, D., 'The battle of Aughrim', in *The Irish at war*, ed. G. A. Hayes-McCoy, Cork, 1964

—, 'The siege of Athlone', in *Journal of the Royal Society of Antiquaries of Ireland*, lxxx. 58–81 (1953)

O'Callaghan, J. C., *History of the Irish brigades in the service of France*, Dublin, 1870

O'Donovan, John, 'The O'Donnells in exile', in *Duffy's Hibernian Magazine*, 1860, pp. 50–6, 106–7

O Finneadh, P., 'Ball Dearg O Domhnaill' in *Béaloideas*, iii. 359–62 (1931–2)

O Lochlainn, Colm, *Irish street ballads from the complete Petrie collection*, Dublin, 1939

O'Sullivan, W., *The economic history of Cork City from the earliest times to the act of union*, Cork, 1937

O Tuathail, E., 'Arthur Brownlow and his MSS', in *Irish Booklover*, xxiv. 26–8 (1936)

Pinard, —, *Chronologie historique-militaire*, Paris, 1760

Power, P., *A bishop of the penal times*, Cork, 1932

Prendergast, J.P., *Ireland from the restoration to the revolution, 1660–1690*, London, 1887

Ranke, L. von, *A history of England, principally in the seventeenth century*, 6 vols, Oxford, 1875

Reid, J. S., *History of the Presbyterian church in Ireland*, 3 vols, Belfast, 1867

Sells, A. L., ed., *The memoirs of James II*, London, 1962

Sergeant, P. W., *Little Jennings and fighting Dick Talbot*, 2 vols, London, 1913

Simms, J. G., 'Dublin in 1685', in *I.H.S.*, xiv. 212–26 (1965)

—, 'Eyewitnesses of the Boyne', in *Irish Sword*, vi. 16–27 (1963)

—, 'A Jacobite colonel: Lord Sarsfield of Kilmallock' in *Irish Sword*, ii. 205–10 (1955)

—, *The Jacobite parliament of 1689*, Dundalk, 1966

—, 'The original draft of the civil articles of Limerick' in *I.H.S.*, viii. 37–44 (1952)

—, 'The siege of Derry', in *Irish Sword*, vi. 271–80 (1964)

—, 'Sligo in the Jacobite war', in *Irish Sword*, vii. 124–35 (1965)

—, *The treaty of Limerick*, Dundalk, 1961

—, *The Williamite confiscation in Ireland, 1690–1703*, London, 1956

—, 'Williamite peace-tactics', in *I.H.S.*, viii, 303–23 (1953)

Smith, C. and Harris, W., *Ancient and present state of the county of Down*, Dublin, 1744

Sterne, L., *The life and opinions of Tristram Shandy*, London, 1914 (Everyman ed.)

Stevenson, D., 'The Irish emergency coinages of James II' in *British Numismatic Journal*, xxxvi. 196–75 (1968).

Stubbs, J. W., *History of the University of Dublin*, Dublin, 1889

Sue, E., *Histoire de la marine française*, 5 vols, Paris, 1835–7

Todhunter, J. H., *The life of Patrick Sarsfield*, London, 1895

Turner, F. C., *James II*, London, 1948

Bibliography

Twomey, M., 'Charles II, Lord Ranelagh and the Irish finances', in
  Bulletin of the Irish Committee of Historical Sciences, 1960
Wall, M., *The penal laws, 1691–1760,* Dundalk, 1961
Went, A. E. J., 'James II's money of necessity, often called gun-money',
  in *Dublin Historical Record,* xvi. 16–21 (1960)

APPENDIX

~~~~~~

JAMES II'S MEMOIRS

MANY REFERENCES to Irish affairs of the period 1685–91 are to be found in J. S. Clarke, *Life of James the second*, 2 vols, 1816. Clarke was librarian to the prince regent, and the *Life* was compiled from four manuscript volumes (now in the Stuart manuscripts at Windsor) which came into the possession of the regent in 1813. They had been in the library of Prince Charles Edward at Florence; were bequeathed by him to his daughter the duchess of Albany; and were left by her to the procurator-general of the English Benedictines at Rome. They were stated to be collected from memoirs written in James II's hand, but were compiled after his death by order of his son James III. The compilation of this manuscript life seems to have taken place between 1707 and 1718, and to have been made by a Jacobite named Dicconson.[1]

The value of the work has been discussed at some length by Winston Churchill in his *Marlborough*. His conclusion is that James's own memoirs do not extend beyond 1660, and that for later years the life has no greater authority than that of Dicconson, the biographer, and in Churchill's opinion that is very little.[2] The biographer appears in Churchill's index as 'Edward

---

[1] Internal evidence shows that the manuscript was written before the death of Mary of Modena in 1718 (James II, ii. 195); for the date 1707 see p. 283 below.

[2] Churchill, *Marlborough*, i. 352–64.

281

Dicconson, Roman Catholic bishop'; he was evidently William Dicconson, a layman and treasurer to the exiled Stuart court, to whom there are many references in the *Stuart manuscripts*.

Churchill's view was challenged in M. V. Hay, *Winston Churchill and James II*. Churchill relied on a letter from the principal of the Scots College in Paris which refers to James's original memoirs as ending at the restoration. Hay points out that the same letter makes it clear that there were other memoirs, letters and papers written by James after the restoration, which were used by Dicconson.[3] The distinction between 'original memoirs', which are pre-restoration, and 'memoirs', which extend to later years, is to be found in the marginal notes of both the manuscript life and Clarke's published edition.

The most recent addition to the evidence is to be found in *The memoirs of James II*, translated and in effect edited by A. L. Sells from the Bouillon manuscript (1962). This manuscript, a French translation of James's memoirs from 1652 to 1660, was discovered in the Château Turenne in France. It was prepared under James II's orders and presented by him in 1696 to Cardinal de Bouillon, a nephew of the great Turenne under whom James had served. The cardinal added a statement that James promised him a translation of those parts of his memoirs that related to Turenne and the fighting of the Low Countries up to 1660. The statement showed that James took an active part in supervising the translation. The editor refers to Churchill's opinion and remarks that evidence has come to light that James 'continued to write memoirs, though not perhaps continuously, after 1660 and even into the 1680s'.[4] He does not specify what the evidence is, but it is presumably James III's order of 1707, to which reference will later be made. The French manuscript has no direct bearing on the point, but comparison of it with Clarke's *Life* shows that the two correspond closely, though some parts of the French version seem to have been abbreviated. The comparison gives a favourable impression of Dicconson's integrity as a compiler.

In the part of Clarke's *Life* that covers the period up to 1660 there are a number of marginal references to 'original memoirs'.

---

[3] Hay, pp. 8–13; Thomas Inese to James Edgar, secretary to James III, 17 Oct. 1740, cited in full in Churchill, i. 361–3.
[4] A. L. Sells, ed., *The memoirs of James II*, p. 20.

These appear to have been a connected account written by James of the first part of his life, and subsequently bound into three volumes. They were destroyed at the time of the French revolution, when the Scots College in Paris made an unsuccessful attempt to get them out of France. The Bouillon manuscript, referred to above, was evidently translated from this account.

In Clarke's *Life* no authority is cited for anything in the period 1661–77. But James II is again claimed as the authority for a number of passages from 1678 onwards. The change in editorial practice appears to be related to an order made by James III on 12 January 1707 for the transfer from the Scots College in Paris to St Germain of James II's 'memoirs and other papers written in his own hand' and relating to 1678 and subsequent years.[5] The first passage dealing with 1678 directly attributed to James cites 'King James 2d., his own memoirs, tom. 7, p. 279, writ in his own hand'.[6] Later references also cite tome 8 and tome 9. There is a good deal of overlapping between tomes 7, 8 and 9 for the period 1678–84, and they do not appear to have formed a continuous narrative. From 1685 onwards only tome 9 is referred to. These volumes are referred to in the *Life*: 'never prince left more monuments of what passed in his time, amounting to nine tomes writ in his own hand and which by a writing under his privy seal he appointed to be lodged in the Scotch College at Paris'.[7] In addition, there are references to 'letters' and 'loose sheets'.

The most important references to Ireland that are attributed to James himself are his landing at Kinsale, with an account of the Irish situation as it then presented itself; his journey northwards to Derry; his confrontation of Schomberg; the Boyne campaign and his flight.[8] These are detailed accounts, which mention an astonishingly large number of names. But the same attention to detail is to be found in James's holograph letters to Hamilton (T.C.D., MS E. 2. 19).

In the portion of the *Life* not attributed to James there are many references to Irish affairs, including some details not mentioned elsewhere. If these portions were not derived from

[5] *James II*, i, p. xxiii; see also *Stuart MSS*, i. 216.
[6] *James II*, i. 515.
[7] Ibid., ii. 243.
[8] Ibid., pp. 327–8; 330–6; 368; 371–84.

James's notes, they were presumably supplied by some of the many Irish at St Germain. Their value as evidence is no less than that of the 'Light to the blind', which was written about the same time (1711).[9] They both present events in Ireland from the point of view of a well-informed Jacobite.

[9] *Jacobite narrative.*

INDEX

~~~~~~

Entries in brackets following the names of places in Ireland refer to counties.

Index

Presbyterians, 5, 8, 11, 50, 100–1, 142
Purcell, Henry, 32
Purcell, Nicholas, colonel, 69, 185, 196, 203, 205, 211, 235, 241, 253
Pusignan, Major-general, 95, 103

Quakers, 11, 13, 35
Quit-rents, 83 n.
Quo warranto proceedings, 35–6, 38 n.

Ranelagh, Roger Jones, 1st earl of, 15
Rapparees, 192, 198–200, 258
Regium donum, 11, 142
Revenue: farming of, 15–16; Jacobite (1689–90), 74, 89–91; Williamite, 121, 137, 142
Revenue commissioners, 35, 242
Rice, Sir Stephen, 25, 40, 53, 63
Rinuccini, Giovanni Baptista, nuncio, 3
Riverston, *see* Nugent
Robartes, John, 2nd Baron, 3
Robinson, William, 137
Roch, James, captain, 108
Rochester, Lawrence Hyde, 1st earl of, 18, 22
Rome, 144, 281
Rooke, George, naval captain, 127
Roscommon, county of, 76, 83
Rosen, Conrad von, marshal, 61, 115, 124, 128, 139; and siege of Derry, 95, 100, 106–8, 110, 112, 116
Rosnaree (Meath), 148, 151
Ross castle (Kerry), 193, 240
Rosse, Richard Parsons, 1st Viscount, 76
Roth, Michael, captain, 59
Russell, Edward, admiral, 174, 231
Ruvigny, Henri de Massue, marquis de, 206
Rye House plot, 11
Ryswick, treaty of (1697), 260, 264

St George's Channel, 69, 155
St Germain-en-Laye, 59, 62, 186, 261, 283
St Johnston (Donegal), 100
St Ruth (Ruhe), Charles Chal-

mont, marquis de, 196–7, 203–5, 207, 210–11, 216–28, 236
St Sauveur, Monsieur, 131–2
Salmon, 14
Sancroft, William, abp of Canterbury, 28
Sarsfield, Honora, countess of Lucan (later duchess of Berwick), 159 n.
Sarsfield, Patrick, earl of Lucan, 33, 47, 63, 73, 76, 156, 160, 188, 211; and Enniskillen, 115–16; and Sligo, 131–2, 238; at the Boyne, 148–9, 151; and resistance party, 158–9, 192, 235; and defence of Limerick (1690), 165–6; and Ballyneety, 167–8, 176, 178; and Kinsale, 184; and defence of Shannon (winter, 1690–1), 194; and Aughrim, 219, 226; and Galway, 233; and defence of Limerick (1691), 246–7, 249–51; and Limerick negotiations, 252–6; and transfer of Irish to France, 259–60; relations with Tyrconnell, 185–6, 195–7, 205, 241–2; relations with St Ruth, 205, 217; created earl of Lucan, 195; death, 260
Savoy, 138, 196–7
Scattery Island (Clare), 259
Schomberg, Friedrich Herman, 1st duke of, 70, 111, 119, 139–40; his expedition to Ireland (1689), 120–32, 134, 283; takes Charlemont, 137–8; at the Boyne, 147, 149; relations with William III, 129, 134, 143
Schomberg, Meinhard, Count, 148, 152, 201–2
Schools, 42–3, 92
Scilly Isles, 68
Scotland, 49, 52, 61–2, 101, 142, 202; Jacobite designs on, 65, 69, 95
Scots, Ulster, 2, 11, 100–1, 123, 149
Scott, Sir Edward, 182–3
Scravenmore ('s Gravemoer), Adam van der Duyn, Heer van, 178, 180
Seignelay, Jean-Baptiste Colbert, marquis de, 59–61, 67, 69, 155, 159, 267

294

IRELAND, 1689-91